Small Business

Legal Tool Kit

(with CD-ROM)

Small Business

Business

Legal
Tool Kit
(with CD-ROM)

Ira Nottonson
Theresa A. Pickner

EP
Entrepreneur Press

Editorial Director: Jere Calmes
Cover Design: Desktop Miracles, Inc.
Production: CWL Publishing Enterprises, Inc., Madison, Wisconsin,
www.cwlpub.com

This publication is designed to provide accurate and authoritative information in
regard to the subject matter covered. It is sold with the understanding that the pub-
lisher is not engaged in rendering legal, accounting, or other professional services. If
legal advice or other expert assistance is required, the services of a competent professional person should be sought.

> —From a Declaration of Principles jointly adopted by
> a Committee of the American Bar Association
> and a Committee of Publishers and Associations

ISBN 13: 978-1-59918-095-3
10: 1-59918-095-2

Library of Congress Cataloging-in-Publication Data

Nottonson, Ira N., 1933-
   Small business legal tool kit / by Ira Nottonson and Theresa A. Pickner.
      p. cm.
   ISBN-13: 978-1-59918-095-3 (alk. paper)
   ISBN-10: 1-59918-095-2 (alk. paper)
   1. Small business—Law and legislation—United States. I. Pickner, Theresa A.
II. Title.
   KF1659.N68 2007
   346.73'0652—dc22

                                        2007003709

Printed in Canada

11 10 09 08 07   10 9 8 7 6 5 4 3 2 1

Contents

INTRODUCTION

Introduction by Theresa A. Pickner

As a practicing attorney who has taught business and legal-related seminars for over ten years, I have always *wanted* to write a book on the legal and tax issues facing businesses today. I never really dreamed that I would be given the opportunity to write just such a book. For that I am thankful to Entrepreneur Press. I am also grateful to my co-author, Ira Nottonson, for his experience, knowledge, encouragement, patience, and more.

From my students, my clients, and in doing research for this book, I have discovered that many of the books out there are very general. In fact, many books just briefly mention topics that deserve to be covered in detail. In that sense, it is my hope that this book is more detailed and thus more educational to the business owner than most. In addition, I constantly hear that there is a lot of information out there, but that no one is putting the legal and tax information in a concise manner that lends itself to the decision-making process of the business owner. I have been told new business owners feel they are drowning in information that is too general and does not lend itself to reaching conclusions. It seems no one wants to actually commit or give advice. It is my goal that reading or referencing this book will provide the business owner with an understanding of the legal and tax requirements of their business as well as the ability to make decisions about their business.

I hope that you find this book filled with practical advice that is useful whether you are starting a business or have been in business for years. The scope of the book covers legal issues every business owner should know in order to form a business and prepare for operation. Also, it covers a fair amount of tax-related matters. I have tried to include practical advice gained from years of operating a business and counseling business clients. I have addressed common questions that I hear over and over again. At the same time, I have tried to address issues that a business owner may not see coming that can cause them problems down the road.

As with any tool used by a business owner, this book should save you time, trouble, and maybe even money. In some cases, it may even allow business owners to simplify their business processes and procedures. Most of all, it is my desire that this book help business owners to be prepared and make decisions. Business owners want answers and it is my hope that this book will provide those answers.

Introduction by Ira Nottonson

The concepts involved in business are not really very complex. Most business owners understand the nature of making money—costs deducted from sales equals profit. There are many books on the subject that go over these concepts from every perspective ... over and over again. Most of the subtleties are lost on the new business owner because they are still caught up in *how to get started*.

The real problems for the new business owner are in the details that most books don't address. How do you start your business? What kind of legal form should your business take? How can you protect against personal liability? How do you file the many forms necessary to make your business legal . . . and keep it that way? How to handle the many, many tax aspects of business? Which states make it easier to operate a business in their area? Which states make it more difficult? How can you do a comparative analysis of tax consequences? And then, how do you address the problems of management in the simplest of ways?

These are the elements of the Toolbox we offer. You can find answers to these details that you won't find anyplace else. You can see what the many forms are that the small businessperson needs to recognize and understand. You can find some basic agreements that will put you on the road to keeping your business professional. This Toolbox is an excellent "starter kit" for the person who is unfamiliar with the real basics of creating a business. This book is not meant to replace professional advice but it is designed to tell you when you need it.

How to Use This Book

This book is intended to serve as guide to understanding some of the common legal and tax issues you as a business owner will face. It is written for the entrepreneur (not the attorney) who wants to understand the business they are developing better from both a legal and tax prospective. Much of the book comes from the experiences I have seen my clients and students face. It is my hope that you can avoid some of the problems and pitfalls these experiences have brought to me over the years.

The book begins with a detailed description of the choice of entities available to a business owner and includes a simple step-by-step analysis for choosing the right entity. In addition, the book presents some of the more complex areas of taxation that every business owner must understand in a manner that can be easily referenced and followed. It includes a state-by-state summary of the rules related to sales and use tax, franchise taxes, and both corporate and personal taxes, not to mention some of the basic tax concepts that every business owner should know. These areas are a bit complex, but they can be understood with just a little help wading through the information and cutting to the chase. I sincerely hope this book helps in that regard.

In addition, the book covers a number of contract issues, ethical concerns, employment matters, franchise-related issues, and exit strategies for the small business owner, including a foolproof way to determine the value of a business. Finally, there are a number of forms that may be used in your business, or if nothing else, they may just serve to help you understand the purpose, language, and issues covered by certain agreements and documents.

Of course, this book is not intended to be a replacement for professional advice, but it should help you to understand your legal and tax advisors better. It should provide you with a good base of understanding, and a good place to start a conversation on just about any topic. If you use the book as a place to start, you can and should get professional assistance if your needs are complex or if you do not understand the ramifications of a transaction with which you are involved, particularly if you are looking at a long-term agreement or contract.

Whether you read this book from cover to cover to help you develop your business or you use it as a reference guide when a particular issue is at hand, I hope that it not only answers your questions, but that it helps you be better prepared to make the legal and tax-related decisions for your business.

About the Authors

Theresa Pickner has operated her own law practice in Colorado since 1989. She practices primarily in the areas of business, taxation and estate planning. Her educational background includes a bachelors of business administration with a major in accounting and a minor in general business from Western Michigan University and a J.D. and L.L.M. in taxation from the University of Denver. Ms. Pickner has been teaching start-up business classes locally for over ten years. And she served on the board of directors of the Boulder Chamber of Commerce from 2003-2005. In February 2006 she was given the member of distinction award by the Boulder Chamber of Commerce.

Ira N. Nottonson is a Law Review Graduate of Boston College Law School and licensed to practice in the Commonwealth of Massachusetts and the State of California. He has practiced general litigation and business/franchise law with partnerships in Boston, Massachusetts and Westwood, California. At present, he confines his consulting practice to the business of buying, selling, evaluation, and reconstruction of small businesses.

Mr. Nottonson has acted in different capacities for many companies, both private and public: chief executive officer, chief operating officer, chief legal counsel. He has also, at various times, been head of marketing, franchise sales, and has acted as consultant for hundreds of companies throughout the United States and the United Kingdom. These companies include International House of Pancakes, Orange Julius of America, House of Pies, PIP Printing, PIP/UK, Quickprint of America, Copper Penny Family Restaurants, The Bryman-Sawyer Schools, United Rent-All, and Icelandic Design.

In his legal capacity, Mr. Nottonson has been responsible as a member of the management committee for all of the above companies. He has been an integral part of the planning and implementation of basic business concepts.

Mr. Nottonson's qualifications are particularly unique, as he has also been an entrepreneur in his own right. He has been the owner of an advertising agency, a television production company, a publishing company, a law practice, and a nightclub. This diverse background has given him a better understanding of the day-to-day problems of business from a very personal perspective.

Mr. Nottonson currently works with both start-ups and problematic situations needing negotiation and reconstruction. He has been appointed as arbiter by the court and has testified on the subjects of small business and business valuations. He has written extensively on the subject of business generally for various newspapers and periodicals and writes a weekly business column for the Boulder Daily Camera in his hometown of Boulder, Colorado. In addition, he has been guest lecturer at various colleges and universities as well as a teacher at the Chamber of Commerce in Boulder under the auspices of the Small Business Development Center. As an articulate exponent of business concepts, he has appeared on radio and television over the years.

He is also the author of the book, *Before You Go into Business, Read This!*

CHAPTER 1

Looking in the Mirror

This book is not designed to help you choose a business. Rather it is for use once you have made the choice to start or purchase a business. This chapter is devoted to the proposition that the first thing you need to know is who and what you are. No author can give you the answers to that. Only you can! This chapter then is your chapter. Handle it carefully. It will help you set the standards that you need to make important life decisions.

You may be very creative, but not a whiz with numbers. You may be brilliant at fixing things but not be very careful at keeping tools where they belong. You may be very quick to speak to friends and family but be very uncomfortable when dealing with strangers. In other words, each of you is better at some things than others. It is important to know what these spe-

> cial talents are. It is even more important, however, to know the things that others can do better than you can. When starting or even running an existing business it is wise to know your strengths and weaknesses and to get help where you need it.

Self-Deception

It is time to look in the mirror. And here is where the problem is with most people. Some people look in the mirror and see, not what they are, but what they'd like to be. This is called self-deception and, in business, it is especially dangerous. Although it is certainly true that you can develop skills that you might not have at any given moment, we are talking, to begin with, about self-realization. It is also true that you can learn the things you don't know, so lack of knowledge at any point in time need not be definitive, or critical. But, don't forget the purpose of the exercise: to understand the talent, the experience, the education, the abilities, and the proclivities that you bring to the table—more importantly, to recognize the things you don't presently bring to the table so you can make arrangements to have them available when you need them. Any other approach would be contrary to the best interests of your business and its future.

> Keep in mind that each question may not pertain to your particular situation. It should, however, keep you ever vigilant on your road.

The following questions are personal. They are questions of self-analysis. Some questions might not seem to fit, but they all represent an element of importance. Don't kid yourself. No one will see the answers ... but you. Be honest, be candid. Then, ask yourself: "If someone else answered these questions in this way, what advice would I give them about starting or owning their own business?" What advice would you give yourself based on your score?

For Those Already in the Business Marketplace

(The numbers in parentheses represent points for the answer to the question.)

1. Have you lost your job and can't find another? (3)
2. Have you been forced to take a position at a lesser salary? (3)
3. Are you in jeopardy of losing your job? (3)
4. Is your job subject to replacement by equipment or computer? (2)
5. Are your family needs increasing while your income remains the same? (3)
6. Have you been forced to liquidate hard assets to maintain your standard of living? (3)
7. Can you see your remaining cash and assets eroding as time goes on? (3)
8. Are you at an age where finding a new job is difficult because younger people are just as well schooled or just as experienced as you? (3)
9. Are you in jeopardy of losing your health insurance? (3)
10. Have you failed to establish any kind of retirement plan? (3)
11. Are you just plain tired of taking orders? (3)
12. Is your job so stressful that it is affecting your health? (6)
13. Do you feel that it's almost too late to change the course of your life? (4)
14. Have you and your spouse been thinking about this for a long time? (5)
15. Do you have a new freedom because the children are now on their own? (2)

If your "Yes" answers added up to 20 or more, it's time to consider a change.

For Those Not Yet in the Business Marketplace

(The numbers in parentheses represent the number of points for the answer to the question.)

1. Have you been harboring a special dream for a business venture? (3)
2. Do you think that you've got talents that are being wasted? (4)

3. Have you run across an interesting business concept lately? (2)
4. Has somebody come to you with a good idea for a partnership? (3)
5. Do you have a particular expertise that could become the framework for a business? (5)
6. Do you have a hobby that can be turned into a profitable business enterprise? (5)
7. Do you want to learn about a whole new field? (4)
8. Do you want to move from your present community? (2)
9. Have you seen a business or a profit margin that got you excited? (3)
10. Are you technically oriented? (2)
11. Are you sales oriented? (2)
12. Are you financially oriented? (2)
13. Are you mechanically oriented? (2)

If your "Yes" answers added up to 20 or more, you may be ready to look for a new adventure.

For Everyone: From a Personal Perspective, How Well Do You Know Yourself?

(The numbers in parentheses represent the number of points for the answer to the question.)

1. Are you able to maintain an objectivity about a business idea? (4)
2. Are you able to candidly discuss your own abilities and inadequacies with others? (4)
3. Are you able to take advice from professionals? (4)
4. Do you know people on whose opinions you can rely? (4)
5. Do you understand the basics of operating a business? (4)
6. Do you understand the basic differences among a profit and loss statement, a cash-flow analysis, and a balance sheet? (4)
7. Do you understand the basic language of a lease and a contract? (4)
8. Do you know what a franchise is all about? (4)
9. Are you a gambler? (4)
10. Are you prepared to make compromises? (3)

11. Are you willing to give up some short-terms goals for a long-term success? (5)

12. Is your family willing to sacrifice in the short term for a long-term success? (5)

13. Is your spouse in sync with your goals and aspirations? (6)

If your "Yes" answers added up to 23 or more, you may be prepared to examine an alternative future.

For Everyone: From a Very Personal Perspective, Is Your Ego a Delicate Thing?

(The numbers in parentheses represent the number of points for the answer to the question.)

1. Are you able to accept criticism from others? (3)
2. Are you capable of delegating responsibility? (3)
3. Can you live with the mistakes of others? (3)
4. Are you willing to accept responsibility for your mistakes? (4)
5. Do you get along with your peers in the workplace? (4)
6. Do you get along with your superiors in the workplace? (4)
7. Do you get along with your subordinates in the workplace? (5)
8. Have you ever been disciplined for any reason as an employee? (2)
9. Are you gullible? (2)
10. Are you an easy mark for a salesperson? (2)
11. Is your marriage strong enough to sustain some frustrating times? (4)
12. Do you mind menial tasks like sweeping the floor or washing the dishes? (4)
13. Are you willing to get your hands dirty? (4)
14. Have you ever served in the military? (4)

If your "Yes" answers added up to 30 or more, you can probably handle most aspects of entrepreneurship.

For Everyone: From a Business Perspective, Have You Ever Examined the Marketplace?

(The numbers in parentheses represent the number of points for the answer to the question.)

1. Have you ever done any research work in business or in school? (4)
2. Have you ever regularly read trade journals in your trade or industry? (4)
3. Do you know how to do a comparative analysis? (4)
4. Have you ever read a disclosure document for the purpose of purchasing corporate shares or a franchise? (2)
5. Have you ever dealt with a lawyer, an accountant, a business broker, a banker, a business consultant? (4)
6. Have you ever done a marketing survey? (3)
7. Have you ever prepared a business plan? (3)
8. Have you ever filled out a resume or a job application? (3)
9. Have you ever applied for a job? (3)
10. Have you ever applied for a loan? (3)

If your "Yes" answers added up to 15 or more, you've got a good start on examining a new future.

How Much Money Do You Have Available for Investment?

The answer to this question depends on the following:

- How much money do you have in liquid assets and cash?
- How much money do you need for personal or family maintenance before you can depend on the profits from the business?
- How much money do you need for working capital if your initial break-even time period does not prove to be accurate?
- How quickly can your other assets be converted to cash?
- How much of a penalty will you have to pay for the privilege of this conversion?
- What effect will this conversion have on your short- and long-term goals?

These questions require a simple "life equation" that must be carefully analyzed with some reasonable objectivity. We suggest discussing these issues with your professional.

Experiential Financial Obligations: Have You Ever Made a Monthly Payment on an Obligation?

(The numbers in parentheses represent the number of points for the answer to the question.)

1. Have you ever paid a home mortgage? (3)
2. Have you ever paid for a car on a time payment plan? (4)
3. Have you ever bought major household appliances on a time payment plan? (5)
4. Have you found it possible to fit such a payment schedule into your monthly budget? (3)
5. Are you prepared to take on the responsibility for this kind of monthly program? (4)

If your "Yes" answers added up to 8, you understand one of the most important elements of owning and operating your own business.

Examining the Priorities: Are You Prepared to Put Your Activity on Your Highest Priority Level?

(The numbers in parentheses represent the number of points for the answer to the question.)

1. Have you discussed this with your spouse? (5)
2. Have you discussed this with your children? (5)
3. Are you prepared to subordinate the emotional needs of your family to that of your business on those occasions when the business demands your time and energy? (5)

Your "Yes" answers need to add up to 15 if you have children. Your "Yes" answers need to add up to 10 if you don't have children.

Are You Ready to Llearn and Delegate? Are You Prepared to Accept Responsibility for Aspects of Business About Which You Have Either Llimited or No Knowledge or Experience?

(The numbers in parentheses represent the number of points for the answer to the question.)

1. Are you prepared to spend the time to learn how to do these things or, at least, to learn enough about them to supervise others? (5)
2. Are you prepared to leave the responsibility to others for those things you are incapable of or ill prepared to handle? (5)

Your "Yes" answers need to add up to 10 to have any comfort in going forward in a new adventure.

Are You Really Ready to "Run over the Hot Coals?"

Have you completely and objectively examined your background, experience, and inclinations with respect to this new business venture? Are you excited, or are you dismayed at the thought of:

- Dealing with retail customers?
- Handling bookkeeping and basic accounting procedures?
- Maintaining inventory and an appropriate ordering system?
- Creating advertising concepts and campaigns?
- Studying a new industry?
- Dealing with employees and employee problems?
- Handling cash at a counter?
- Maintaining strict hygiene discipline?
- Doing outside sales calls?
- Doing cold calls?
- Doing telephone solicitations?

You need to be excited about more of the questions than dismayed in order to understand the focus necessary to be an entrepreneur.

Have You Examined the Harsh Realities of Ownership?

Are you looking at a business because it looks like fun or because it looks like it would make a lot of money?

- Can you afford to buy a business and treat it like a hobby?
- Can you afford to buy a business that generates less money than you or your family needs to live on?
- Have you got either an auxiliary income or a deep reservoir of savings in case the business is something less than anticipated?
- Are you sure you have done enough homework to ensure that the dollars you see are the dollars you'll get?

You need three "Yes" answers here to have a realistic perspective on the problems of owning your own business.

Have You Analyzed the Practical Aspects of Your New Environment?

If you are moving to a new community or a new climate, have you considered the following:

- Have you examined what all four seasons are like?
- Have you looked for a church or social group with which you will have something in common?
- Have you examined the price of housing (rental or purchase) and determined that you can afford it?
- Have you examined the school system to ensure that it satisfies the needs of the family and its growth potential?

You need to answer all four questions with "Yes"—if you can't, you're not ready to move.

What Do You Really Know About the Business?

Have you examined the industry you are entering?

- Does the industry have a future?

- Does your industry (and your business) maintain state-of-the-art products and services?
- Are you sure that the marketplace is not saturated?
- Have you asked a person who owns one like it?
- Do you know the level of responsibility you will be taking on?
- Are you totally prepared for the realities of the business?
- Do you know what comprise the aggravations and the frustrations of the business?

You need to answer all seven questions with a "Yes." Or, do more homework!

Getting Closer to the Truth: A Real Comparative Analysis

Have you examined your personal finances in order to be sure of the following:

- Do you have enough money to keep the business going in the event that it brings in less cash (or even a great deal less cash) than you anticipated?
- Do you have a reservoir of dollars that you can draw upon if the business continues to be disappointing for an extended period of time?
- Will these dollars (to help the business survive) be taken away from the needs of your personal living expenses?
- Have you analyzed just how much money you will need to properly support the family during the early, and possibly unprofitable, period of the business?
- Have you discussed this with other responsible family members?
- Have you anticipated some of the extraordinary expenses that the family may need to accommodate during the early days of your new business activity?
- Do you realize that you can see a clearer picture of the cash flow and profit of a business that is already in existence than you can conjecture about a business that has not yet opened?
- Do you need to feel comfortable about cash flow in order to properly function in your new role as an entrepreneur?

- Have you ever been in the position of entrepreneur before this venture?
- Have you spoken to others who have had the experience of this kind of venture?
- Do you feel that you have as much ability and confidence in your ability as they have?

If you are contemplating the purchase of a franchise:

- Have you asked the franchisor about these subjects?
- Have you asked other franchisees about these subjects?

If you have more than three "No's" to these questions, you should do a reappraisal of your finances, or do more homework.

Examining What Competition Is All About

Do you understand the nature of the competition in your business?

- Have you ever been in a competitive situation before, even in the corporate world?
- Were you able to cope with the disappointment of losing to a competitor?
- Were you able to bounce back and continue to function well after such a disappointment?
- Were you able to objectively analyze the reason for having lost to your competitor?
- Were you able to correct the elements that were noted as the cause of the loss?
- Do you have the ability to learn from your mistakes?
- Do you have the ability to absorb and utilize that learning to be more effective next time?
- Do you understand the nature of healthy competition?
- Do you believe that it can be to your advantage?
- Have you found it comfortable to spend time, on a business level, with your competition?
- Have you found it uncomfortable to spend time, on a personal level, with your competition?

- Have you ever tried to work out a mutually advantageous arrangement with your competition?
- Do you think such an arrangement can be helpful in the right circumstances?

If you are contemplating the purchase of a franchise:

- Have you asked the franchisor about these subjects?
- Have you asked other franchisees about these subjects?

If you have more than three "No's," you should devote some time to the study of competition in the marketplace.

What Kind of an Entrepreneur Are You?

- Are you interested in taking a risk for a high reward, or are you more interested in getting a good day's pay for an honest day's labor?
- Does your background suggest that you have preferred one direction or the other with regard to the previous question?
- If you have taken the conservative road before, has this been a satisfactory one for your family?
- If you were to choose to be less conservative in the future, would your financial portfolio really allow you to take that road?
- Would your family be able to maintain their style of living in the event the road turned out to be a rough one?
- Is the family willing to make such an adjustment?
- Have you candidly examined this alternative with the other members of your family?

If you answered "No" to more than one question, you may want to revisit your thinking about becoming an entrepreneur.

Some Specific Business Questions About Leases

Do you understand the reasons for having a particular kind of location in the trade or industry you are entering?

- Have you done a competitive analysis of the location?

- Have you done any market research on the location in terms of your customer base?
- Have you examined the municipal records to ensure that there will be no building or demolition in your immediate neighborhood, if owned by the same landlord?
- Have you examined your lease to ensure that there will be no surprises in the future?
- Does your lease offer protection from a competitor opening in your immediate area?
- Have you sought the advice of a professional with regard to all aspects of your lease?

If you are considering the purchase of a franchise:

- Have you asked the franchisor about these subjects?
- Have you asked other franchisees about these subjects?

You must answer all these questions in the affirmative. If you can't, you are not ready to sign a lease.

Some Additional Business Questions

On whose information have you relied to make your final judgment?

- If you are considering a franchise, have you sought information from sources other than the franchisor?
- Have you sought the advice of professionals in each field that is appropriate: an accountant for financial, a lawyer for legal, a marketing person for the marketplace?
- Have you sought information from competitors and vendors in the same business?
- Have you sought information from independents as well as franchisees of other franchises in the same trade or industry?
- Have you examined and compared the numbers with any vendors in the industry?
- Have you inquired of the vendors about the state-of-the-art-equipment and supplies?

- Have you read any trade journals about the business you are about to enter?
- Have you done an analysis of the future of the industry?
- Are you satisfied that your personality and experience is compatible with the requirements of the business you are examining?
- Have you examined other businesses to ensure that you are taking the best advantage of your personal and business assets?

If you can't say "Yes" to most of these questions, you are not yet ready to take on the responsibilities of a new business.

The above questions represent the beginning of your personal exercise. No single section is definitive. Don't be afraid to seek professional advice. The small dollars spent early on will save many big dollars and a multitude of disappointments later in the game. Whatever you do, be honest with yourself!

CHAPTER 2

Limited Liability Protection

Limited liability protection is a legal concept that essentially separates the assets of a business from the personal assets of the owners of the business, thereby insulating personal assets from the debts and obligations of the business. This is a key issue in determining what form of entity you should choose for your business. The only way to get limited liability is by forming a limited liability entity of some kind, usually a corporation or limited liability company. As you may know, there is no distinction between the sole proprietor or general partners and the business itself, meaning the proprietor or general partners are personally responsible for the debts and obligations of the business. When a limited liability entity of some kind is formed there is a clear distinction between the business and the owners of the business, and thus the personal assets of the owners and the business assets are kept separate. Limited liability protection is the number one reason for forming a corporation or a limited liability company. While tax issues and business image are also important, often a close second or third in the decision-making process, it is this limited liability protection that is paramount when choosing an entity.

What Is Limited Liability?

Generally, what is meant by limited liability is that the owners are liable only for what they have contributed or put into the business. For example, if you started a catering business and put $30,000 into the business to purchase the equipment and tools you would need to run the business, under the concept of limited liability protection, your liability would be limited to $30,000 even if you caused the entire guest list to the Smith/Jones wedding to get food poisoning. Keep in mind that as the business grows the business assets always remain at risk for the debts, obligations, and judgments of the business. The only way to protect the business assets of any business is through insurance, and we all know that insurance premiums keep going up, so this can be costly. There is a difficulty, moreover, in determining how much insurance to get. Should you get enough insurance just to cover your personal assets, or should you be looking more at compensating for the potential harm your business could cause?

While forming a limited liability entity involves a cost, it can be a relatively inexpensive way to protect your personal assets. And you can deduct the cost of incorporation on your taxes as a business deduction. Conventional wisdom recommends a combination of limited liability protection (forming a corporation or an LLC) and insurance. This can provide two levels of protection. It is also important to note that business owners can never limit their liability for negligence. This is another reason why insurance can come in handy even for a limited liability entity. When in doubt, protect yourself by forming a limited liability entity and obtaining some insurance. Also be aware that many states have additional liability requirements for licensed professionals such as doctors, lawyers, accountants, architects, and veterinarians.

What You Should Be Asking

When determining whether your business should be incorporated or whether a simpler business form may suffice, there are two specific questions you should be asking. The first one has to do with the protection you feel you need for the assets you own or will own in the future. You should ask, "What do I need to protect?" Really, what you are asking is "do I have assets that I would want to be protected from the debts, obligations, and judgments of the business?" If you own a home or investment portfolio, limited liability should be high on your list of priorities. You might say at this point, "I don't have any assets." One man called his attorney to say, "You have to hurry and make me an S corporation." The attorney asked, "What assets did you want to protect?" After some discussion, it was determined that he owned an old VW Bug and a really nice pair of skis. While this client did not have assets at the time, it was clear that, through the business, it was likely that he would accumulate wealth and assets fairly quickly. So after looking at the tax issues and his plans for the business, the attorney formed a corporation for the client's business. Keep in mind that while you may not have assets today, a judgment once obtained against you can be enforced in practically all jurisdictions for a period of 20 years or more. In other words, you can't run away from it. This fact alone may cause you to look more closely at a limited liability entity.

How Will You Operate Your Business?

The second question is "How risky is the business activity?" Be honest and come up with a worst-case scenario. Determine what could go wrong and how your business might be held responsible for errors, mistakes, and mishaps. Look at how your client or customer could be hurt. The riskier the business the more likely a limited liability entity would be beneficial in protecting your personal assets. If you are making hand-knit sweaters as opposed to opening a restaurant or maintaining computer equipment, the risk would certainly be less problematic. To date, I have not heard of anyone being seriously injured by a hand-knit sweater; however, running a restaurant is a riskier endeavor because it involves food. If you are manufacturing or designing a product, risks are higher than if you are just reselling the product, although the problem of risk is not absent. It is a good idea to confirm that a manufacturer has product liability coverage for the products you are purchasing. The gentleman with the skis was going to be providing management consulting services to his clients, which could involve certain risks. This determination helped make the decision to form a corporation. Along those same lines, another issue to take into consideration when looking at limited liability protection is whether or not you are going to be hiring employees or independent contractors. Having others involved in your business activity can increase your risk of something going wrong. Remember: to a large extent, you can be held responsible for the acts of your employees and contractors. If you are going to have employees or independent contractors working for your business, a review of the risks involved would be appropriate in determining whether or not you need to form a limited liability entity of some kind.

Can You Do It Later?

The question often comes up as to whether a business can start as a sole proprietorship or a general partnership and later change to a limited liability entity of some kind. While this is possible, keep in mind that, during the time that you are a sole proprietor or a partner in a general partnership, your business will not enjoy limited liability protection. Be aware that some licenses, such as sales tax licenses and business registrations, cannot be transferred between a sole proprietorship and a corporation or an LLC. Forming a limited liability company or a corporation later will not protect your personal assets or your business retroactively. Your personal assets will always be at risk for the time you remained a sole proprietorship or general partnership. This option should be chosen only if you determine that the risks involved in your business are minimal and the protection of assets is not an immediate concern.

Limited Liability Can Be Lost

While the concept of limited liability is a strong one in the eyes of the law, it is not a 100-percent guaranty that you would not be held personally responsible for an obligation of the business. A limited liability entity can lose its limited liability protection in two ways. First, some or all of the owners can sign what is called a *personal guaranty*.

This is a document that guarantees the payment of a debt or obligation by the owner even if the business fails. Personal guarantees are common when signing leases, obtaining bank loans, and when purchasing an existing business.

> To help protect yourself when signing any type of contract or agreement, always include the name of the corporation or LLC and your title along with your signature to be clear that you are acting on behalf of the business and not signing personally. This does not apply to the signing of checks.

The second way a limited liability entity can loose its limited liability protection is by having its corporate veil pierced. This means that the owners, managers, officers, or directors could be held personally responsible for the debts and obligations of the business. This is another reason to obtain insurance. For example, a business may want to look into directors and officers liability insurance.

Limited Liability Can Be Lost

1. Co-mingling of funds. This occurs when a business owner mingles corporate money with personal monies. For example, you are accepting payment from a client, so you say to the client, "Just write that check out to me personally rather than to the corporation or company." Operating your business out of a personal bank account can create the same kind of problem. Corporations and LLCs (and general partnerships) are required to have a separate bank account and all funds have to be properly run through the entities' accounts. This is technically not required of a sole proprietorship or a one-member LLC; however, all businesses should have separate bank accounts for the business. It is just good business practice. This does not mean that you cannot purchase something for the business using your personal funds or credit card. It just means that you have to do it properly, such as using written expense reports to reimburse yourself. Make sure there is a good audit trail of what you are doing so that you will always be in the position to explain or defend your actions.

2. Misrepresenting your product or service to your client or customers. This can be especially problematic when it is intentional. On the other hand, even an inadvertent misrepresentation can create liability.

3. Not properly maintaining corporate records. The many examples include: not filing annual corporate reports with the secretary of state, not filing tax returns, and not holding corporate meetings when required. Take the following as a good example. A group of engineers had developed several inventions. These engineers formed a corporation (without the benefit of counsel), obtained patents on those inventions, and then borrowed money from a bank using the patents as collateral. Later, in a bankruptcy case, the engineers accused the bank of using unfair and unethical lending practices. The judge agreed with the engineers and actually referred to the bank as "a very bad bank." Even though the court found that the bank had, in fact, used unfair and unethical lending practices, there was a problem. The engineers had not properly formed or maintained their corporation. They did not have bylaws, did not hold corporate meetings, did not properly elect officers and directors, and did not properly file their taxes. The judge determined that he could not give limited liability protection to the corporation since the corporation had not been maintained as required by law. Therefore the judge ordered that "the very bad bank" got the patents. This cost the engineers millions!

4. Not paying payroll or trust fund taxes. The IRS and state departments of revenue tend to get a little testy about payroll taxes, particularly the trust fund or employee portion of such taxes. If these are not paid, the taxing authority will look for the "responsible person" (basically the person who makes the decision not to cut the check) and that person can be held personally liable for the taxes and their associated penalty and interest. Also, the IRS rules are pretty particular when it comes to qualified pension or retirement plans on behalf of employees.

5. Doing anything illegal can lose you your limited liability protection. So, if you were planning on laundering money or any other such chicanery, forming a corporation or an LLC will not afford you any protection.

This is a partial list. If you "do the right thing," it is unlikely that a court would be inclined to pierce your corporate veil.

Judges, Customer Service, and Human Nature

The only person who can pierce your corporate veil is a judge. Therefore, the best advice is, don't find yourself in a courtroom and you should never be in a position to have your corporate veil pierced. This leads into the customer service category. If you have an unhappy or unsatisfied client or customer, it would behoove you to fix the problem (even if it costs you) or, if that is not possible, give them their money back. Mistakes happen even to the most careful entrepreneur. Generally, people do not sue those who have worked hard to correct a problem or those who have made a refund or even a partial refund. Even if your client or customer is being a bit ridiculous, it is best to make them happy or, in some cases, just satisfy them enough to avoid legal action. Remember: if someone likes what you do for them, they will tell two people and, if they don't like what you have done for them, they will tell ten people. That is human nature.

If it is at all possible, fix the problem—just do it. For example, one lawyer had completed an entire estate plan for her client's elderly mother. The client subsequently informed the attorney that she was talking with her neighbor who worked at a local title company and that the title company could have done the same thing for her for $8. To begin with, title companies should not be preparing wills, medical directives, or living wills for their clients, let alone for $8. While a title company may have a standard power of attorney form for real estate transactions, anything more than that would likely constitute the unauthorized practice of law. However, since the attorney had not been in practice for a long time, she made a full refund to the client, not because the client was right, but because the attorney did not want the client out there bad-mouthing her services or business. What is it they say about celebrities, that, "even bad press is good"? This does not apply to businesses, particularly new businesses.

Once you have determined whether limited liability is desirable for your business, you can check off certain entities from your list of choices. The sole proprietorships and general partnerships do not provide the business owners with limited liability protection. They should not be considered as options for a business that has risks associated with it or a situation where the business owner has personal assets that need to be protected. Starting with this issue can actually simplify your choice of entity analysis. Again, when in doubt, protect yourself and your assets. And, don't forget: a little insurance can go a long way.

Insurance and the Duty to Defend

When obtaining insurance, it is wise to make sure the policy includes the duty to defend. This means that the insurance company will provide the business with a defense attorney to represent it if a legal action is brought against the business. While this may increase your premiums, it can save a business owner thousands of dollars. And isn't that what you get insurance for?

Bonded or Insured

You have seen the businesses that advertise that they are bonded or insured, or both. The terms "bonded" and "insured" are often misunderstood. Both involve protection against financial risk or loss, and in some instances there may be little difference between the two. However, bonding generally refers to a type of surety guarantee that a project or job will be financially covered if performance is not complete, if work is unsatisfactory, or if there are cost overruns or damage to a customer's property. Insurance, on the other hand, generally refers to a set amount of financial coverage for risk to a tangible item, such as a building, vehicle, inventory, or shipment of goods. Some types of insurance, such as errors and omissions coverage (E&O) or product liability insurance, are more like bonds, because they provide financial protection for acts performed or not performed, in contrast to protection for risks to a tangible item. When considering becoming bonded, talk with your bonding company, insurance agent, or other financial advisers about any potential overlap of protection. There's no need to become bonded if you're already adequately covered by insurance.

The Personal Guaranty

Personal guarantees are being used more and more these days. Generally, when you sign a personal guaranty you are agreeing to personally complete the transaction or pay the obligation in the event the business fails to. Make sure you are clear on whether you have made a personal guaranty, because it will make a big difference to your personal financial position if the business cannot pay its debts or obligations. Also, be aware that some states make the personal guaranty subject to the Statute of Frauds, which requires that such an agreement is only enforceable if it is in writing and signed by the guarantor.

Review Questions

1. Do you currently have personal assets (or plan to have assets in the future) that will need to be protected?
2. How risky is the business activity?
3. How could my client or customer be hurt?
4. Are you going to hire employees to perform services or are you going to use independent contractors?
5. What kind of insurance is available for your business activity?
6. Do you know why your corporate signature is different from your personal signature?
7. Do you know what a personal guaranty is?
8. Why is it best to stay out of the courtroom?

CHAPTER 3

Sole Proprietorships, General Partnerships, and Limited Partnerships

Sole Proprietorships

The sole proprietorship is the most common and simplest form of business. It is defined as one person in business for profit. There is no distinction between the sole proprietor and the business itself, which means that the personal assets of the sole proprietor are at risk for the debts, obligations, and judgments of the business. Thus, the sole proprietor does not have limited liability protection. While a sole proprietorship is easier and simpler, it is also riskier. The sole proprietor is in complete control of the business and gets to make all the decisions. The sole proprietorship is freely transferable, which means that it can be sold. However, some, sole proprietorships are harder to sell than others. Often, the proprietor is the business, particularly in small service-based businesses. As a practical matter, it may be difficult to find a willing buyer, since transferring client loyalty is often problematic. If the sole proprietor passes away, the business is automatically dissolved. Of course, its assets may be sold, thereby creating a new business for the purchaser.

Federal Employer Identification Number and Identity Theft

If you are operating a sole proprietorship under any name other than your legal name you will need to file for a trade name. While each state is different, the trade name is usually filed with the department of revenue or secretary of state. This is also where you would obtain a state sales tax license and a state wage-withholding license if your sole proprietorship is going to have employees or independent contractors. Yes, a sole proprietorship *can* have employees and independent contractors. If a sole proprietorship is going to have employees or independent contractors, the business is required to obtain a federal employer identification number (FEIN) from the Internal Revenue Service. *See Chapter 6 for more information on federal employer identification numbers.* Technically, a sole proprietor may operate his or her business using his or her own social security number if they are not going to have any employees or independent contractors. However, it is wise for all sole proprietors to get a federal employer identification number regardless of whether or not they are going to have employees or independent contractors. This allows them to maintain the security of their Social Security number. With identity theft a growing concern, using the federal employer identification number may better protect your personal credit. Often clients, vendors, government agencies, and other businesses will need some sort of tax identification number from your business. It's better to give them access to a FEIN for the business than a Social Security number, which is personal. Finally, the sole proprietor is likely to have to register their business with the city or county, and the business may need to obtain a separate city sales tax license with the city where the principle place of business is located. *See Chapter 7 on sales tax for more details.*

The Government As Your "Partner"

The sole proprietorship reports its income for tax purposes by filing a Schedule C, which is an additional schedule attached to their 1040 Individual Income Tax Return. Thus, the sole proprietorship's taxes are due on April 15 of each year. This return can be automatically extended for six months by filing an extension (IRS Form 4868) on or before April 15. Please note that many states require an additional extension form if you will owe tax. The Schedule C looks like any other income statement, sometimes referred to as a profit and loss statement. The basic equation is gross revenue minus cost of goods sold (if you have it) minus operating expenses equals net profit. On the net profit, the business owner will pay income tax at their personal income tax rate. In addition to income tax, if net profits are over $400, the business owner will pay 15.3% self-employment tax on the net profits of the business each year. The self-employment tax covers FICA, which is Social Security taxes (12.4%) and Medicare taxes (2.9%). As you probably know, when you are an employee, your employer pays one-half of the FICA (7.65%) and the employee pays one-half (7.65%). As a self-employed individual, you pay the whole thing. This can be a chunk of change and is often the most painful check to write.

Each year, the sole proprietorship is deemed to take all the profits out of the business; thus, the only way to keep money in the business is to purchase assets, inventory, or supplies. In some cases, the business may prepay expenses as a way to increase tax deductions and reduce tax liability. Taxes are paid in through the quarterly estimated tax payment system. For each calendar quarter, the sole proprietor is required to estimate the net profits of the business and pay to the IRS any income tax and self-employment tax estimated to be due. Because the self-employment tax is a federal tax, estimated income taxes should only be paid to the state on a quarterly basis. If the state where you operate your business does not have an income tax, then state estimated tax payments need not be made. The estimated tax payment system is not optional. It is a mandatory system and the sole proprietor can incur penalties for not properly making estimated tax payments to either the federal or the state systems. Keep in mind, however, if you have no profit, then you owe no tax, as is often the case with a new business. The estimated tax payment system is actually useful to the business owner for cash flow purposes because it requires the business owner to pay taxes throughout the year rather than discovering on April 15 that a large amount of tax is due. While it may seem obvious, it is easier to pay $3,000 each quarter than to pay the entire $12,000 in April.

Cash vs. Accrual, Calendar vs. Fiscal

The sole proprietorship generally will be considered a cash-basis taxpayer as opposed to an accrual-basis taxpayer. Cash-basis taxpayers report income when they receive it, while accrual-basis taxpayers will report income when earned, even if they have not received it. The business will be a calendar-year taxpayer, which means that the business tax year begins on January 1 and ends on December 31, rather than a fiscal tax year taxpayer, which means that the tax year begins and ends on any day of the year other than January 1 and December 31, respectively. For a sole proprietorship to be a fiscal year taxpayer, it must get permission from the IRS. Generally, this is done for certain types of businesses, such as seasonal businesses. The cash basis and calendar year are easier for the sole proprietor to keep track of and to remember deadlines.

It All Belongs to You ... the Good and the Bad

Ease of formation is the big advantage of the sole proprietorship. Because the sole proprietorship is easy to form (just an FEIN and state or city registration, if required), the costs related to forming the business are relatively low. Just set up your office, intend on making a profit, and you're good to go. Another advantage to the sole proprietorship is that the owner has complete control over the business and is able to make all the decisions related to the business. The biggest disadvantage to a sole proprietorship is the lack of limited liability protection. Remember: your personal assets are at risk if anything goes wrong in the business, and you are personally responsible for the debts and obligations of the business. You should look at the assets you would like to protect and how risky the business activity can be for you, your customers or clients, and your vendors before you make this decision.

Some Good Things to Keep in Mind

Bob has a sole proprietorship, and his business is doing so well that he hires Kim. Kim, it turns out, is a fabulous employee, and Bob decides that he is going to sell 25 percent of the business to Kim to keep her involved in the business. Once Kim agrees and purchases her 25 percent, Bob and Kim have just formed a general partnership by operation of law. Definition: two or more people in business for profit. Be aware that husbands and wives are considered two people, and, if they are in business together and they have not formed any other type of entity, they will be considered a general partnership. Like the sole proprietor, general partners do not have limited liability protection. In fact, they are jointly and severally liable for the debts, obligations, and judgments of the business. Joint and several liability means that a creditor may collect all or part of the debt from any of the partners. And it gets worse. General partners are agents of the partnership with equal rights to be involved in the management of the partnership. Thus, they can legally bind one another without consent. This means that Kim could go out and obligate the general partnership for $100,000 without Bob knowing anything about it and—guess who is liable for the obligation? Bob is and Kim is, but Bob is probably the deeper pocket, and the creditor could collect the whole amount from him. In addition, each partner is liable for the wrongful acts of the other partners. While each partner owes a fiduciary responsibility to the other partners as a matter of law, it can be difficult to prove that a partner acted in bad faith or ignored this responsibility. As a result, the general partnership is not recommended. There are other entities better suited for co-ownership that afford each owner limited liability protection and do not allow owners to bind one another without consent. In the interest of being thorough, a description of the attributes of a general partnership follows, but be clear that it is not recommended that you form a general partnership.

General Partnerships

Unlike the sole proprietorship, the general partnership can be owned by individuals, corporations, trusts, estates, or LLCs. However, partners are typically individuals. Technically, the partnership terminates upon the death, disability, withdrawal, or addition of a partner. However, the partners can provide for continuation of the partnership under a partnership agreement. While a general partnership is not required by law to have a partnership agreement, it is a very good idea. The partnership agreement, at a minimum, will dictate the general rules of the partnership and how profits and losses are to be shared by the partners. Most partnership agreements will provide for continuation of the partnership and issues of ownership transfer, such as a requirement that, to sell an interest in the partnership, there must be unanimous consent of all existing partners. There is no restriction on the number of partners. However, the ownership interest of the general partnership will always equal 100%. For example, if you have four partners each owning 25 percent and one partner wants to reduce her ownership interest by 15 percent, then either the existing partners or a new partner must purchase the 15 percent interest from the partner who is reducing her share. Thus, any money paid for such an interest is paid to the partner, not the partnership itself. Because the partnership assets are held as tenancy in partnership, as opposed to tenancy in common or joint tenancy (see below for definition of these legal concepts), an individual partner cannot transfer specific assets or an undivided interest in the assets. Theoretically, a partnership interest is transferable; however, the new owner of the partnership interest does not necessarily become a partner entitled to management and control. He or she is simply entitled to the profits the interest would accrue and a proportionate share of assets upon dissolution. Interestingly, this new partner is also vulnerable to partnership obligations just as any other partner referenced above in the Bob and Kim story.

The Tax Picture

The general partnership must file a partnership tax return, usually federal (Form 1065) and state for the business, which is due on or before April 15 of each year. The return can be extended for six months by filing an extension (IRS Form 7004), postmarked on or before the due date. Generally, the general partnership is a cash-basis and calendar taxpayer. The partnership rules can be quite complex. Rather than confuse you with complex issues that may or may not apply to you, it is more important that you understand the basic aspects of the partnership rules. The partnership is what is called a pass through entity. This means that the entity itself does not pay income and self-employment tax. Income taxes and self-employment tax on the business income is required to be paid by the individual partner. The partnership return is informational only. From the partnership return, a K-1 is generated for each partner. The K-1 contains each partner's share of income and deductions. Each partner then places the information from their K-1 on their individual income tax return. For those who care to know, the K-1 information appears on Schedule E of the 1040 Individual Tax Return. It is also important to note that partnerships may make special allocations or guaranteed payments in allocating income and deductions in order to take full advantage of each partner's income tax rates.

Other Filings for the General Partnership

A general partnership will usually need to operate under a trade name, which will need to be registered with the state. This registration will likely need to be filed with either the state department of revenue or secretary of state. Depending on the state, city, and county rules, the business may need sales tax licenses at the state and city level. A federal employer identification number is required for all partnerships regardless of whether they will have employees or independent contractors. A state wage withholding license will be necessary if the partnership is going to have employees. Creating a general partnership can be less expensive than forming a corporation; however, the cost of creating a comprehensive partnership agreement may increase the cost significantly.

The Positives and the Negatives

Remember: the general partnership is not recommended. To review, the disadvantages of the general partnership are many and include:

1. Lack of limited liability protection for the debts and obligations of the business

2. Liability for another partner's wrongdoing
3. Ability of a partner to legally bind the other partners without consent
4. Restrictions on the transferability of partnership interests
5. Difficulty of resolving disputes between or among partners
6. Difficulty of attracting outside investors

The advantages to the general partnership are few but, to be fair, should be mentioned here:

1. Simplicity of formation
2. Relatively low costs for formation
3. Ability to pool resources

Clearly, the disadvantages of the general partnership outweigh the advantages. When choosing an entity, even if a partnership would be possible, the business owners should look seriously at creating a limited liability entity of some kind.

Limited Partnerships

Another entity option is the limited partnership. The limited partnership combines some characteristics of a general partnership with some of the characteristics of a corporation. Generally, the limited partnership must have one or more general partners who are involved in the day-to-day operations and management of the business and one or more limited partners who have limited liability and limited participation in management. The purpose of the limited partnership is to allow one or more individuals (or entities) to invest in the business without incurring the unlimited liability of the general partner(s). However, the limited liability protection afforded the limited partner can be lost if the limited partner holds himself out as a general partner, or if the limited partner participates in the management of the business. Because of the unlimited liability of the general partner in a limited partnership, the same concerns apply here as those for the general partnership. Like the general partnership, the limited partnership should also have a partnership agreement. Most states will require that the limited partnership be registered with the state, usually the secretary of state. Unlike the general partnership, the withdrawal of a general partner in a limited partnership does not cause the dissolution of the partnership as long as another general partner remains or as long as obtaining a new general partner is provided for in the partnership agreement.

The Passive Investor

The role of the limited partner in a Limited Partnership is that of a passive investor. Limited partners have the right to inspect the books or have an accounting of the partnership affairs, and they usually have the right to be informed about all matters concerning the business. However, the management decisions and their level of participation in the activities of the limited partnership will generally be dictated by state statute. The withdrawal of a limited partner does not affect the continuation of the business or dissolve the limited partnership. Unless otherwise provided in the partnership agreement, the interest of either the limited or general partners is freely transferable. Such a transfer of limited partnership interests may be required to be reported to the state and therefore may be somewhat cumbersome. As with any entity that enjoys limited liability protection, the corporate veil may be pierced if the proper formalities and the duties of the limited partnership are not maintained. This can expose limited partners to the *unlimited liability* suffered by general partners.

The Tax Consequences

For the most part, limited partnerships are pass-through entities and are treated like general partnerships for tax purposes. A limited partnership needs to be particularly careful that it does not act too much like a corporation, or the IRS could treat the limited partnership as a corporation, which could result in higher taxes. Income tax is paid at the individual partner level rather than at the entity level. Limited partners are subject to self-employment tax only on guaranteed payments, such as salary and professional fees for services rendered to the limited partnership by the limited partner. The limited partnership is also generally considered a cash-basis and calendar-year taxpayer.

Additional Consequences

There may be restrictions on the use of limited partners' names in the name of the Limited Partnership itself. The limited partnership must apply for a federal employer identification number regardless of whether or not it is going to have employees or independent contractors. If employees or independent contractors are hired, the limited partnership is likely to need a state wage withholding license. Sales tax licenses and business registrations may be required at the state, city, or county levels. Again, see the chapter on sales tax for details.

The advantage of the limited partnership is clearly the limited liability protection afforded the limited partners; however, this advantage is really only an advantage over general partnerships. The main disadvantage remains the lack of limited liability protection for the general partner of the limited partnership. As with the sole proprietorship and the general partnership, it is recommended that you take a serious look at entities that provide limited liability protection to all of the owners before adopting the limited partnership structure.

Limited Liability Partnerships (LLPs)

Another type of partnership is the limited liability partnership (LLP). The LLP is a partnership that is statutorily created by the state and that generally gives limited liability to all partners for some of the debt and obligations of the partnership. This entity is often used for large professional firms such as accounting, law, and architectural firms, where the professionals act independently for each of their clients. However, the extent to which the LLP gives limited liability to each partner and restrictions on the type of business (accountants and attorneys only or some similar restriction) vary from state to state. For example, some states limit liability for debts and malpractice-type claims while affording no protection for non-malpractice or tort liabilities. All LLP statutes provide that the LLP partner is personally liable for his or her own negligence or wrongdoing. In addition, capital contribution requirements, insurance requirements, and cash reserve requirements vary from statute to statute. Most of the LLP statutes impose liability for the wrongful acts and misconduct of any person under the "direct supervision and control" of the LLP partners. Currently, the LLP is not recognized in all fifty states, but the eventual enactment in all fifty states is anticipated. Because LLPs are relatively new entities, there are many issues that will be decided or clarified by the courts, and this fact alone may leave a LLP partner at risk. Many of the states that have enacted LLP statutes allow that a business operating as a general partnership may become an LLP by filing the appropriate registration with the state (usually the secretary of state) and the LLP is not considered to be a *new* entity, a concept unique to the LLP. For tax purposes, the LLP is treated like a partnership. Income tax and self-employment tax is owed by each partner for their share of the net profits of the business. The LLP may be a disadvantage for a new business, as there may be better entity choices available for a new business. But this disadvantage may be less of an issue for an existing general partnership that is considering changing to an LLP. Some limited liability is better than none.

In Conclusion

The entities described above have in common either the lack of or a limitation on the limited liability protection afforded their owners, not to mention the uncertainty currently surrounding some of the newer types of partnerships (LLPs and LLLPs). Please reserve your decision on the type of entity that would suit your business until you have read the next chapter, which describes the characteristics and attributes of the limited liability company, S corporation, and C corporation. Surprisingly enough, a review of these entities may simplify your decision rather than make it more complicated.

Local Assistance

Small Business Development Centers and other local resources for new and existing businesses may be available in your area. These can often provide free counseling services and low-cost seminars on a variety of topics. Check with your local chambers of commerce or colleges and universities for available programs.

Separate Bank Accounts

For the sole proprietor and partner signing anything on behalf of your business, this means you are signing personally and will have personal responsibility for the debt or obligation. All businesses should maintain separate bank accounts. The sole proprietorship will generally open what is called a DBA (doing business as) account, which will allow it to keep separate bank records for the business and accept payments under their DBA or trade name. Generally banks have a minimum deposit requirement for opening a business account and they will request a copy of your trade name registration. The bank will also likely run a credit check on the owner(s) of the business to open the account.

Property Ownership

The term *tenants in common* refers to two or owners who each own a portion of an undivided estate or property. If one owner dies, the other owners do not automatically take the entire estate. Whoever is designated in the owner's will inherits their individual share of the property. *Joint tenants* or *joint tenancy* refers to ownership where when one person dies, the ownership passes to the survivors. This is common among married individuals or related parties.

Review Questions

1. Do you need limited liability protection for yourself or your business?
2. Do you know that a sole proprietorship affords you no liability protection?
3. How many owners will be involved in the business?
4. Do you know that you could be responsible for the financial foibles of your partners?
5. Have you determined who will manage the business operations?
6. Do you know that the general partner in a limited partnership is liable for all debts of the business?
7. Will all owners generally work with all clients or customers?
8. Do you know that active participation by a limited partner could create liability for that partner?

9. Who will manage the business?
10. Do you know how to protect yourself from identity theft?
11. Will the business be hiring employees or independent contractors?
12. Do you understand joint and several liability?
13. Do you know that an LLP is created generally for professional partnerships?
14. Does your state have a limited liability partnership (LLP) statute?
15. Does your state allow for limited liability limited partnership (LLLP)?
16. Do you know the differences between cash and accrual? Do you know the differences between calendar- and fiscal-year taxpayers?
17. Do you know how to limit the involvement of any investors in the day-to-day operations of a limited partnership?
18. Do you know the positive and negative aspects of a general partnership?
19. Do you know the other owners of the business well?
20. Have you worked with the other owners of the business in a professional or industry setting?
21. Do you know what it means to "pierce the corporate veil"?
22. Is your business a general partnership?

CHAPTER 4

Limited Liability Entities:
Limited Liability Companies, S Corporations, and C Corporations

All legal entities described in this chapter afford their owners limited liability protection. You will recall that this is the legal concept that limits the liability of the owners of a business to the value of their investment in the business. It is important to note that the assets of the business itself are always at risk for the debts, obligations, and judgments incurred. Limited liability protection is a way of separating and insulating the business owner's personal assets.

Capital Contributions

When forming a limited liability entity, whether it is a limited liability company or a corporation, the owners do not get their ownership interest for free. LLC members and corporate shareholders must contribute something to the entity in exchange for their ownership interest in the entity. The contribution can be cash, equipment, furniture, fixtures, inventory, supplies, or other tangible assets. The assets are simply transferred to the entity in exchange for the ownership interest. This transaction is called a 351 transfer (Internal Revenue Code §351), and it is a nontaxable event. Services can also be given in exchange for corporate stock or a membership interest; however, if services are contributed it is a taxable event. Payroll taxes on the value of the services must be paid. Because of the taxable nature of this transaction, if at all possible, services should not be used as a capital contribution. See your accounting professional to ensure that such a situation is handled properly.

Creating an Equality

All that you need to do is make a list of assets that you intend to contribute to the business and assign a fair market value to the assets. If you have owned the asset for a while, keep in mind that the fair market value may not be what you paid for it. Each owner should be making a capital contribution that matches their proportionate share of the ownership in the business. For example, if Karen and Joe want to form a corporation and be 50/50 owners, they should each make the same capital contribution. They could each contribute $1,000 in cash, or Karen could contribute a computer, a chair, a desk, and a file cabinet worth $2,500 and Joe could contribute $1,500 in cash, a printer, a scanner, and a fax machine valued at $1,000. In some circumstances, potential business owners may find that one or more of them have more cash or equipment to start the business and one or more may have little cash. As another example, Karen may have $18,000 in cash and assets to contribute while Joe has only $2,000. In this situation, Karen could contribute her $18,000 and get a 90 percent ownership interest and Joe could contribute his $2,000 in exchange for a 10 percent interest. However, if Karen and Joe wanted to be 50/50 owners in the business, it would seem unfair for Karen contribute $18,000 for 50 percent of the business while Joe contributed $2,000 for his 50 percent ownership interest. One way to resolve this issue would be for both Karen and Joe to contribute $2,000 for a 50% interest and then Karen could loan the business an additional $16,000. It is advisable that your ownership interest in the corporation or the LLC have *economic reality*. As a matter of fact, this is required by the IRS for LLCs. Corporations do not technically have to meet this "economic reality" requirement; however, it makes sense to have that economic reality to avoid potential problems between owners in the future.

A Working Capital Reservoir

There is no specific dollar amount required for a capital contribution. There is no rule that says you must put in a specific amount to form a corporation or an LLC. That being said, you will need to properly capitalize your business. For instance, you will need more to start a manufacturing business then you would need to start a small consulting business. Not properly capitalizing your business may mean that the business might not succeed. You will need to look at the sales cycle for the business and determine the amount of money you will need to open and operate the business until you can begin generating revenue. Many business advisors recommend that you capitalize your business by having enough cash to cover a 6- to 12-month period of operating expenses. While it is important to be properly prepared, something less may be reasonable for certain types of business, such as service providers or consultants with a short sales cycle. When looking at this issue, it is important to properly plan for costs and to keep your overhead low.

Reinvesting

Be aware that corporate shareholders and LLC members are not entitled to a return of their capital contributions unless and until the business is dissolved and all liabilities are paid. Additional capital contributions may be made at any time after the business is formed. In fact, the owners can make such additional contributions mandatory or optional by agreement. When making additional contributions the owners should be cognizant of the effect such additional contributions may have on their ownership percentages.

The Limited Liability Company

The limited liability company (LLC) is an entity created by state statute that combines aspects of a corporation and a limited partnership. Although some people refer to LLCs as "limited liability *corporations*," the correct terminology is, in fact, a "limited liability *company*." The owners of the LLC are called members. All states permit an LLC to be organized with a single member. The member(s) of the LLC then elect one or more managers to run the day-to-day operations of the business. The member(s) and manager(s) may or may not be the same people. In many states, the LLC may elect to have officers; however, this is not generally required. The most important aspect of the LLC is that every member is afforded limited liability protection.

The Specifics for Tax Purposes

The LLC is a pass-through entity. This means that profits and losses for the business are passed through the entity to each member's individual tax return. Historically, the LLC was required to file a partnership return for income tax purposes (Form 1065). This meant that the LLC filed a partnership return that is informational only. No income tax is paid with the partnership return. A K-1 is generated by the partnership return for each member of the LLC, which shows the individual member's share of the LLC's income and deductions. This K-1 information is then placed on each individual member's personal tax return (Form 1040, Schedule E). Today, the IRS has put in place what is called a "check-the-box regulation," which allows an LLC under certain circumstances to choose how it will be taxed. If an LLC has one member only, it may elect to be treated as a "disregarded entity" for tax purposes. This permits the one-member LLC to file a Schedule C for income tax purposes. You may recall this is what the sole proprietorship files. The election can be made either on Form SS-4 (Application for Employer Identification Number) at the time of formation or by filing Form 8832 (Entity Classification Election) at a later date. The advantage of the "disregarded entity" classification is that it is simpler and, in most cases, the cost of tax preparation will be less than that of a partnership return. Under the "check-the-box regulation," an LLC that has two or more members is still required to file a partnership return unless it elects to be treated as a corporation. Again, this election can either be made when forming the entity on the SS-4 Form (Application for Employer Identification Number) or can be made at a later date by filing Form 8832 (Entity Classification Election). While the LLC may elect to be treated either as an S corporation or a C corporation, it usually elects to be treated as either an S corporation, in which case a Form 2553 (Election for a Small Business Corporation) will also need to be filed. It is important to note that, if an LLC is electing to be treated as a corporation, it must meet certain corporate characteristics. In the case of the S corporation, it must meet all S corporation requirements. See below for details regarding corporate characteristics and S corporation requirements.

Watch for the Pitfall When Converting

When changing the tax classification of your LLC after the entity has been formed, timing may be a factor. For example, Susan can form a one-member LLC (disregarded entity) and later decide that she wants her LLC to be taxed as an S corporation. This can be done at any time but, if it is done in the middle of the year, she will need to file two tax returns: 1) a Schedule C for the time before she makes the S corporation election; and 2) an S corporation return (Form 1120S) for the period after she makes the election. Because this can increase the costs for tax preparation and accounting services, it may be wise to elect S corporation status in timely fashion. In order to make that election for January 1, Susan would have to make her request for the S Corporation election by filing Forms 8832 and 2553 on or before March 15 of the year she wants the election to take effect. Susan could also file the paperwork in one year to take effect on January 1 of the next year if she wants to get a jump on the election. When an LLC is changing from a one-member LLC (disregarded entity) to a two-member LLC (partnership), a Form 8832 (Entity Classification Election) should be filed before the due date of the tax return for the new entity classification. LLCs that are required to file a Schedule C or a partnership return must file their return on or before April 15; while LLCs electing to be treated as a corporation (either C corp. or S corp.) must file their respective return on or before March 15. The corporate and partnership returns may be extended for six months by filing Form 7004 (Application for Automatic 6-Month Extension) on or before the April 15 due date. LLCs that file a Schedule C for tax purposes may also extend for a period of six months by filing Form 4868 (Application for Automatic Extension).

Basic Flexibility of the LLC

The LLC is very flexible in that there are no restrictions on (1) who can become a member of the LLC; and (2) the number of LLC members. LLC members can be individuals, corporations, trusts, estates, partnerships, or other LLCs. This flexibility may make the LLC the right entity for your business, depending on who your owners will be.

The LLC is formed by filing articles of organization with the secretary of state. While this document can be customized for your business, most states have a simple articles of organization form that can be filled out and filed. Using the secretary of state form is a good idea because the state-prepared form contains the minimum information required by your state. Also keep in mind that the information in the articles of organization becomes public record. When possible, it is smart to keep the formation and inner workings of your entity private. Filing fees for the LLC vary from state to state, but research shows them to be between $25 and $600.

All states require the LLC to have a registered agent with a physical street address located in the state of formation. A registered agent is an individual or entity designated by the LLC (or corporation) to accept *service of process* and other official documents on behalf of the LLC (or corporation). Service of process means the delivery of court documents or filings to a party or person having a stake in a particular legal action. You can serve as your own registered agent, but keep in mind that the registered agent should generally be available to accept service or receive documents during standard business hours.

Someone other than you may serve as your registered agent as long as they maintain a street address in the state where your entity has been formed. There are professionals and other businesses (such as attorneys and accountants) that will act as your registered agent if you do not want to or if you are away from your office most days. You will need a professional registered agent if you do not have a physical office in the state where you are forming. Fees for such a service can range from $125 to $350 per year.

The Operating Agreement

The governing document used and required by many states for an LLC is called the *operating agreement*, which provides the rules, rights, duties, and operational procedures for the members and managers of the LLC. While some states do not require an operating agreement, it is wise to have one in place, as it is the primary agreement between or among the members and can help to resolve future issues and dictate important procedures. You should check the requirements of the state where you are forming your LLC. The operating agreement should also include the details of what happens if a member transfers his interest, dies, retires, or becomes disabled, often referred to as *exit strategies*.

Below are some common issues that should be addressed in the operating agreement:

1. Issues relating to any conflicts between the articles of organization and the operating agreement
2. Listing of initial capital contributions and percentage of membership interest for each member
3. Provisions related to additional capital contributions and whether they are mandatory or optional
4. Allocations of profit and losses and maintenance of each member's capital accounts;
5. Issues related to member loans
6. Provisions on how assets may be distributed
7. Rules relating to members: procedures for admission of new members,

voting rights, issues relating to calling meetings of members, member indemnification, use of proxies, and what constitutes a quorum

8. Rules relating to managers: the number and qualifications of managers; general powers, duties, and responsibilities; voting rights; what constitutes a quorum; procedures regarding manager meetings; treatment of conflicts of interest, and indemnification of managers

9. Procedures related to the keeping of the books and records of the LLC: location of books and records, rights of members to review the books; details regarding the keeping of the books, authorization to hire a CPA, whether the entity is a cash-basis taxpayer and calendar-year taxpayer, and a statement as to the type of tax return to be filed for the entity

10. Dissolution-related issues and exit strategies: what constitutes dissolution (e.g., bankruptcy of a member, insolvency of the business); member withdrawal; death, retirement, and expulsion of a member; life insurance for members; continuation of the business

11. Procedures for the sales of membership interests

12. General provisions: modifying the agreement, notice requirements, and governing law

Getting the Money to the Members

The LLC member may or may not materially participate in the day-to-day operations of the LLC. Regardless of participation, the way an LLC member is paid is by taking a member draw for their proportionate share of the profits of the LLC after all other expenses are paid. These draw payments can be made at regular or irregular intervals, but must be made to all members in accordance with their ownership interest. For example, Bob, Tom, and Kim are all members of a small consulting LLC that earns $360,000 in annual revenue and incurs commensurate expenses of $120,000. This would leave the members with $240,000 available as distribution of profit. If they each have a one-third ownership interest in the LLC, then they are each entitled to $80,000 in draws from the LLC for the year. These draw payments are gross payments. There are no taxes withheld from the draw payment on behalf of the member. As a result, each member would then be responsible for paying income tax on the draw at their personal income tax rate. In addition, if the member participates in the operations of the LLC, he or she will owe self-employment tax of 15.3 percent on the amount of draws received throughout the year. Each member will need to make quarterly estimated tax payments to cover the taxes due on their draws. Each year, the members are deemed to take all of the profits from the business; this means that even if they do not take all profits out of the business in the form of a draw, they will still owe the taxes on the profits left in the business accounts based on their percentage of ownership

Registration

In most states, the LLC is not required to have annual meetings of its members, which means the LLC can be slightly less cumbersome than a corporation. A review of the statutes in your state is a good idea. The LLC is generally going to be a cash-basis and calendar-year taxpayer. Registration of your LLC with the state, city, and county in which you operate your business may be necessary. A few states require that the LLC publish in a local newspaper notice of the formation of the LLC. (Some states require that corporations do the same.) You can check with your county clerk and recorder's office to determine if your state has such a requirement. As with other entities your business may need state and city sales tax licenses. The LLC is required to obtain an FEIN (federal employer identification number) regardless of whether it is hiring employees or independent contractors. This is true except when you are operating as a disregarded entity (one-member LLC), although it is recommended that even the one-member LLC obtain an FEIN in order to keep the owner's Social Security number private. (See section on identity theft in Chapter 6.) Some states charge what is often (but not always) called a franchise tax. The franchise tax is an annual tax charged to a corporate entity or LLC for the privilege of doing business in a state. The tax can be based on asset values, number of owners, or authorized shares and, in some cases, it is based on the amount of revenue an entity generates. Check your state department of revenue or secretary of state to determine if your state has such a tax. See Chapter 8 on franchise taxes.

Corporations in General

A corporation is a legal entity that is separate and distinct from its owners and is formed in accordance with state statutes. A corporation generally has the following four corporate characteristics:

1. Continuity of life: the death, disability, or withdrawal of any owner does not cause the dissolution of the business.
2. Centralized management: the corporation has a designated person or group of persons who run the business and make all of the management and business decisions.
3. Limited liability: each owner has limited liability to the extent of their investment in the business.
4. Free transferability: each owner may freely assign his or her beneficial interest in the profits, assets, and control of the business.

The Corporation as a "Person"

The owners of the corporation are usually called *shareholders* or *stockholders*. The shareholders of a corporation have limited liability, which limits their liability to the amount they invested in the corporation. Corporations are generally treated as "artificial persons," as they can own property, incur debts, and sue or be sued. With the exception of the right to vote and the right to the pursuit of happiness, they have the same rights as you under the laws of the United States. The organizational chart of the corporation begins with the shareholders who are the owners. The shareholders elect the board of directors, which then elects the officers who run the day-to-day operations of the business. Most states will specify by statute which officers are mandatory. Today, all states allow a corporation to be formed by one person. That person can be the only shareholder, serve as the only director on the board of directors, and be the president, secretary, and treasurer of the corporation. The corporation is formed by filing articles of incorporation with the secretary of state. Similarly to the LLC, it is a good idea to use your state's preapproved articles of incorporation due to the minimal nature of the disclosure. Filing fees can range between $25 and $600.

Authorized vs. Issued Shares

The articles of incorporation will usually require you to state the number of shares authorized for the corporation. The authorized number of shares is the highest amount of shares that the corporation is authorized to issue. It is a somewhat arbitrary number, because it is the *issued* shares that determine ownership, not the *authorized* shares. A corporation can authorize as little as one share (not recommended, see example below) or millions of shares. Remember, it is the number of issued (not authorized) shares that will determine the ownership percentage of each shareholder. You will want to authorize more shares than you plan to issue in order to leave room for growth.

As an example of what not to do, consider the group of four men who formed a corporation, without the assistance of an attorney, and then authorized one share of stock. When it came time to issue stock to the shareholders, each engineer received one-fourth of a share of stock. While they each owned 25 percent of the corporation, they soon found out that, in some cases, fractional shares were not recognized, and this became a problem for the business. In addition, this format left them no room to grow.

If you authorize more shares than you plan to issue, the corporation can always maintain for growth purposes an amount of stock that is authorized but unissued. This is useful when new capital is needed and new shareholders are brought into the corporation. While a small business is unlikely to need millions of shares of stock, a nice round number of 100,000 works well. One word of caution: if your state has a franchise tax based on the number of shares authorized or issued, you may want to use lower numbers for authorizing or issuing stock. An approach that leaves the corporation plenty of flexibility would be to authorize 100,000 shares and then issue only 60,000 shares to current stockholders, leaving 40,000 shares authorized but unissued for use in the future. Be clear that those authorized but unissued shares might not ever be used by the corporation and that is fine.

Dilution

Whether you are investing in a small, *closed corporation* or a larger, more sophisticated company, you need to be concerned about the shares you hold and the percentage of ownership that those shares represent. You want to make sure that subsequent investors do not undermine your percentage of ownership. For example, you may invest $10,000 for 10,000 shares of stock, which represents 10 percent of the company's ownership if there are 100,000 shares "issued and outstanding." Under some circumstances, the next investor may also acquire 10,000 shares of the company for $10,000. But if the company has issued another 100,000 shares, then the 10,000 shares represent only 5 percent of the issued and outstanding shares. What the company has essentially done by doubling the number of shares is reduce the value of your shares by half. Your 10,000 shares of stock now represent only 5 percent of the issued and outstanding shares instead of 10 percent. This means that your 10,000 shares now represent only 5 percent of the company's ownership. It may not be what you had in mind or what the company had promised for your investment. Be sure that you understand the short-term and long-term goals of the company's management team.

Classes of Stock

Corporations can have more than one class of stock. The two primary classes of stock are common and preferred. Some companies divide these classes into subclasses. The intent is to give voting rights and dividend rights to different groups of stockholders. Generally preferred stock provides a set dividend that is paid before any dividends are paid to common stockholders, and preferred stock takes precedence over common stock in the event of liquidation. Like common stock, preferred stocks represent partial ownership in a company, although preferred stock shareholders may not enjoy any of the voting rights given to common stockholders. Though a preferred stock will usually pay a fixed dividend, the corporation does not have to pay the preferred dividend if it lacks the financial ability to do so. The main benefit in owning preferred stock is that the investor has a greater claim on the company's assets than common stockholders. Preferred shareholders always receive their dividends first and, in the event the company goes bankrupt, preferred shareholders are paid off before common stockholders. Common stockholders, on the other hand, exercise control by electing a board of directors and voting on corporate policy. Common stockholders are on the bottom of the priority ladder when it comes to the ownership structure. In the event of liquidation, common shareholders have rights to a company's assets only after bondholders, preferred shareholders, and other creditors have been paid in full.

Bylaws

The governing document for the corporation is its bylaws. Bylaws are the rules and regulations adopted by a corporation for its internal governance. They usually contain provisions relating to shareholders, directors, officers, and general corporate business. The bylaws are adopted at the organizational meeting of the directors and are a private document that is not filed with the state. Generally, the bylaws are more detailed and easier to amend than the articles of incorporation. Common provision and issues included in the bylaws are:

1. The location of the principal office and the registered agent or office
2. The types and classes of stock (i.e., preferred or common)
3. Provisions relating to annual or special meetings of the shareholders: voting rights and procedures, what constitutes a quorum, notice requirements of meetings; use of proxies, provisions relating to waiving notice, action by consent of shareholders, and who can call meetings
4. General powers and duties of directors: number and qualifications of directors, term of office, procedures for resignation, filling vacancies or removal of a director, provisions relating to board of director meetings, indemnification, compensation, and provisions governing the use of executive committees

5. General powers and duties of each officer position: term of office; election issues, procedures for removal and filling vacancies, bonding requirements, and compensation-related matters
6. Provisions related to banking and shareholder loans
7. Details related to stock certificates and procedures to replace lost or stolen certificates
8. Dispute resolution processes and indemnification for directors and officers
9. Provision regarding the transfer of shares and any restrictions on such transfers
10. General provisions: modifying the agreement, notice requirements, and governing law

Annual and Special Meetings

Every state requires the shareholders to have a minimum of one annual meeting, the primary purpose of which is to elect the board of directors of the corporation, but may include other matters as dictated by state law or by the corporate bylaws. Any corporate issue or matter may be considered at an annual meeting. Written notice of the annual meeting is generally required to be given to all shareholders. Notice issues may vary from state to state, so check your state's corporate statutes for notice and meeting requirements. The annual meeting does not have to occur on the same day every year, and it just needs to be held once every calendar year by December 31. Keep in mind that even one-person corporations will need to comply with the annual meeting requirements. An annual meeting of the board of directors is customarily held following the annual meeting of the shareholders; the primary purpose of the meeting of the board of directors is to elect the officers of the corporation.

Calling the Meetings

Any meeting of the shareholders that is not an annual meeting is called a special meeting. Unlike an annual meeting, the only topic that can be considered at a *special meeting* is that set forth in the notice of the special meeting.

Common reasons for holding a special meeting include: corporate mergers or reorganizations, a sale or transfer of substantially all the assets of the corporation, amendment to the bylaws, the issuance of certain corporate securities or stock option plans, the transfer of stock or issuance of additional stock, or the dissolution and winding up of the affairs of the corporation. In fact, many states require these matters be evidenced by either an annual or special meeting or by written consent of the shareholders. The annual meeting is generally called only by the board of directors; however, a special meeting can be called by the board of directors, the president of the corporation, a shareholder or group of shareholders who own at least 10 percent of the issued corporate stock, or other persons authorized to do so in the corporate bylaws. Directors may also call a special meeting of the board of directors. If your shareholders and directors are the same people, your meetings can be combined.

Confirming the Meetings

A corporation must keep written minutes of its meetings and such minutes should be open to inspection by any shareholder or director. The corporate meeting minutes at a minimum will need to be certified by the secretary of the corporation or other authorized officer. For smaller corporations, if it is feasible, getting signatures from all shareholders and directors on the minutes and any waiver of notice may be desirable. Actions of the board or the shareholders by consent should also be reflected in any corporate meeting minutes or by individual corporate resolutions authorizing the action and signed by all parties.

Prerogatives of Voting

Most states allow for one vote per share of stock. (Check with your professional to be sure that this is the case in your state.) Therefore the shareholder(s) with the greatest number of shares tend to determine issues that are put to a vote. A *record date* is the date set by the board of directors on which those who own shares may vote at a particular meeting. The record date is a bigger issue for corporations with many shareholders than for a smaller *closely held* corporations. For the most part, corporate action that must be voted on cannot be taken unless there is a quorum at a meeting. The quorum for shareholders is based on the number of shares issued and outstanding—either a majority vote, two-thirds of the issued and outstanding shares, or, in some cases, the unanimous vote by all shareholders. What constitutes a quorum should be set forth in the corporate bylaws. In most states, if the bylaws are silent on this issue, the default quorum will be a majority of the outstanding and issued shares. Finally, every state allows for voting by proxy. A proxy is a written authorization for a person to vote on behalf of a shareholder. The person voting by proxy must vote in accordance with the direction of the shareholder authorizing the proxy.

Taxes Are the Only Difference Between an S Corporation and a C Corporation

The terms C corporation and S corporation, and you probably wondered what the difference was. Actually, C corporation and S corporations are created exactly the same in accordance with state law. The only difference is how the two entities are taxed.

C Corporations

C corps., as they are often referred to, file their own income tax returns (Form 1120) and pay income taxes at the corporate level using a graduated tax rate.

C Corporation Income Tax Rate Schedule

Over	But Not Over	Tax Is	Of the Amount Over
$0	$50,000	15%	$0
$50,000	$75,000	$7,500 + 25%	$50,000
$75,000	$100,000	$13,750 + 34%	$75,000
$100,000	$335,000	$22,500 + 39%	$100,000
$335,000	$10,000,000	$113,900 + 34%	$335,000
$10,000,000	$15,000,000	$3,400,000 + 35%	$10,000,000
$15,000,000	$18,333,333	$5,150,000 + 35%	$15,000,000
$18,333,333	—	35%	$0

Issues Related to C Corporations

There are no ownership restrictions on C C\corporations. The shareholders can be individuals, other corporations, LLCs, trusts, estates, or partnerships. This allows for flexibility of ownership in much the same way as an LLC. Corporate tax returns are due on the 15th day of the third month following the end of the tax year. An automatic six-month extension can be requested by filing Form 7004. For calendar year taxpayers, the corporate return is due on March 15. C corporations can elect either a calendar tax year or a fiscal tax year (a tax year ending any day other than December 31). The type of accounting method used by a C corporation will depend on whether the entity has inventory or is a manufacturer. There is also a hybrid method of accounting, which is a combination of both cash and accrual methods of accounting. Anyone forming a C corporation should get individual tax advice regarding the method of accounting their business should use. See Chapter 2 for a description of cash and accrual accounting methods.

Double Taxation

The biggest issue with the C corporation, for most business owners, is that of double taxation. When a C corporation files its tax return, it pays taxes at the corporate rate on its net income. If there is money left over after expenses and taxes, *net profit after taxes*, the corporation may pay a dividend to its shareholders. When the shareholders receive the dividend, each shareholder is then required to claim the dividend as income on his or her personal income tax return. Thus, the same dollar is taxed twice. This can be very expensive, particularly for a small business.

If you who are thinking about avoiding this secondary tax by not declaring dividends, you should be aware of the *accumulated earnings tax*. While it is possible for a C corporation to pay out all income in tax-deductible expenses, particularly shareholder salaries, this can be difficult for a larger corporation with many shareholders or a corporation that generates large amounts of revenue. The accumulated earnings tax is an additional tax of 15 percent on corporate earnings that are accumulated for purposes other than bona fide business purposes. Business growth is a bona fide business purpose but is subject to scrutiny and substantiation. Generally, $250,000 in accumulated earnings will be considered reasonable for most businesses. However, for a business whose principal function is performing services in the fields of accounting, actuarial science, architecture, consulting, engineering, veterinarian services, other health services, law, or the performing arts, the acceptable amount of accumulated earnings is only $150,000. The fact that a corporation has an unreasonable accumulation of earnings is enough to create liability for the accumulated earnings tax. It will be the C corporation's burden to prove that the accumulated earnings were reasonable and not held just to avoid the additional income tax. Remember: the accumulated earnings tax is in addition to the corporate income tax rate paid by the C corporation on its net income. It is also important to note that if a C corporation operates at a loss, those losses are generally locked into the C corporation and generally cannot be used by the shareholders to reduce their personal incomes. Such losses are called *net operating losses* and can be carried forward or back to reduce the tax liability of the corporation in other years.

S Corporations

S corporations are corporations that were filed as C corporations, but then requested special tax treatment for the entity. The election is generally made by filing Form 2553 with the IRS (Election for a Small Business Corporation) within 75 days of forming the corporation. In some circumstances, the IRS will grant the election if Form 2553 is filed late. (See the instruction to Form 2553 for details.) The election can be made by a C corporation after the year of formation by filing Form 2553; however, timing is important and business owners should be aware that there can be costly tax ramifications to changing from a C corporation to an S corporation. Once an S corporation election is terminated or lost, the entity cannot make the election again for five years. The S corporation is a pass through entity much like the LLC. The S corporation files an S corporation return (due on March 15), which is informational only. No income tax is due with the return. The S corporation return generates a K-1 for each shareholder, who puts their respective information on their individual tax return (Form 1040, Schedule E). Thus, the taxpayer pays income tax on the earnings of the business at their personal tax rate. Because individual income tax rates tend to be lower (10 percent to 35 percent) than corporate rates, the S corporation election is usually a benefit to most shareholders. In addition, *if the S corporation operates at a loss, the individual shareholders may use their proportionate share of such losses from the S corporation against other income claimed on their individual tax return.*

The S corporation has some restrictions that may prevent certain businesses from making the S corporation election. To qualify for the small business election (S Corp. election), the business must:

1. Be formed in one of the 50 states of the United States
2. Maintain no more than 100 shareholders and have only one class of stock (usually common stock) (Voting common stock and nonvoting common stock are not considered two separate classes of stock for S corporation purposes,)
3. Be comprised of shareholders who are individuals, estates, or certain qualified trusts that consent, in writing, to the small business corporation election
4. Have no shareholder who is a nonresident alien (a foreigner who is living outside of the United State or who is not legally living in the United States)

If your business is unable to meet the above requirements, your corporation cannot make the S corporation election. In addition, if your S corporation meets these requirements initially and later does not, then the S corporation election can be lost.

More often than not, the shareholders of the S corporation are hired as employees and are paid a salary. The IRS requires that this salary be reasonable and that full employment-related taxes must be paid on the gross wages. If there are profits after business expenses, including shareholders' salaries, then the S corporation may make distributions to its shareholders. Distributions are different than dividends. However, like dividends, distributions must be made in accordance with each shareholder's respective ownership interest. They can be made at regular or irregular intervals throughout the year and, because distributions are gross payments and no taxes are withheld, the shareholder may be required to make estimated tax payments to cover the taxes due as a result of the distribution. Like the LLC, all of the profits of the S corporation are deemed to be distributed to the shareholders each year. This does not mean that the shareholders have to go to the bank and remove all the money on December 31, but that the shareholders will pay income tax on any money left in the corporation at the end of the year whether distributed or not. Employment taxes and self-employment taxes are not paid on distributions as long as the shareholder is an employee and paid a reasonable salary or if the shareholder does not materially participate in the business. This offers a tax savings over LLCs and C corporations, making the S corporation an attractive entity choice.

Other Issues Related to S Corporations

The S corporation is generally going to be a cash-basis and calendar-year taxpayer. Registration of your S corporation or C corporation with the state, city, and county in which you operate your business may be necessary. Like the LLC, a few states require that corporations publish in a local newspaper notice of their formation, regardless of whether the corporation has made the S corporation election or not. Remember to check with your county clerk and recorder's office to determine if your state has such a requirement. As with other entities, your business may need state and city sales tax licenses. The corporation, whether it is an S corp. or C corp., is required to obtain an FEIN regardless of whether it is hiring employees or independent contractors. Also check with your state to determine if it imposes a franchise tax on corporations.

Signatures

When signing on behalf of your corporation or limited liability company you should always include your title and the name of the corporation or company with your signature.

For example: as the owner of the LLC, your title would be Managing Member. The signature line should look like this:

_____

William Smith, Managing Member
ABC Consulting, LLC

As a corporate officer, the signature line should be similar,

_____

William Smith, President
ABC Consulting, Inc.

Your title is not required on checks. The above signature block should be used on agreements and documents that you are signing on behalf of the corporation or in your capacity as an officer or manager of the business. This will avoid any confusion as to whether you are signing personally or as a representative or agent of the entity. This could become an issue if a debt or obligation is not paid by the business. This will not apply to personal guaranties, which are often required for leases and bank loans and which use the personal guaranty as a separate document. Send signature as an indication of personal responsibility.

Banking

All corporations (S corps and C corps) and limited liability corporations (except one-member LLCs) are required to obtain a separate corporate bank account. We recommend that even the one-member LLC get a separate corporate bank account to better separate the business assets from the personal assets. Most banks will require a minimum deposit to open the business bank account. The minimum deposit can range from $100 to thousands of dollars. The banks will require certain documents to open the account; this will vary from bank to bank. It is a good idea to call the bank and ask what documents they require.

At a minimum, they will need your articles of incorporation or organization, your federal employer identification number, and, in many cases, a certificate of good standing from your secretary of state. This is a certificate indicating the entity has complied with the requirements of the secretary of state and is in good standing. Please note that many states will allow you to obtain this document online while other states require that the certificate be ordered through the mail. This can take time, so plan accordingly. Many banks will also require a banking resolution, which is document that authorizes the entity to open the bank account and is signed by a corporate officer or a manager of an LLC. Some banks will want copies of the operating agreement, bylaws, and organizational meeting minutes of the entity. These days, most banks are pretty competitive. Assuming prices are similar, pick a bank based on convenience. Banking becomes more important and a more frequent occurrence when you own a business. Do not cross town to save a few dollars, as you will discover that your time has become a precious commodity.

Business Names

One thing every business must do is come up with a name. Your name should be distinct. The secretary of state and department of revenue in your state will not allow your business to file a name that is the same as or deceptively similar to another business name. Many states may restrict the use of particular words in a corporate name, such as Bank, Financial Institution, Credit Union, Insurance, Trust, Surety, Federal, National, Reserve, or United States. You will need to check for these types of restrictions in your state.

Most states will require that you include a corporate designation at the end of your corporate name, such as Incorporated, *Company, Corporation, Limited*, or an abbreviation of the above. LLCs often have similar requirements such as Limited Liability Company, Limited Company, or an equivalent abbreviation. If you use a name that is similar to another business, you may receive a cease and desist letter claiming infringement and asking that you change your name or risk a lawsuit. Generally, the first to use a name has the rights to the name. You do not want to have to change your name nor do you want to defend against a lawsuit. Do at least a preliminary search on your name to determine if anyone is using the name or something similar. Do a name search with your secretary of state or department of revenue. Search the trademark registered with the U.S. Patent and Trademark Offices at *www.uspto.gov*, and do an Internet search and see what comes up. You will also want to see what is available in the way of domain names if you are planning on having a Web site. Pick a name wisely since you will, hopefully, want to live with it for a long time. Once you have picked a name, you can use the TM or SM symbol at the end of your name to put others on notice that you consider the name to be a trademark (usually used for names of products) or a service mark (usually used for names of services). *This can be done even if you have not filed a state or federal trademark application.* Do not use the ® symbol unless you have a registered federal trademark granted by the U.S. Patent and Trademark office. The right to use a name continues indefinitely as long as you continue to use the name in commerce. However, federal trademarks have an initial term of ten years and can be renewed for additional ten-year terms. Be aware that, between the fifth and sixth year, the USPTO requires an affidavit that you are still using the mark. *And the USPTO office does not send out a reminder of this requirement.*

Par Value

A corporation must sell shares of stock in order to capitalize the corporation, that is, provide the corporation with capital. Shares of stock sold by the corporation represent proportionate ownership interests held by shareholders in the corporation. Par value is a dollar value assigned to shares of stock, which is the minimum amount for which each share may be sold. There is no minimum or maximum value that must be assigned. Shares may also have no par value, which means that the board of directors will not assign a minimum value to the stock below.

Review Questions

1. Do you need limited liability protection as the owner of a business?
2. Have you estimated how much your business will have in Revenue, Expenses, and Profits?
3. How many owners will be involved in the business?
4. Have you determined who will manage the business operations?
5. If an owner leaves the business, will the business continue?
6. Will all owners directly participate in the business?

7. Will the business be hiring employees or independent contractors?

8. Have you chosen a name for your business and done a preliminary search on the name?

9. Would you like to limit the involvement of investors in the day-to-day business?

10. Have you considered exit strategies for the business owners?

11. Have you considered each owner's percentage interest in the business and what capital contribution will be made?

12. Will you have more than 100 owners? Are any of the owners of the business nonresident aliens?

13. Will your business be owned by individuals only? Corporations? LLCs? Or any other entities?

14. Do you know what would be a reasonable salary for the work you would be doing on behalf of the business?

15. Have you determined who will serve on your board of directors or be your officers or manager(s)?

CHAPTER 5

Choosing an Entity

Now that you know a little something about the various entities that you may choose from, it is important to look at which entity is right for your business. One way to begin this choice of entity process is to look at the advantages and disadvantages of each entity. There is no one best form of ownership for a business. You will need to determine the most advantageous legal and tax structure in order to accommodate your overall business objectives. This will be different for each business. Issues that should be considered include: limitation of liability, asset protection, tax treatment, investors, creditors, insurance needs, transferability of assets, flexibility of sharing profits, continuity of life, management issues, formalities of formation or existence, self employment taxes, and state taxes.

Start with Limited Liability Protection

Look at the choice of entity options available to you on a sort of continuum from the simplest structure to the most complicated one. Picture the continuum as follows:

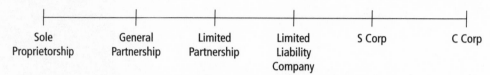

| Sole Proprietorship | General Partnership | Limited Partnership | Limited Liability Company | S Corp | C Corp |

A good place to start is with limited liability. Does the business owner want or need limited liability protection? The riskier the business activity, the more likely a limited liability entity of some kind would be appropriate. For example, if the business is hand-painted note cards to be sold at craft fairs and in shops by a local artist, then the sole proprietorship may be the right structure for the business as opposed to, say, a manufacturer of computer components. The business owner should also look at the need to protect personal assets.

The more personal assets a business owner has, the more need for separation and protection of those assets. What if you have worked all your life as an employee and you are now starting a business? Do you really want your home or stock portfolio to be at risk if something goes wrong with your business? Keep in mind that the number-one reason business owners form corporations and limited liability companies is for that limited liability protection. The use of insurance, either for your products (product liability) or your services (malpractice insurance or errors and omission coverage), should be considered here. Perhaps insurance would insulate you from liability and protect your personal assets. If you are going to be producing hand-made furniture from your garage, one piece at a time, a simple product liability policy may be all the protection you and your business needs. The trick is determining how much insurance coverage to get. Keep in mind that insurance can be expensive and may be needed even if you create a limited liability entity of some kind.

More often than not, limited liability protection is desirable. Once you determine whether your business needs limited liability protection, you can start to eliminate some of the legal structures on the continuum. The fewer entities you have to choose from, the easier the process of choosing an entity will be. If a business owner wants to have limited liability protection (and insurance alone will not be enough), then the sole proprietorship, general partnership, and limited partnerships are not appropriate entity options. Remember: the general partnership not only has unlimited liability, but has the additional issue of partners being able to legally bind one another with out the other's consent. As a result, the general partnership is not recommended. For the most part, only small businesses that involve very little risk should consider forming an entity that does not give its owners limited liability protection.

Who Is Going to Own the Business?

Another issue that needs to be considered is that of ownership. The number of owners and the legal structure of those owners will also help to determine which legal structures you should consider. If your business will have one owner who is an individual, you can consider the sole proprietorship, the limited liability company, or the corporation, but not the general partnership or the limited partnership. If your business will have two or more owners, the sole proprietorship is not available as an option, but you could form a partnership, a limited liability company, or a corporation. Generally, the more owners your business will have, the more likely a limited liability entity of some kind would be the better choice for your business. Also, identifying who your business owners are and their legal structure may help to identify which entities are available. Remember that the S corporation cannot have nonresident aliens as shareholders. If your business is going to be owned by a U.S. citizen living in Colorado and an Australian citizen living in Sydney, the business could not operate as an S corporation. However, assuming limited liability is desired, the business could be formed as a limited liability company or a C corporation, because there are no restrictions as to who can be a member of a limited liability company or a shareholder of a C corporation. Shareholders could be other entities, such as corporations or limited liability companies. S corporation shareholders are generally individuals.

Financing the Business

How the business is going to be financed or capitalized may also play a part in determining who will be owners of the business, and therefore should be considered when choosing an entity. If you are the only owner and you will be providing all the capital to start and operate your business, you may choose any of the entities, except the general or limited partnership. If you are planning to have other individuals or entities share in the profits of your business and contribute capital to the business, a limited liability company or a corporation is advisable. Because your investors may dictate which entity is right for your business, it is a good exercise to try to identify, in theory at least, who those investors might be. For example, if you think your investors will be venture capitalists, the limited liability company or C corporation will allow for the most flexibility. If you are sure your investors will be individuals, an S corporation is an option provided you meet all of the requirements of an S corporation.

Management and Size of Your Business

How the business is going to be managed, the size of the business, and the number of employees should also be considered when looking at the choice of entity. If your business will have many owners, a limited liability company or a corporation may be better to provide structure and readily accepted procedures for operating the business. If only some of the owners will be involved in the day-to-day operations of the business, the corporation (S corp. or C corp.) or a limited liability company provides centralized management through the board of directors or the managers, respectively. This may help to keep too many cooks in the kitchen, particularly if you are interested in having investor-only types involved in the business. In addition, whether the business plans on hiring employees and what type of work the employees will be performing should be taken into consideration. Because a business owner will have less control over the individuals performing services for the business, it may be wise to look at a limited liability entity of some kind. This may not be an issue for a consultant hiring an administrative assistant but could be an issue for a handyman service that will be hiring technicians to enter the customers' homes or businesses. If your business is going to have many employees or if the work the employees will be performing is risky, a limited liability entity should be seriously considered. Keep in mind: if the business starts as a sole proprietorship, it can change its legal structure if the business grows. For some business owners, starting small and keeping the business simple at the beginning may be best. Remember that the business will not have limited liability protection during the time it operates as a sole proprietorship, even if it later changes into a corporation or a limited liability company. Limited liability protection is not retroactive. Once again, limited liability protection is the key.

Sharing Profits

Before choosing an entity, the business owner will want to understand how profits are shared among the participants of the various entities. Profits can be defined as the earnings of the business after all expenses of the business are paid. Therefore, profits are a net figure rather than a gross figure. The sole proprietor is entitled to 100 percent of the profits of the business. Partnerships, limited liability companies, and corporations will need to share profits in proportion to the ownership interests set forth by the entities' governing documents (partnership agreement, operating agreement, or bylaws). For example, if Tom and Darlene each own 50 percent of a partnership or limited liability company, they will share profits and losses 50/50. If Tom owns 20 percent and Darlene own 80% of the common stock of a corporation, Tom will receive 20 percent of the profits and Darlene will receive 80 percent of the profits. Generally, profits are shared in accordance with each owner's percentage ownership, or by the percentage of shares of stock owned, or the membership interest owned. Corporations have a little more flexibility in how owners who work for the business are paid. They can hire the business owner and pay salaries, whether the same or different. For example, let's say two owners, Kim and Susan, are forming a limited liability company to run a massage therapy practice. Assuming Kim and Susan own 50 percent each of the membership interest of the limited liability company, they will share profits equally. If Kim does 965 massages a year and Susan does only 678, the normal sharing of profits would seem a bit unfair to Kim. The use of a corporation could alleviate this issue, because Susan and Kim could each be paid a salary based on the number of massages each provides. Kim could be paid a salary of $35,000 per year and Susan could be paid a salary of $25,000 per year, then the remaining profits could be split 50/50. This would compensate Kim for the extra work. As you can see, knowing how profits are distributed for each of the entity choices could make a difference in the entity you choose.

Exit Strategies and Freely Transferable Interests

The next issues that should be considered are those of exit strategies for the business owner and the ease with which the ownership interests in the business may be transferred. While it may seem a long way off, it is wise to have some idea as to what it is you want to accomplish with the business. *See Chapter 17 for more on exit strategies.* Are you just looking for a business that allows you to work for yourself, or are you trying to build a business for generations to come? Corporations and limited liability companies can have a perpetual existence, while sole proprietorships and partnerships tend to dissolve upon the death, bankruptcy, or retirement of an owner. In addition, change of ownership of a partnership or sole proprietorship can cause the business to dissolve and a new business to form. Free transferability of interests allows the business owners to sell their ownership interest without restriction. Transfer of ownership tends to be more flexible with the corporations and the limited liability companies, with the exception of the ownership restrictions imposed on S corporations. Those restrictions may or may not be a concern for your business. Exit strategies may be an important part of your planning for the business. If you are 52 years of age and are starting a business, it is unlikely that you will want to be working for 20 more years, so it would be wise to consider what you would do with the business in the future. If you are 28 and starting a business, the issue may still be very relevant. For example, you might grow the business for five years and then sell it to a com-

petitor. Because corporations and limited liability companies can continue forever, a retiring owner could sell his or her shares or membership interest to
others and walk away. Or perhaps the business owner would prefer to just stop
working and forgo a salary, but remain an owner who shares in the profits.
This could provide an income stream during retirement. Also consider, if you
wanted out of the business, who would you sell the business to? Are there
other owners who would want to purchase your interest? Is the business a
family business that could be continued after your death? Perhaps there are
key employees who would want to purchase your interest and continue the
business. While these issues may be unknown at the time you start your business and may not alone determine the type of entity you choose, they should
be considered and kept in mind throughout the life of your business.

Choosing Your Entity

Once you have determined the issues discussed above, you should have a better idea of which entities you should be considering. For most small business
owners, the choice begins with whether the business should have limited liability protection. For a one-owner business, if limited liability protection is
not a concern, the business can be operated as a sole proprietorship. Keep in
mind that the current "check-the-box" regulation allows a one-member limited liability company to file a Schedule C for tax purposes. This is a way to
keep the business as simple as possible and yet give the owner limited liability
protection. It is a "best of both worlds" kind of scenario. The only drawback
is that pesky self-employment tax. Once you are looking at having more than
one owner, you really should be looking at a limited liability company or a
corporation. Remember the general partnership is not recommended.
Limited partnerships may provide some protection to owners but, depending
on the rules of your state, one owner may have to serve as a general partner
and may have to forgo limited liability protection. Since the limited liability
company affords limited liability protection to all of its owners, it is a good
place to start when considering the choice of entity. Now might be a good
time to go back to your continuum:

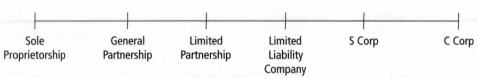

Assuming you have determined that you want to have this all-important limited liability protection, in all likelihood you can eliminate the sole proprietorship, general partnership, and any type of limited partnership. This would leave you with a continuum that looks like this:

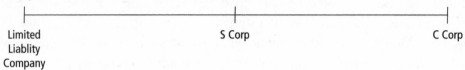

This should be getting easier and perhaps a little less scary for you. Next, I would look at the far end of the continuum, at the C corporation. While the C corporation has a great deal of flexibility in ownership and distribution of profits through dividends, there is the matter of double taxation. Because of the potential for a higher tax, you will want to look at the expected tax rate for the corporation as opposed to the individual tax rate of the shareholders to determine which is lower. A pass-through entity may be a better entity for your business from a tax perspective. Also, if you will be offering shares in your C corporation to investors (outside of your friends and family) to more than 35 people, you may have to comply with Securities and Exchange Commission (SEC) regulations and this could complicate things. What you should ask is whether there is *any* reason your business should consider a C corporation. For example, if you know you will be going public soon, a C corporation will need to be seriously considered. Keep in mind that, while a business can change its form of entity, there can be serious tax implications from making such a change, not to mention the costs involved in switching entities. Also, there can be significant costs in the way of a built-in-capital gains tax, a tax imposed on appreciated assets and retained earnings of a C corporation when the C corporation changes to an S corporation. You will want to get this right from the beginning. For many closely held (privately owned) businesses, the concern with double taxation and more complicated compliance issues is enough to take the C corporation out of the running. If this is true for your business, that leaves you with a continuum that looks more like a choice between two entities: the limited liability company and the S corporation.

Comparing the LLC and the S Corporation

Many business owners can find it difficult to decide between the limited liability company and the S corporation. The two entities often appear to have more similarities than differences. Because both entities afford limited liability protection to all of their shareholders or members, this factor will not help you choose between the limited liability company and the S corporation. The ownership restrictions imposed on S corporations can be a deciding factor. It is best to address this issue first.

Remember that the S corporation can have only one class of stock (usually common stock) and no more than 100 shareholders. Also, the shareholders of an S corporation will be individuals who are U.S. citizens or resident aliens legally living in the United States. If your business cannot comply with these requirements then your business will not be able to operate as an S corporation. The most common reason not to elect the S corp. status is if a business wishes to have foreigners or entities other than individuals as shareholders, either at formation or in the future. Obviously, if your business will not be in a position to comply with all of the S corporation requirements, then your business should be a limited liability company and there is no need to continue the comparison. However, if your business will comply with all of the S corporation requirements, the comparison must be continued.

Both the S corporation and the limited liability company are freely transferable and both entities have perpetual existence. Assuming that future transfers will not jeopardize your S corporation status, these factors will not help you choose between the limited liability company and the S corporation. Also be aware that ownership changes may be restricted by state law or internally through operating agreements and shareholder agreements.

Costs of Formation and Operation

A look at the costs related to formation and ongoing compliance issues should be considered at this point. Both the limited liability company and the S corporation will have state law requirements for formation. In fact, every state requires that a formal document be filed with the state to form either entity. Filing fees vary from state to state but, more importantly, the filing fees can differ for corporations and limited liability companies within a particular state. Every state requires the corporation (S corp. or C corp.) to maintain corporate bylaws and to hold annual meetings. Limited liability company requirements vary from state to state, but it is wise to have an operating agreement in place, at a minimum. This is one of the reasons it is important to be aware of your particular state requirements. Your state may or may not require annual meetings of the members of a limited liability company. If your state does not require annual meetings for the limited liability company, this is certainly simpler. But, as many small business owners have learned (the hard way), an annual meeting of your members may serve as a useful tool in maintaining communication with any members who are not involved in the day-to-day operations of the business. Therefore, you may want to hold an annual meeting of members even if it is not required. The cost of ongoing compliance will, of course, depend on your state rules.

You will want to determine if there is an annual reporting requirement for either entity. Many states have some kind of annual reporting requirement that allows for updating corporate and LLC data on file with the state. Often, this requirement will be the same for corporations and limited liability companies. At this point you will want to know if your state has a franchise or value-added tax on corporations or limited liability companies, and you will want to determine if there is a difference in such tax based on the type of entity. Another issue you will want to consider is the cost of tax preparation for the business. Excluding the cost of maintaining payroll, which would be the same for either entity, most tax preparers will charge about the same for a partnership return or an S corporation return. More often than not, this cost will be based on the volume of transactions and the number of owners more than on the type of entity. However, a one-member limited liability company that is being taxed as a disregarded entity (Schedule C filer) may find that the cost of tax preparation is less expensive than that of a two-member limited liability company or an S corporation. Just about every other cost related to the business will fall into the same category as the cost of payroll preparation. The costs would be the same for either the limited liability company or the S corporation.

How the Owners Get Paid and Self-Employment Tax

Because the factors discussed above may not necessarily help you choose between the limited liability company and the S corporation, you may be thinking—does it matter? It does.

The biggest difference between the S corporation and the limited liability company is how monies are paid to the owners and what taxes are paid on those monies. Let's start with the limited liability company.

Generally, the members of a limited liability company are paid draws, which are gross payments (no taxes are withheld), which can be made in regular or irregular amounts throughout the year. This means you could make a draw of $1,000 one month and $5,000 the next or you could even make draws more sporadically. These draws may be paid to the members if the company has revenues in excess of expenses and is operating at a profit. The individual member(s) will pay income tax and probably self-employment tax on the draws. The income tax rate will be at each member's individual tax rate and the self-employment tax rate will be 15.3 percent on the first $97,500 taken in draws and 2.9 percent on all draws taken over $97,500. (This line of demarcation changes every year. This is the amount for 2007.) This is because there is a wage limit on social security taxes (12.4 percent), but not on medicare taxes (2.9 percent). The members of the limited liability company will need to pay quarterly estimated tax payments to the IRS and, in most cases, to the state. Remember: the estimated tax payment system is not optional. Failure to pay enough estimated tax or at a minimum 90 percent of your previous year tax liability can result in a "failure to pay" or "late payment" penalty. It can also cause a cash crunch at tax time.

What the Savings Look Like

With the S corporation, the monies paid to the owners are usually handled differently. The S corporation will generally hire an owner as an employee of the corporation and pay them a salary. The IRS requires that this salary be reasonable. Basically, the IRS is concerned about you paying a salary that is too low. To determine a reasonable salary, you will have to look at the work being performed and the going rates for such work in your area of the country. A good rule of thumb is—how much would you have to pay for someone else to perform the work?

On the salary paid to any shareholder, you will have to pay payroll taxes and you will pay unemployment insurance on a portion of the gross wages (both federal and state). *See Chapter 10 for more details on employment-related matters.* The actual tax paid on the salary will vary from state to state depending on the unemployment insurance rate, but the total payroll-related tax can be as much as 16 percent of the gross wages. Be aware that, in most states, it will be difficult for an owner to collect unemployment benefits unless they can prove the loss of employment was due to no fault of their own, like a hurricane that has shut down the business. While the payroll tax can be a little higher than the self employment tax paid by a member of a limited liability company, this may not be a big concern, as you will see shortly.

After the S corporation has paid its expenses and paid reasonable salaries to its shareholders, the corporation can make a distribution to its shareholders if there are any additional profits. The distribution must be made in accordance with the ownership percentage of the S corporation. For example, if an S corporation has four shareholders who each own 25 percent of the issued shares and, after all expenses and salaries are paid, the S corporation still has $30,000 in profit, it may make a distribution to its shareholders in the amount of $7,500 each. On the distributions made, each shareholder will pay income tax *only*. This could be a tax savings of up to 15.3 percent on the distributions made by the S corporation and may clearly be an advantage of the S corporation over the limited liability company. Put as simply as possible, the S corporation can enjoy a tax savings of 15.3 percent on all distributions until each owner has earned $97,500 (between salary and distributions) each year, then the tax savings goes down to 2.9% on any remaining distributions made by the S corporation in any given calendar year. As you can see, the tax savings with the S corporation is a large percentage initially and is reduced to a lower percentage as the business makes more money. Keep in mind, however, that even a 2.9% tax savings may be significant to you and your business. Clearly these tax savings are an advantage of the S corporation over the limited liability company, as is shown in the example table on the next page.

Don't forget the dangers involved. While the above example shows the potential tax savings enjoyed by an S corporation, there a few issues that a business owner should be aware of and take into consideration. The IRS would like to close this loophole (for lack of a better term). As you can imagine, there is a temptation to make the shareholder salary very low and pass most of the profits from the S corporation to the shareholder as distributions. In years past, the IRS has looked closely at S corporations that were paying their shareholders very low salaries; we will call these the "piggy cases." The IRS would then recharacterize some or all of the distributions as salary/wages, on which the shareholders would then owe payroll tax, not to mention penalties and interest. Today, most S corporations have learned the lesson of the "piggy cases" and are setting shareholder salaries at more reasonable levels. Remember, you want to set those shareholder salaries as low as you can get away with without incurring the wrath of the IRS. This would be fine except that the IRS has, in recent years, been looking more closely at S corporations that have, as their only employee, one shareholder. Under these circumstances, the IRS is arguing that all of the income generated by a one-shareholder S corporation should be considered the salaries/wages of that shareholder. This is particularly true in the area of service-based businesses. Currently, there are plenty of businesses taking advantage of this potential tax savings, but be clear about the fact that there is some risk for certain S corporations. In fact, the IRS is warning all businesses, when it grants the S Corp. election, that it could recharacterize distributions as salaries/wages.

Comparative Analysis of LLC and S Corp.

LLC		S Corporation
$150,000	Gross Revenue	$150,000
($70,000)	Cost of Goods Sold, Nonowner Salaries, Operating Expenses	($70,000)
$80,000	Net Profit (before owners are paid)	$80,000
Draws are made to members in accordance with the ownership interest (one owner = 100%)		If the corporation pays its only shareholder a salary of $40,000, income taxes on the salary will be $4,000 and total payroll taxes will be approximately $6,300 for both employer and employee portions. However, in this example there is still $40,000 that can be paid out to the shareholder as a distribution. On the distribution, only income tax will be paid, $4,000 in income tax.
Owner receives $80,000 in draws and will pay income tax (using a 10% income tax rate) of $8,000 and self-employment tax of $12,400.		Owner receives $80,000 in salary and distributions and will pay income tax (10%) of $8,000 and payroll tax (instead of self-employment tax) of approximately $6,300 (depending on the state unemployment rates).
Total tax due is $20,400		**Total tax due is $14,300 S Corp savings: $6,100**
Quarterly estimated tax payments are required to be paid on all draws because taxes are usually not withheld on draws.		Quarterly taxes should be paid on all distribtutions, because taxes are generally not withheld on distributions.

Making the Final Decision

This issue should not be a big concern for S corporations that will have non-shareholder employees as long as the S corporation is paying its shareholders (who are employees) a reasonable salary. This is because, when you hire employees, you will usually pay them a wage that is less than the revenues they generate. The theory is that the distributions are by the efforts of your employees and not your owner(s) and are truly profits and not wages. Consequently, payroll or self-employment tax would not be warranted on the distributions. It is unknown how this issue will ultimately play out in the courts or otherwise, but it should be considered when choosing the S corporation as a choice of entity. *If your entity will employ shareholder and nonshareholders alike, the S corporation will likely be the entity for your business.* In a similar vein, you should also consider, as a shareholder, what your "reasonable" salary would be. This may affect your decision between the limited liability company and the S corporation because, if your reasonable salary is higher than what you think you would earn through the business, perhaps it would be best to form the limited liability company to keep things simpler (i.e., potentially no payroll).

An Interesting Example

Take, for example, the case of Karen, a chemist who worked for the same chemical company for 15 years, making $175,000 annual salary. When Karen decided to start a consulting firm, doing virtually the same work for several chemical companies, and it came time to analyze her choice of entity options, they were quickly narrowed down to the LLC or the S corporation. When comparing the two entities, it became clear that her earnings from the consulting business would probably never be much more than her previous salary. Because Karen was not going to have other employees and her previous salary was so high, she formed a limited liability company rather than an S corporation. This was a fortunate choice in Karen's case, because that same year, she was audited by the IRS on an unrelated matter (an issue with her 401(k) retirement plan from her previous employer). Had Karen attempted to form the S corporation and pay herself a low salary, she may have been in a position where she would have had to pay the FICA-related taxes anyway and could also have been assessed penalty and interest.

Another issue is whether or not you, the business owner, will be keeping another job for which you earn W-2 income. If you are earning more than $97,500 annually at that other job, you may want to take a closer look at the limited liability company, because the self-employment tax will be only 2.9 percent on all draws or profits of the limited liability company, whereas an S corporation may end up paying more in payroll taxes on a reasonable salary than the LLC will pay in the reduced self-employment tax.

In Conclusion

A final issue to keep in mind is that there is no time limit on when you have to start paying a shareholder as an employee of the S corporation. There is no rule, for example, that the entity must start paying its shareholders within six months. It could take years to be in a position to pay owner salaries. With the S corporation, if you are not paying your shareholders a salary and you have profits, each shareholder will pay income tax and self-employment taxes on those profits (or distributions) whether you actually pay it out in the form of a distribution or not. Thus, until you are paying your shareholders salaries or wages, the tax effect of the S corporation and the limited liability company are virtually identical for most businesses. Clearly, conventional wisdom is partial to the limited liability company or the S corporation. And between those two entities, the S corporation is favored under many circumstances. But remember, each business is different and you should review the issues and factors individually for any business opportunity you are considering. The following table summarizes many of the points made in this chapter.

Type of Entity	Advantages	Disadvantages	Taxation
Sole Proprietorship	No formality to form and maintain Inexpensive to create	No limited liability protection Business as a whole cannot be transferred or sold One owner only	Schedule C Self-employment tax paid on net profits
General Partnership	No formality to form although a partnership agreement is recommended Pass-through tax treatment	No limited liability protection for partners Partners can legally bind each other without consent	Partnership Return Self-employment tax paid on net profits
Limited Partnership	Limited partners have limited liability protections provided they don't participate in management Pass-through tax treatment	General partner does not have limited liability protection Limited partners may not participate in day-to-day operations of the business Formation is more complex; filing with state is required	Partnership Return Self-employment tax paid on net profits
Limited Liability Company	Limited liability for all members Pass-through taxation Unlimited number of members (owners) No limitation on who or what type of entities may be members	Formation requirements are more formal; filing with the state required	Schedule C (one member) Partnership Return (2 or more members) May elect to be a corporation for tax purposes (S corp./C corp.)
S Corporation	Limited liability for all shareholders Pass-through tax treatment Annual meetings generally not required	More complex to form and maintain; filing with state required Ownership restrictions One class of stock Annual meetings required	S Corp. Return Individual tax returns by shareholders

Type of Entity	Advantages	Disadvantages	Taxation
C Corporation	Limited liability for all shareholders Unlimited number of shareholders and no ownership restrictions May have more than one class of stock	More complex to form and maintain; filing with state required Double taxation Annual meeting required	C Corp. Return Individual tax returns on recipients in addition to coporate tax

Restrictive Covenants

A corporation or a limited liability company may include in its governing documents a restrictive covenant requiring unanimous consent of all owners for any transfer of ownership or issuance of additional stock. Another common restrictive covenant is a provision requiring that the remaining owners be given the right of first refusal on any transfer of ownership to another party. These types of restrictions are commonly put in the bylaws or shareholder agreements for corporations and in the operating agreements for limited liability companies. This is often wise for closely held entities, as it may spare the business owner the headache of waking up one day and learning that his or her co-owner had a gambling problem and someone in Las Vegas is now part owner of the business.

Attorneys Fees for Formation

Legally, you do not need an attorney to incorporate. It is, however, recommended. Attorneys' fees for incorporation or for the formation of a limited liability company vary widely; however, most attorneys who do provide corporate formation services will have a flat fee for the service. Research has shown that attorneys' fees can be range between $800 and up through $3,500 for the formation of a corporation or a limited liability company, depending on the complexities involved. This figure does not include the state filing fees. It is best to specifically ask what documents the attorney will be preparing and filing as part of their fee. If you are going to use an attorney, shop around a bit to see what is common in your location. It is easy to make a mistake that can come back to haunt you. If you are going to form your entity yourself, do your homework!

Good in All Fifty States

There are many Internet companies that claim they will form your corporation or limited liability company for a small fee (as little at $99.95 plus filing fees.) A few issues with this approach should be mentioned. First, not all documents are good in all fifty states even when they are claimed to be. Second, Internet formation does not generally include the application for state or local licenses that may be required (i.e., sales and other tax licenses and business registrations). Third, in some cases, they do not file the required forms with the IRS. And fourth, if you have questions, it is unlikely that the Internet fee would cover such questions. In addition, all documents are the same for all businesses. This cookie cutter approach may or may not be appropriate for your business. You should research thoroughly and shop around before you take the Internet formation plunge. It is this author's considered opinion that you will probably need an attorney at some time during the life of your business and it wouldn't hurt to establish a relationship with a good attorney before you need one.

Review Questions

1. Does your business need limited liability protection for the owner of the business?
2. Do you know what types of entities will be included in the ownership of your business? (i.e., individuals, corporations, LLCs, trusts, estates, etc.)
3. Will there be more than 100 owners of the business?
4. Will any owners be foreigners not legally living in the United States?
5. Are all owners U.S. citizens?
6. Do you plan to have more than one class of stock?
7. Do you have any expectation as to how long you plan to be involved with the business?
8. Could your business continue without you?
9. Is there a market or possibility of selling your business to a competitor or other unrelated party?
10. Have you considered what would be done with the business in the event of your death or retirement?

11. Do you expect that any of the owners will receive W-2 income from another employer?

12. Have you determined what a reasonable salary would be for the work each owner performs for the entity?

13. Have you evaluated such a salary in terms of the potential earnings of the business?

14. Have you prepared projected revenues and costs in order to best evaluate potential income, payroll, or self-employment taxes due from each owner?

15. Have you reviewed the statutes in your state pertaining to LLCs and corporations or gotten assistance from a professional?

16. Have you considered restricting all owners' ability to transfer their interest in the business?

17. Have you considered how your business would be valued in the event of a transfer of interest, death, or retirement?

CHAPTER 6

Federal Employer Identification Number

The federal employer identification number (FEIN) is like a Social Security number for your business. It is also referred to as Employer Identification Number (EIN) or taxpayer identification nNumber (TIN). Like the Social Security number, it is a unique nine-digit number written in the following format: 00-0000000. The Internal Revenue Service issues and uses the number to identify taxpayers who are required to file certain business tax returns and to track employment-related taxes. Generally, most businesses will need to apply for an EIN. If your business will be hiring employees or is operating as a corporation (C corp. or S corp.), partnership, or two-member limited liability company, you are required to obtain an EIN. Sole proprietorships and one-member LLCs may operate their business using their Social Security number as long as they do not have employees or independent contractors. However, they may then be required to give their Social Security number to customers, contractors, vendors, and other individuals or businesses they do work with. Having an EIN may help to protect the business owner's Social Security number. This may help to safeguard a business owner from personal identity theft. Therefore, it is recommended that *all* businesses obtain an EIN.

Identity Theft

Today, the nation's fastest-growing crime is that of identity theft. The information age, the ease of obtaining credit, and the inability to control and safeguard sensitive information, such as Social Security numbers and driver's license numbers, have fueled the increase in this crime. Identity theft covers a range of crimes, from credit card fraud to more complicated cases where the victim's identity is assumed completely, and it can result in problems securing not only credit, but housing and employment. It is estimated that approximately 8.9 million individuals were victims of identity theft in 2005. While most victims are discovering the crime faster, the experts say it can take up to 600 hours of time to repair the damage caused by identity theft. While consumers cannot remove all risk of identity theft, there are some steps that can be taken to minimize the risk. Consumers should take the steps described below and make them part of their daily routine:

Rule One: Be Defensive with Your Personal Information.

Give out personal information in person, online, or over the phone only when you are certain of the people with whom you are communicating or when you, yourself, have initiated the contact. Keep your Social Security number private. Use it only when required and do not carry it in your wallet or print it on your checks. When on line, give only information that is required—often marked by an asterisk. Do not leave mail with sensitive data in unlocked or unprotected mailboxes.

Rule 2: Protect Your Credit and Your Cash

Carefully check all financial statements each month for any unusual charges. Contact the bank or creditor immediately if there is any suspicious activity. Check your credit report with the three credit-reporting agencies at least once a year. Do not leave receipts with any vendor or at any ATM. Shred all credit cards, bank statements, solicitations, and other records that contain sensitive financial information.

Rule 3: Create and Use Passwords or Personal Identification Numbers (PINs)

Manage your passwords and do not write them where they can be located by others. As a step in the right direction, create and use one set of passwords for financial purposes and one for all other needs. Always protect your computers and laptops with passwords.

While identity theft may have devastating effects on its victims, it is important to note the effects on the business community itself. Besides the cost of direct losses related to fraud, there is the issue of inadequate security and poor business practices, which could create liability, fines, or the loss of clientele for a business. Again, it is impossible to completely prevent identity theft, but there are steps a business can take to minimize the risk. Businesses collecting personal data are the first line of defense against identity theft. A business should determine whether the information it is collecting is truly necessary and put in place proper procedures that ensure that the information cannot be overheard or seen by unauthorized individuals. Issues like storage, security, disposal, and personnel access should also be considered. Background checks on personnel who will have access to private information, either clients or other employees, might be wise.

How to Apply for an Employer Identification Number

Fortunately, the Internal Revenue Service makes it easy to apply for an EIN. Form SS-4 (Application for an Employer Identification Number) is used to apply and this can be done by mail, phone, fax, or online. The information you supply on this form will establish your business tax account with the IRS and will be used by the IRS to determine the tax returns required for your business. It will also be used to determine whether you will need employment tax forms. New employers that have a federal tax obligation will be preenrolled in the Electronic Federal Tax Payment System (EFTPS). The EFTPS allows employers to make tax payments online at *www.eftps.gov*. Instructions regarding the EFTPS are sent out shortly after you have been assigned your EIN if you plan on hiring employees.

The SS-4 form is one page and simple to complete. If you are having any trouble, there is a six-page set of instructions that should answer any questions you might have about the form. The form is required to be signed by an individual owner, officer, managing member, or partner of the business. You can authorize a third-party designee to receive your EIN and answer questions regarding the SS-4 form, but you must still sign a completed form and it should be kept for your records or by your third-party designee. If you are filing by phone, only someone who is authorized to sign may make the call. File only one SS-4 form or you may end up with more than one number and this can be a problem for you and the IRS.

Ways to File

Online at *www.irs.gov*. Insert "SS4" into the search line on the home page of the IRS Web site. Scroll down until you get to the online application and click. You will then be allowed to fill in the form and submit it to the IRS for an immediate assignment of an EIN. The EIN will be confirmed by mail in approximately ten days. Print your number and the completed SS-4 form for your records. If you are filing online do not use any punctuation (i.e., commas, periods, the number sign, or dashes) as the form cannot be submitted with those symbols.

Phone at (800) 829-4933. It is wise to fill out the form before calling because an IRS representative, after verifying personal data on the caller, will virtually ask you to read the form. The agent may request that you fax or mail a copy of the signed SS-4 to the IRS within 24 hours. The representative will assign an EIN right then and there. Hours are 7:00 a.m. until 10:00 p.m. local times (Pacific-time for Alaska and Hawaii). International filers should call 1-215-516-6999.

Fax or Mail. To receive an EIN by fax takes 4 to 5 days. Make sure you include your fax number so the IRS may return your assigned number. They will do so without putting a cover page on the return fax. By mail, it can take 4 to 5 weeks. Complete, sign, and date the SS-4 Form and submit either by fax or mail as indicated below:

Where to File

If your principal business, office, or agency, or legal residence in the case of an individual is located in:	Fax or file with the "Internal Revenue Service Center" at:
Connecticut, Delaware, District of Columbia, Florida, Georgia, Maine, Maryland, Masschusetts, New Hampshire, New Jersey, New York, North Carolina, Ohio, Pennsylvania, Rhode Island, South Carolina, Vermont, Virginia, West Virginia	Attn: EIN Operation Holtsville, NY 11742 Fax-TIN: (631) 447-8960
Illinois, Indiana, Kentucky, Michigan	Attn: EIN Operation Cincinnati, OH 45999 Fax-TIN: (859) 669-5760
Alabama, Alaska, Arizona, Arkansas, California, Colorado, Hawaii, Idaho, Iowa, Kansas, Louisiana, Minnesota, Mississippi, Missouri, Montana, Nebraska, Nevada, New Mexico, North Dakota, Oklahoma, Oregon, South Dakota, Tennessee, Texas, Utah, Washington, Wisconsin, Wyoming	Attn: EIN Operation Philadelphia, PA 19255 Fax-TIN: (859) 669-5760
If you have no legal residence, principal place of business, or principal office or agency in any state:	Attn: EIN Operation Philadelphia, PA 19255 Fax-TIN: {215) 516-1040

After you have submitted your SS-4 form, you will receive written confirmation of the EIN from the IRS along with the type of tax return your business will be required to file. Also, with that form, you can make any corrections necessary to your tax account. You will want to get your EIN after you file your articles of incorporation or articles of organization (corporate or entity charter) from the secretary of state as you will want to be sure of your entity or business name. However, you should file for the EIN before you file any sales tax or other business registrations with your city, state, or county because those forms often ask for your EIN Number. Also if you are making the S corporation election, you will need your EIN to file Form 2553 (Election by Small Business Corporation).

Common Reasons for Rejection of an SS-4 Form

The IRS has indicated the following as the top five reasons for the rejection of an EIN application as:

1. The taxpayer identification number (TIN) supplied on Form SS-4, line 7b doesn not match the name on line 7a.

IRS checks the name on line 7a against the Social Security number (SSN), individual taxpayer identification number (ITIN), or employer identification number supplied on line 7b. Do not include the individual's title on line 7a. Adding a title to an individual's name on line 7a will cause a mismatch and result in a rejection of the automated application. A transposition of the numbers in the TIN will also cause a mismatch. Use the exact name connected to the individual's Social Security number on 7a. Review these entries before transmitting your application.

2. The TIN on Form SS-4, line 8a, does not match the name on lines 1, 2, or 3.

After transmission of your application, IRS completes a cross-check between the SSN and ITIN supplied on line 8a with the name on line 1, 2, or 3. A mismatch will result in a rejection of the automated application. Please double check these entries for typographical errors before transmitting your application.

3. Third party designee's address matches the mailing address on Form SS-4, lines 4a and 4b.

A Form SS-4 must show the applicant's mailing address on lines 4a and 4b.

A third party designee (with taxpayer authorization via signed Form SS-4) is able to receive the EIN issued during the online application process. However, the EIN confirmation letter *must* be sent to the taxpayer if there is not a valid Form 2848, Power of Attorney and Declaration of Representative, on file with the IRS. If you wish to receive IRS correspondence on behalf of the taxpayer, please complete the Form SS-4 and Form 2848 and use the telephone, fax, or mail options to obtain an EIN.

4. This entity already has an EIN.

An EIN was previously issued for this entity. If the IRS locates another EIN for the same entity (and entity type), any online EIN you receive will be voided.

5. The entity type is unknown.

In all cases, an entry must be made on line 8a to successfully process your application. Do not check the box labeled "Other" unless none of the other types of entities are applicable (e.g., Sole Proprietor, Trust, Estate, etc.). A limited liability company (LLC) is not an entity type. If you are an LLC, the following entity types are available to you:

- Sole proprietor (one member only)
- Partnership (multi-member only)

If you are a one-member LLC and you want to file as a disregarded entity (Filing a Schedule C for tax purposes), you can either mark the box for the sole proprietor or "Other" and type in "1 Member LLC" on the line provided.

Review and Record-Keeping

Please review your SS-4 form (or any forms submitted to government agencies) carefully before you submit them. It can be time consuming and often frustrating to correct information with such agencies in the future. Remember to always keep a copy for your records of anything you file.

Review Questions

1. Do you need an EIN? (This is a trick question to determine if you have been retaining what you have read.)
2. Will your business have employees?
3. If yes, when do you plan to start paying wages?
4. Do you have a corporate name for your business?
5. Will your business operate under any other names (trade names)?
6. Do you have a physical address for your business?
7. Will you be using a mailing address for your business?
8. Have you determined what type of entity your business will be?
9. If you are operating as an LLC, have you determined how it will be taxed?
10. If you are operating as a corporation, will you be electing S corporation status?
11. Have you ever applied for an EIN number before?
12. If yes, you will need to know for what business (name); previous EIN; approximate date you filed, and city and state where you filed for the previous EIN.
13. Will you be authorizing a third party to receive your EIN or answer questions regarding your Form SS-4?
14. Have you determined the closing month of your business tax year? (This will be December for most businesses.)
15. Do you have a short description of the type of business?
16. Have you completed the SS-4 form?
17. Have you determined who is authorized to sign your SS-4 Form?
18. Before submitting your application, have you carefully reviewed all information on the SS-4 form?'

CHAPTER 7

Sales Tax

Besides income tax and employment-related tax issues facing business owners there are additional taxes a business owner needs to be aware of and understand. The most complicated of these additional taxes are the sales and use tax as imposed by most states and local governments. Sales tax issues can often seem more complicated than issues with the Internal Revenue Service for income taxes because there are thousands of taxing authorities involved in administering and collecting sales and use taxes around the country. Sales tax rules can be different for every state, county, and municipality. You will need to investigate the rules for your state, city, and county.

The difference between a sales tax and a use tax is basically in the time frame within which the tax is assessed or collected. If the tax is imposed at the time of the purchase, it is considered a sales tax. If, on the other hand, for any reason, the tax is not assessed or collected at the time of a sale, a use tax is assessed for the privilege of use and ownership.

The sales and use tax is, perhaps, one of the most complex of all business taxes assessed, since each state has exercised its prerogative of taxing events that take place within its borders and, in some cases, even beyond. This is further complicated by the fact that some items may be involved in a conflict in which an item may be taxed by more than one state authority as well as by local authorities. In addition, further complications may occur when states have the prerogative of taxing the out-of-state individual or the business that is doing business within its borders. This combination of taxes, designed to make funds available for community services, may suggest that it's advantageous to do business in one state rather than another. If the federal income tax is added to this aggregate tax picture, you can understand why the question of all taxes needs to be constantly monitored by the entrepreneurial community.

Generally, a sales tax is a tax imposed on the retail sales of tangible personal property, often referred to as goods or products sold to the actual consumer. In addition, many states tax the sales of certain services. There are generally two types of licenses referred to as sales and use tax licenses: (1) a retail license and (2) a wholesale license. Many states and municipalities will distinguish between sales made to the actual end user or consumer (retail) and sales made to those who will resell the goods or services (wholesale). Often, the state will not require that a business get both licenses but rather choose the license for which the business will make its primary sales.

> Most states require sales tax to be collected only at the time the retail sale is made to the consumer.

Furthermore, a wholesale license, sometimes called a *reseller's exemption certificate*, will allow businesses to purchase goods that will be resold without paying any sales tax at the time of the purchase of such goods. The wholesale license or reseller exemption certificate should not be used to purchase goods that will be consumed by a business or will not be used for resale purposes as a way of avoiding sales tax.

Many local or city governments have their own sales and use tax requirements. There are two types of cities when it comes to sales and use tax: home rule and non-home rule. The home-rule city collects its own sales and use tax. The non- home-rule city lets the state collect its portion of any sales and use tax. The state then remits the tax due to the city. While the issue of home rule versus non-home rule will not impact the amount of tax ultimately paid, it will determine whether your business must report and file separate tax returns for the state and city. While many states collect any county or transit taxes related to the sales and use tax, it is wise to confirm this with your state or county governments.

An Issue of Nexus

A use tax is a tax on goods or services purchased from out-of-state vendors that are not required to collect sales tax on such sales. Thus use tax is collected on taxable sales when made by a business that is not required to collect tax in its own state or the state where the sales took place. The use tax generally becomes the problem for the purchaser rather than the seller. *The issue here is one of nexus, which is a substantial physical presence within a state.* Once a business has established a nexus within a state or jurisdiction, it may be required to collect sales tax in that state. What constitutes a nexus or substantial physical presence differs from state to state and may differ from county to county or city to city. Generally, if you have a physical business location within a state or if you have employees living and working in the state, you have established a nexus. In some cases, even an itinerant worker or traveling sales representative soliciting within a state may establish a nexus. A common question arises regarding Internet sales.

Just like for any other sales, the business owner must determine whether the business has a nexus or substantial physical presence in the state where the goods or services are to be shipped or delivered. Remember, if a business is not required to collect tax for states in which it has no nexus, use tax may still be due on the sale. *The obligation to pay the use tax usually falls upon the purchaser of the goods.* This is important to remember because your business may make purchases from out-of-state vendors and may therefore owe use tax on such sales. If, for example, your Wyoming business purchases some software from a California company that does not have a nexus in Wyoming, there should be no sales tax collected when the item is shipped. However, the Wyoming business may owe use tax on the purchase of the software. Use tax is generally assessed at the same rate as sales tax.

When making a taxable sale, you are required to collect the tax for the state in which you deliver the goods. Therefore, if a product is shipped to the customer, the tax should be collected for the state of delivery. If the customer picks up the product from your location, then the tax collected should be for the state where you are located. For example, if a Colorado business that does not have any connection to Nebraska sells dishes to a resident of Nebraska, the Colorado business would not have to collect the Nebraska sales tax when it ships the product to Nebraska. However, if the customer was visiting Colorado when the purchase was made, Colorado tax would be collected at the time of the sale. If the same business hired a Nebraska salesman to go door-to-door selling the dishes, it is likely that the business would have to register as a retailer in Nebraska (this would constitute a nexus), and collect Nebraska sales tax on each sale that took place in Nebraska, even if the item was shipped from Colorado.

Most states will require reporting of sales and use tax on a monthly, quarterly, or annual basis. For example, Colorado retail license holders must report and remit the tax monthly if the business collects more than $300 in sales tax per month. All other retail license holders are generally required to report and remit the tax on a quarterly basis. Colorado wholesale license holders are only required to report annually because they are not generally going to collect any tax. Because each state is different, you will need to check with your state and local governments to be sure you understand the sales and use tax rates and rules. See Appendix A of this book for a discussion of the sales and use tax currently imposed by your state. Rates change frequently, in some states every year, so you will want to make sure that you are staying up-to-date on any changes your state may make. Every business should be sure to check the local rules and rates as they are in addition to the state rules and rates. Also, exemptions should be reviewed at both the state and local levels. *It is important to know your state and local rules because some states and local governments will shut down a business that gets behind on its sales tax.*

Some Lease and Rental Payments May Be Taxable

Some states consider lease and rent payments on tangible personal property to be taxable sales and therefore require that sales tax be paid on the transaction. It is appropriate to note that the phrase "lease and rental payments on tangible personal property at retail" appears in just about all the states' definitions of items subject to sales tax. The reason for this is that the concept of leasing is somewhat complex, since a true lease is like a rental when the item is returned at the end of the lease term. There are other leases that are actually sales since the lessee has the right to acquire title to the property at the end of the lease term for a modest payment. This payment is sometimes based on the residual value, the market value, or the depreciated value of the property at the end of the lease. In fact, in some cases, there is merely the payment of $1.00. In order to avoid the confusion of whether these situations represent a true lease or an actual sale of some kind, the taxing authority will impose a tax as if it were a sale. *See Appendix A for a state-by-state comparison.* Note the specific prerequisites defined in the Nebraska law. Note also the reference to a "taxable sale" in Nevada.

Internet Sales—the Saga Continues

In 1967, the U.S. Supreme Court voided an Illinois statute that required mail-order firms selling to Illinois customers to collect a sales tax on their orders. The Court ruled that the seller could be forced to collect a sales tax only if it had a physical presence (nexus) in the state in which its sales took place. A "seller whose only connection with customers in the state is by common carrier or the United States mail" lacked the requisite minimum contacts with the state, the Court pronounced in its opinion. The Court's decision was based, in large part, on the significant burden of having to deal with the complexity of, potentially, as many as 30,000 taxing jurisdictions.

In 1992 the Supreme Court revisited its 1967 decision. The North Dakota Supreme Court had upheld a state statute similar to the Illinois law overturned by the U.S. Supreme Court. The U.S. Supreme Court overruled the North Dakota Court and reaffirmed its 1967 decision. The Supreme Court agreed with North Dakota that technological changes virtually eliminated the interference-with-interstate-commerce argument. But the Court found that a major industry (mail order) had been built in large part on the basis of that ruling, and it would be unfair to change the rules in midstream.

It is important to note that the Court decisions related to the collection of sales taxes, not the payment of sales taxes. Therefore, the person buying from the Internet may be responsible for paying a "use" tax to the state. However, it is so administratively complicated for states to identify such persons that the vast majority of people do not voluntarily pay the tax; in fact, most people don't even known they are required to pay a use tax. The Court did specifically say that Congress has the authority to subject interstate mail-order (or Internet) sales to state sales taxes by implementing laws to change the rules. To date Congress has not done so.

However, the National Governors Association has developed the Streamlined Sales Tax Project (SSTP). Under this project states have been working to streamline and simplify their sales tax rules. Currently, 42 states have approved a model interstate agreement that establishes uniform sales tax rules and definitions and 20 of these states have actually enacted implementing legislation. Under the SSTP, state and local governments would still determine whether to charge a sales tax and at what rate. But they would lose their ability to have more than one tax rate for different kinds of goods. All jurisdictions would have to agree to the same definitions and the same forms, and to make changes to their tax systems at the same time. Software is being developed and an amnesty program is also being discussed. In fact, in February 2003, Wal-Mart, Target, and other major retailers agreed to start collecting sales taxes for purchases in 37 states and the District of Columbia in return for amnesty on any back taxes that the retailers might owe. Online taxation has been a thorny topic for years. The problem, then and now, is how to implement a fair system for all involved—the states, businesses, and consumers. Many states think that streamlining and simplifying their sales tax systems will encourage passage of a Federal Sales Tax Fairness bill that would require out-of-state companies to collect sales tax on Internet and mail-order sales.

A number of national retail chains have established an Internet department ("click and mortar") and they contend under the Supreme Court ruling that their e-commerce operation is a distinct legal entity, unrelated to their bricks-and-mortar stores. This practice is known as *entity isolation*. Six states—Alabama, Arkansas, Kansas, Indiana, Louisiana, and Minnesota—have amended their sales tax nexus laws to clarify that entity isolation does not absolve Internet retailers of state sales tax obligations; however, three states—Ohio, Pennsylvania, and Connecticut—have upheld entity isolation as a means of avoiding state sales taxes. The U.S. Supreme Court has never heard the issue.

This Internet sales issue has been on the table in some form or other for many years. How it will be resolved remains unclear. For now, if you have a presence or nexus in a state, you should collect sales tax from your customers within that state. But be aware that that could change at any time. You would be served well by keeping your eyes and ears open on this issue.

In Conclusion

All businesses should check the local rules and rates as they are in addition to the state rules and rates. In addition, exemptions should be reviewed at both the state and local levels. Finally, make sure you are clear on reporting requirements for your state and municipality as many states and cities require reporting even if no sales take place. Penalty and interest on unpaid or unfilled returns may add up quickly.

Sales Tax Deposits

License fees tend to be relatively small for sales and use licenses. However, some states will require a business to pay a deposit to the taxing authority at the time it applies for a license.

Some local governments and counties require that a sales tax application be completed even for businesses that are not required to hold a sales tax license as a type of general business registration.

Check the Local Rules!

In most states, contractors and builders do not collect sales tax from their customers, but are required to pay tax on the supplies and materials they purchase for the structures they build.

Businesses that travel from location to location or mobile businesses may require more than one local sales tax licenses. This can be messy, and each new city or county should be checked and researched to determine its particular rules and rates. For example: some local governments do not want a business that is not located within its city limits to obtain a sales tax license at all, even if an occasional sale takes place.

Special Rules for Licensed Professionals

Often states have special regulations or rules that apply to a specific profession or industry. For example, Colorado allows photographers who contract with each client to take a specific photograph (like family portraits) to be treated as a service-based business and therefore, to avoid the sales tax issue as long as the photographer pays sales tax on all film materials and supplies used to produce the photograph. Knowing if your state has a special rule may save you a lot of time and effort, not to mention money.

Selling Products Overseas

If your online company sells certain products overseas, you should be aware that the European Union is enacting a law requiring the collection of taxes on digital goods like software and music downloads. If you sell such digital items abroad, you will have to collect the EU's Value Added Tax (VAT) based on where the buyer is physically located.

Some States Are Doing More to Collect Sales Tax

Some states are employing a different strategy to encourage companies to collect the sales tax. North Carolina and South Dakota require state agencies to purchase goods and services only from companies that collect sales tax on all sales in their state.

Review Questions

1. Have you determined in which state(s) you will be doing business?
2. Have you determined if you are a retailer, a wholesaler, or a service provider offering taxable services?
3. If your business sells both wholesale and retail, does your business need to get separate wholesale and retail licenses or permits?
4. Will your business have a nexus in more than one state?
5. Is your product or service exempt from sales tax at the state level?
6. Does your state or city require registration or a permit of some kind for all businesses or just for those that will be collecting tax?
7. Do you know your state tax rate?
8. Do you know your city tax rate?
9. Do you know if your city collects its own tax (home rule) or if it lets the state collect the tax on behalf of the city (non-home rule)?
10. Does your county or borough have any sales tax? If so, who collects this tax?
11. Do you know if your business is located in a special taxing district? Have you reviewed the sales tax application for the state and the city to determine the information needed?

12. Have you determined the filing fees and/or deposits necessary to get the proper licenses or permits?
13. Have you determined how often you will need to file tax returns and remit the tax?
14. Does your state or locality have a requirement that the sales or use tax needs to be stated separately on invoices, billing statements, or receipts?
15. Have you checked to see if your state, city, or county has any special rules or regulations that apply to your business or industry?

CHAPTER 8

Franchise Tax and Personal Property Tax

Now that you have a good handle on sales and use tax, there are some additional taxes that you should know about.

Franchise Taxes

The first of those taxes is what are called *franchise* or *privilege taxes*. A franchise tax is a tax on the privilege of carrying on business as a corporation or LLC in a state. The amount of the franchise tax may be measured by amount of earnings, total value of capital or stock, or by the amount of business done. In some states, like California, the franchise tax is simply an income tax, and in other states it is more like an annual report fee used to keep the corporation or LLC records updated. All states view a corporation or LLC that is not formed in their state as "foreign." This may be important

> because the fees may differ depending on whether your entity is considered domestic or foreign. In Nebraska for example, the rates are double for foreign corporations operating in Nebraska. *See Appendix B for a state-by-state discussion of franchise taxes.* As you will see, franchise (or privilege) taxes are handled a little differently by each state, and some states really do not have such a tax but have reporting and filing fee requirements. At the same time, some states will refer to their income tax as a franchise tax, which can cause new business owners some confusion. Check your state for common terms and rates as they may change more frequently than you would guess. *Again the issue is one of nexus, which is a substantial physical presence within a state.*

Once a business has established a nexus within a state or other jurisdiction, it may be required to register in that state and may then become responsible for the franchise taxes and any annual reporting required by the state. Each state has different rules as to what constitutes a nexus and when registration is required. Not only does a nexus or substantial physical presence differ from state to state, it may also differ from county to county or city to city. Generally, if you have a physical business location within a state or if you have employees living and working in the state, you have established a nexus. In some cases, just making sales or soliciting sales within the state may establish a nexus. A common question arises regarding Internet sales. In general, an Internet sale alone will not give a business a nexus within the state for franchise tax and annual reporting purposes. As for any other tax, the business owner must determine whether the business has a nexus or substantial physical presence in the state where the goods or services are to be shipped or delivered. It will be your responsibility to determine if registration in any state you do business in is required. Because fees can be expensive and the time it would take to register in every state could be substantial, it is not a good idea to just automatically register in every state. If you are doing business in more than one state (not including Internet businesses) or if you plan to do business in other states, you should find out the rules in those states and register accordingly. A register-as-you-go approach may very well save you time and money.

Every state has different rules and rates. You will need to check with your state and local governments to be sure you understand the franchise tax and the rules. *Again, see Appendix B of this book for a discussion of the franchise tax currently imposed by your state.* Be advised that rates change frequently, in some states every year, so you will want to make sure that you are staying current on any changes your state may make.

Personal Property Taxes

Another common tax that businesses need to be aware of is the personal property tax. This is tax on tangible personal property used in a business to generate business income. The tax is much like the real estate tax in that it is a tax on the value of the property, in this case other than real property. The taxing authority requires the taxpayer to provide a list of property along with the value, and then tax is assessed in proportion to that value. Forms of property tax vary by county or other jurisdiction. Often the tax is imposed at the city, county, or district level by a tax assessor's office. Of course the rates will vary from location to location, so checking with your local authorities would be wise. This tax is more often than not what is considered an ad valorem (of property) tax and is based on the current fair market value of the property.

Generally, the business will have to provide the municipality or jurisdiction with an annual list of assets and their value, which is then multiplied by a tax rate to determine the amount of tax due. The tax will usually be assessed where the principal place of business is located and can be on vehicles, boats, equipment, furniture, fixtures, inventory, stocks, bonds, and other goods or intangible personal property. Of course, the rates will vary from jurisdiction to jurisdiction and from state to state. Most jurisdictions will allow for certain exemptions, such as items valued at under $250 or a total exemption amount of $2,500; this is another reason to check the rules at your state or local level. In addition, there should be a right of appeal should you feel that the taxing authority is overstating the fair market value of your business property. Personal property tax audits typically involve three to five tax years retroactively.

Many businesses have a problme with ghost assets—assets that no longer exist physically within the organization, yet remain on the books. As a result, businesses should do an annual review of any property disclosure statement they have on file with the local or state government or carefully amend any disclosure being filed to ensure that only assets actually owned and used by the business are being reported. Incorrect disclosure can negatively impact everything from depreciation schedules to insurance payments, personal property tax rates, and even earnings calculations.

Real Estate Taxes

Most local governments also tax real property owned by individuals or businesses. Generally the taxing authority will value a piece of real estate using one or more of the normally accepted methods of valuation (i.e., income approach, fair market value, or replacement cost). In most, if not all jurisdictions, the determination of value made by the assessor is subject to some sort of administrative or judicial review, if the property owner appeals the determination. The local tax assessor then applies an established assessment rate to the fair market value of the property to determine the tax due. These taxes are collected by municipalities, such as cities, counties, and districts in many locations in the United States. They provide an excellent tax base to fund municipal budgets for school systems, sewers, parks, libraries, fire stations, hospitals, and local government services. Be aware that some jurisdictions have both ad valorem and non-ad valorem property taxes, the latter representing a fixed charge (regardless of value) for items such as street lighting and storm sewer control.

> **The Difference Between Biannual and Biennial**
> *Biannual* means twice in one year's time. Please note that the year referred to may be either a calendar year (January–December) or a fiscal year (any 12-month period that is not a calendar year.) *Semiannual* can also be used to describe a biannual requirement. The term *biennial* means every two years.

Useful Life

Personal property tax and real estate tax rules may differ from the IRS rules as they pertains to the useful life of a piece of property. For example, the IRS may dictate that new carpeting has a useful life of seven years and the personal property taxing authority may dictate that the useful life of carpeting is ten years. Make sure you, or your accountant, are aware of such discrepancies.

Vehicle Taxes

Many states include in the cost of registering vehicles or obtaining license plates any property taxes, and often sales taxes. Make sure you are aware of your state or local rules before listing automobiles or other licensed vehicles on a personal property declaration report or tax return.

Review Questions

1. Do you know if your state has a franchise tax?
2. When is the franchise tax due to your state?
3. Is your business operating in more than one state?
4. If yes, have you identified which states?
5. Are you aware of the foreign registration requirements for any states other than the one in which you have incorporated?
6. Have you identified to whom the franchise tax is paid and what reporting or return requirements are in place for each state where the business will be operating? And, with regard to any state in which you are obligated to pay a franchise tax, consider the following:
   (a) Is there an annual requirement to update corporate information with the secretary of state?
   (b) When does such information have to be updated?
7. Are you aware of whether your state will administratively dissolve your entity if such information is not filed?

8. Does your state or local government impose a personal property tax on business property?
9. Are you aware of what is required to report personal property taxes and when such taxes are due?
10. Do you know the tax rate for your locality?
11. Are you familiar with any property exemptions or limits that could reduce the personal property tax paid by your business?
12. Will your business own real estate?
13. If yes, do you know approximately what the real estate taxes for the property will be?
14. Are vehicle property taxes paid with the vehicle registration in your state?

CHAPTER 9

Income Taxes

While it would be impractical to try to cover all aspects of taxation in one chapter, it may be useful to you to have a basic understanding of certain tax issues. Remember: what you don't know can hurt you, so plan on getting professional assistance when dealing with accounting and tax issues with which you are unfamiliar.

Some Basic Tax Issues

One of the most common questions put before accountants and tax professionals is "What costs or expenses are deductible?" Generally, trade or business expenses are tax-deductible, which means they can be used to reduce your gross revenue (total revenue) to net income (profit) and thus reduce your taxable income. A good rule of thumb is that a cost or expense will generally be deductible if it has a legitimate business purpose, "legitimate" being the operative word here. Just because something can be deducted on your tax return doesn't mean it is a good idea. Remember that in most cases to get the deduction you have to spend money. Therefore, taxes remain only part of the decision to incur a cost or expense in business.

Another common, but extremely complex, issue is that of depreciation. On a basic level the question becomes "When can I deduct (write off) certain costs or expenses?" Usually a cost or expense will be written off in the year in which the business pays for the item. This is called *expensing* the cost. However, if an asset (or expense) has a useful life of more than one year, it will be considered a capital asset and will need to be written off over its useful life. This is called *depreciating* an asset or, in some cases, *amortizing* an asset. Be aware that the IRS dictates the useful life of most assets by placing them into classes (e.g., carpeting has a class life of seven years). Capital assets do not include, for example, the case of paper purchased on December 23 that will be used by the business through the end of March; this cost should be expensed in the year it is purchased. Furthermore, the depreciation of assets should not apply to small, insignificant purchases; no one, including the IRS, expects you to depreciate the cost of a stapler. Many businesses will set a dollar limit for items that will be expensed rather than capitalized, or depreciated. For a small business, $100 to $300 is probably reasonable.

No discussion of capital assets and depreciation is complete without a mention of the useful tax tool known as Section 179. The Section 179 election allows a business to elect to expense up to $112,000 of certain equipment and capital assets in the year of purchase rather than depreciating them over time. This is an important tax planning tool, especially for pass-through entities such as partnerships, S corporations, and limited liability companies. Because pass-through entities are deemed to take all the profits or net income out of the business each year, Section 179 can be used to reinvest in the business and avoid income taxes. It is wise to look at the potential income to owners and cash on hand in early December of each year to determine if a business should make an equipment or asset purchase before December 31 of each year to take advantage of the Section 179 election. Again remember, while you may see a tax savings, both at the corporate level and the individual level, you still have to spend the money to purchase the equipment or asset.

Finally, a short discussion of start-up and organizational expenses incurred by new businesses might be helpful. Start-up expenses would usually include, but are not limited to: the cost of travel, trade shows, educational or training seminars, accounting and legal fees, consulting fees, building costs, and supplies or materials needed to get your business started (not inventory or raw materials). Organizational fees include the costs relating to forming or creating the business: fees paid to obtain licenses, and accounting or legal fees for formation of the entity.

Generally, a business can expense in the year purchased up to $5,000 each of its start-up costs and up to $5,000 of its organizational costs (that's $10,000); any cost over that $5,000 maximum must be amortized over 15 years. Often start-up costs and organizational costs are incurred prior to the actual formation and operation of the business. This will be important to know from day one, because it could affect when and how a business owner decides to incur a cost. For example, a new business owner who wants to attend a trade show might form her business (i.e., incorporate) prior to paying for the trip and trade show fees ($8,000). That's because if she incurred those expenses before forming her business, they would be considered a start-up expense: (only $5,000 would be deductible in the first year and the remaining $3,000 would have to be written off (amortized) over 15 years). But if she pays the costs after forming her business, they will be considered a regular trade or business expense and will be expensed in their entirety in the first year. A similar example might be legal fees—a new business may have several legal costs, such as incorporation (organizational cost), customer agreements, and a lease review (start-up cost). If the business incorporates first, the cost of incorporation will be an organizational expense and the first-year deduction will be limited to $5,000. The same goes for the customer agreement and a review of the lease, if the owner paid for them prior to forming his business the costs may have to be treated as a start-up expense, rather than expensed in full, as they would be if the fees were paid after the business was formed.

Federal Income Taxes

Income taxes for businesses are complex primarily because there are lots of ways to tax business income. Below is a brief summary of the way income taxes are assessed for the various entities. Sole proprietors file a Schedule C and pay income tax and self-employment tax (15.3 percent) on their net income or profits. An LLC may be taxed like a sole proprietorship if it has only one member or like a partnership (Form 1065) if it has two or more members. LLCs may also elect to be taxed as corporations (either an S corporation or a C corporation). LLCs' members, regardless of how they choose to be taxed, will pay income tax and self-employment tax (15.3 percent) on their net business income or profits that flow to their individual returns. Like the LLC, partnerships file a partnership return (Form 1065) and pass the earnings on to the individual partners, who will pay both income tax and self-employment tax on those earnings. The S corporation also passes its earnings through to their individual shareholders, who will pay income tax, but self-employment taxes or payroll taxes may be avoided in certain cases. C corporations file a corporate return and pay income tax. Any distribution of dividends to shareholders will be taxed as part of their total income.

State Income Taxes

Every state has different rules and rates. You will need to check with your state and local governments to be sure you understand the rates and the rules. *See Appendix C of this book for a discussion of both the corporate and personal income tax rates currently imposed by your state.* Rates change frequently, in some states every year, so you will want to make sure that you are staying up on any changes your state may make.

Taxes Are Not Necessarily the Only Issue

While tax issues are important for a business to take into consideration, they are not always the only issue to address when making business decisions. For example, when choosing an entity, limited liability may outweigh any tax advantage or disadvantage.

Don't Get Carried Away

A tax savings alone may not justify the expense. Before incurring an expense just for the tax savings make sure you have considered other issues facing the business with regard to the expense. For example, when deciding to buy a piece of equipment for the Section 179 deduction, you will want to make sure whether the cost of the equipment is justified or if perhaps taking the money out of the business and paying some tax wouldn't be more prudent. Even when facing a significant tax break, you should still perform a thorough analysis of the matter before making your final decision.

Statute of Limitations

Generally, the statute of limitations on most tax returns is three years, which means after three years, the return cannot be amended or, if the return is incorrect, the IRS or tax authority will not be able to make changes or charge additional tax. However, if you do not file or if the return is fraudulent, there is no statute of limitations. Thus, it is best to file a zero-based tax return even if it is not required, to start the clock on the statute of limita-

---

Once You Start a Payment Plan with the IRS, Stick with It

The IRS imposes both a penalty for failure to file and a penalty for failure to pay. So, if you cannot pay the tax due, it is still best to file the return to avoid the failure-to-file penalty. You will always pay interest on any amount due. The IRS allows people to enter into installment agreements or payment plans. Be aware that once you start a payment plan with the

IRS, it is best to never miss a payment or they will place you into a collection process that may be pretty aggressive and may include a levy on your bank accounts or a lien on your home.

Always report income. The IRS gets particularly uptight when taxpayers do not report all of their revenue. In fact, if you underreport revenue by 25 percent or more, the IRS will automatically consider your return fraudulent and assess penalties accordingly. Penalties for fraud are steeper than for mathematical errors. Also there is no statute of limitations on a fraudulent return.

Review Questions

1. Do you know your personal income tax rates (federal and state) and have you considered how the business will affect your personal tax rate?
2. Do you understand the federal and state income tax rules and how they will affect your business?
3. Do you know what forms you will need to be filed and the due dates for the forms?
4. Have you determined if any particular entity for your business would give you a tax advantage?
5. Have you checked with your local government to determine if there is a local income tax?
6. Will you hire a professional to prepare the required tax returns?

CHAPTER 10

Employment Matters

As a business owner, you will have to determine if you need help to run your business. If the answer is yes, then you have to determine if the individual who will be performing services to the business is an employee or an independent contractor. Many business owners believe that they get to choose whether someone is treated as an employee or an independent contractor; unfortunately, that is not necessarily the case. The determining factor generally is going to center on the amount of control the employer has over the individual who is performing services for the business. It costs less for the business to hire an independent contractor than to hire an employee because of the employment taxes that must be paid by the employer for anyone who is classified as an employee. Chances are the IRS has already made a determination about the particular job you are trying

> to fill. While most workers are going to be considered employees, a business owner might be able to create a position that would be more likely to be classified as an independent contractor if he or she understands the rules.

Control of the Details vs. Control of the Results

Before you can determine whether someone is an employee or an independent contractor, you need to be aware of a few definitions. A person performing services for your business may be a *common-law employee*, an *independent contractor*, a *statutory employee*, or a *statutory non-employee*. A common-law employee is anyone who performs services for your business if you have the right to control what work will be done and how the work will be performed. An independent contractor is anyone who performs services for your business who has the right to control the means and methods of accomplishing the result of the work that will be done. If you, the payer, have the right to control or direct only the results of the work but not the details of how the work will be done, the service provider would generally be deemed an independent contractor. You might compare this to someone cleaning a house as opposed to someone building it.

Some Very Specific Examples: A Statutory Employee

Even if someone is an independent contractor, he or she may still have to be treated as an employee if designated as a statutory employee. The following individuals are generally treated as statutory employees: (1) a driver who distributes beverages or meat, vegetables, fruits, or bakery products (other than milk); or who picks up and delivers laundry or dry cleaning, if the driver is your agent or is paid on commission; (2) a full-time life insurance sales agent whose principal business activity is selling life insurance or annuity contracts, or both, primarily for one life insurance company; (3) an individual who works at home on materials or goods that you supply and that must be returned to you or to a person you name, if you also furnish specifications for the work to be done; and (4) a full-time traveling or city salesperson who works on your behalf and turns in orders to you from wholesalers, retailers, contractors, or operators of hotels, restaurants, or other similar establishments, if the goods sold are merchandise for resale or supplies for use in the buyer's business operation. The work performed for you must be the salesperson's principal business activity. In addition, the statutory employee must meet the following three conditions:

- The service contract states or implies that substantially all the services are to be performed personally by him or her.
- The person does not have a substantial investment in the equipment and property used to perform the services (other than an investment in transportation facilities).
- The services are performed on a continuing basis for the same payer.

Statutory Non-Employees

There are two categories of statutory non-employees: direct sellers and licensed real estate agents. These individuals are treated as independent contractors or self-employed for federal tax purposes, if: substantially all payments for their services are directly related to sales or other output, rather than to the number of hours worked, and there is a written contract that states that the individual will not be treated as an employee for federal tax purposes.

The Definitions to Use

The big issue is the right to control the individual who is performing services for the business. Evidence of the degree of control or the degree of independence must be reviewed. Facts that provide evidence of the degree of control and independence fall into three categories: behavioral control, financial control, and relationship of the parties.

Behavioral Control. This generally includes the type and amount of instruction that the business gives to the worker. Because the amount of instruction given to a worker will vary for different jobs, what's important is whether the business has retained the right to control the details of a worker's performance or, if it has given up that right, not whether the instruction is actually given to the worker. The types of behavioral control to consider include:

1. When and where the services would be performed
2. What equipment, tools, or supplies would be used to perform the services and where such items would be obtained
3. What work must be performed by a specific individual
4. What order or sequence is to be followed in completing the tasks
5. What additional workers are needed to assist with the work and, if any, who is to hire those additional workers
6. The amount of training necessary to perform the services (generally, the more training, the more likely the worker would be considered an employee)

Financial Controls. Things to consider when determining whether a person is an employee or an independent contractor determination are:

1. Whether the worker has unreimbursed business expenses. While both employees and independent contractors may have unreimbursed expenses related to their work, independent contractors are more likely to incur such costs, especially fixed costs that are incurred regardless of whether work is currently being performed.
2. The extent to which the worker makes his or her services available to a relevant market, such as if the worker performs similar services for other businesses or to the general public. This is a big issue. *In fact, many companies require that independent contractors form a business entity (limited liability company or corporation) and offer their services to others before they can work for the company.*
3. How the business pays the worker is also relevant. Employees are generally paid a guaranteed wage for a specific time period (hourly, weekly, or other time period), while independent contractors are often paid a flat fee for a specific job or project. Some professions are commonly paid an hourly fee; this alone will not make an independent contractor an employee. An employee can be paid a commission, which varies depending on performance. This factor, by itself, does not change the status of

employment. The extent to which a worker can make a profit or loss performing the services is an important factor. Generally, independent contractors can control their profit or loss by adjusting the amount of time spent on performing services, or controlling the costs and expenses related to such services. Whether or not an independent contractor has made a significant investment in the facilities he or she uses in performing services is a factor to be considered. However, this is not a requirement.

The Relationship of the Parties. Whether the parties have a written agreement or contract describing the relationship they intend to create is an important facto. For example:

1. Do the parties have an employment contract or an independent contractor agreement?
2. Is the business providing employee-type benefits to the worker (e.g., health insurance, life insurance, vacation pay, sick pay, or retirement planning)?
3. What is the duration of the relationship? The independent contractor usually works on a specific project or for a specified period of time, while an employees usually works for an unspecified or indefinite period of time.
4. Does the worker performs services that are a key aspect of the regular trade of the business?For example, if a software development firm hires a programmer, the programmer's work would be more likely to be presented as the work of the business; therefore, the work would be more likely to be directed and controlled by the business. This would certainly be more so than if a department store hires the same programmer to develop a Web site for its retail operations.

And if Your Determination Is Unclear

Once the behavioral controls, financial controls, and the relationship of the parties have been reviewed, the business owner can make a determination of whether a worker is an employee or an independent contractor. For those cases that are unclear, the business owner can submit a Form SS-8

(Determination of Worker Status for Purposes of Federal Employment Taxes and Income Tax Withholding) to the Internal Revenue Service for an official determination.

The Devil Is in the Details

It is important that you, the employer, determine correctly whether an individual providing services is an employee or independent contractor because the employer must withhold income taxes and employment taxes from the employee's wages. In addition, the employer must pay Social Security and Medicare taxes and unemployment insurance on some of the wages paid to an employee. *See below for details on employment agreements.* Generally, there is no withholding on the earnings of the independent contractor; however, there are reporting requirements. If you pay an independent contractor who performs services for your business more than $600 in a calendar year, you must file a Form 1099 with the Internal Revenue Service to report those payments. *If an employer misclassifies an employee as an independent contractor, the employer may be held liable for all of the employment taxes for that worker. In addition, the employer may owe a penalty and interest on the unpaid taxes.* This can cost you a pretty penny.

In addition, issues with qualified benefit and retirement plans may be created by the misclassification of employees as independent contractors. This could occur because most qualified benefit and retirement plans require that the employers not discriminate among employees and many have participation requirements for employers who offer such benefits to employees. For example, if a business has 15 employees and 60 independent contractors and the IRS reclassifies 25 independent contractors as employees, the benefit plans may no longer be qualified and therefore eligible for favorable tax treatment. As a final note, it is important that you be aware that the IRS does perform 1099 audits. *See the Independent Contractor Agreement and the Consulting Service Agreement in the Forms Section of this book.*

A Good Example to Remember

Another issue relative to treating a worker as an independent contractor who should be classified as an employee is that the worker can get the employer into trouble. Here is a scenario that happens all too often.

Bob runs a restaurant and hires a manager to run the business for him when he is not there. Both Bob and the manager agree in writing that the manager will be paid as an independent contractor. All of Bob's other workers are kitchen or wait staff and are treated as employees. Bob pays the manager $35,000 per year, regardless of the amount of time he is actually at the restaurant. After about a year, Bob determines that the manager is not doing that great of a job and decides to let him go. Immediately after being dismissed, the manager contacts the IRS and the state department of revenue and tells them, "Bob treated me as an independent contractor, and I should have been an employee." The manager also makes an unemployment claim against the business with the department of labor. The government agencies then swoop in on Bob to determine whether the manager should have been an independent contractor or an employee. Bob is required to fill out the SS-8 form and respond to the IRS and the state department of revenue requests for information. It is determined by the IRS (and the state follows suit) that the manager should have been treated as an employee because his services were completely controlled and directed by the restaurant owner. Bob now has to pay for the taxes that should have been paid on behalf of the manager in excess of $13,000, including federal withholding, Social Security, and Medicare taxes (both employee and employer portions), not to mention penalties and interest. All this for an employee who earned $35,000 per year. Clearly, you do not want this to happen to your business.

How to Get It Right

The bottom line is that you want to do this right to avoid problems down the road. If controlling the details of the job for those who are performing services to your business is necessary, then you will need to treat them as employees. Keep in mind that, while there is no penalty for treating an independent contractor as an employee, the cost of doing so can easily exceed 10 percent of the wages paid to such an individual. It is better to do your homework and, if you are going to pay someone as an independent contractor, you should have an independent contractor agreement in place. Set the job up so that it is more likely to be found to be an independent contractor arrangement. Contract provisions that should be included, in addition to the general terms of your arrangement, are:

1. a provision that the independent contractor can hire others to perform the services or to assist
2. a statement that there is no employer/employee relationship and that no taxes will be withheld
3. a statement that that no workers compensation or unemployment insurance will be paid
4. a statement that indicates that the independent contractor does similar work for others
5. a provision that the business will not control how the work is to be completed beyond general direction on the results of the project or job.

Be aware that an independent contractor agreement in and of itself will not necessarily protect you from the IRS determining that a worker is an employee, but it will help determine the intent of the parties. Another common way of helping to ensure that your worker will remain classified as an independent contractor is to require that the worker form an entity, such as a limited liability company.

Hiring an Employee

Once you have determined that you will be hiring an employee, you will need to understand the employment-related issues you will face. The first thing you will need to do is to find your potential employee. This can be done by word of mouth, ads in newspapers, or advertising through employment-related agencies. You may have potential employees complete an employment application.

Once you have found the right candidate for the job, a job offer should be made. It is wise to do this in writing in the form of an offer letter. The letter

Be sure that your application form does not ask questions that are illegal, such as age, sex, race, religion, marital status, or if the applicant has children. In addition, these types of questions should not be asked during any interview process.

should set forth the basic terms of employment, such as: a description of the work to be performed, the wages that will be paid and how they will be paid, the expected hours to be worked, start date, vacations and sick days, any benefits offered by the employer, any dress or uniform requirements, and any other issues specific to the job. Also a statement that the employment is considered at-will should be included, which means that the employment can be terminated at any time, for any reason, by either party. An example of such language is "The parties recognize the employee's right to resign at any time for any reason; similarly, the employer may terminate the employee at any time, with or without cause." Be aware that some state courts have limited the at-will doctrine, which may make it wise for an employer to terminate for good cause only. As an employer, you are not required to offer you employees benefits such as health insurance, but be aware that once you offer such benefits to one employee, you should plan to offer the same or similar benefits to all employees to avoid discrimination issues among your employees. *See the Application for Employment-Short Form on the CD that accompanies this book.*

Maintaining Employment Files

As soon as your candidate has accepted the position, you will need to start a file on that employee, starting with the written offer of employment and including a copy of the employee's Social Security card and driver's license. (Make sure the address on the driver's license is current.) Also, have the employee fill out the IRS Form W-4, Employee's Withholding Allowance Certificate, which sets forth the number of allowances claimed by the employee for income tax withholding purposes. Be aware that the employee should be allowed to change this form at any time.

It is a good idea to keep all employee files in a locked or secure location that can be accessed only by you or authorized personnel. The employee file should be maintained on the employee for as long as he or she works for you. Moreover, you should be adding any significant events or notices to your employees' files, especially any job performance-related issues. This could be helpful to document events should the employment relationship be terminated. In addition, if an employee has a medical issue, complaint, or problem while employed in your business, it should be well documented in the employee's file. Documentation may be as simple as handwritten notes of meetings or reprimands (put a date on everything) or formal evaluations, notices, or letters. Employees do have the right to review their file and to add written material. A request to view an employment file should be accommodated within 30 days (sooner if possible). The review should be done by the employee or his or her representative and should be done in the presence of a supervisor, if possible. If a copy of an employment file is requested, the file should be provided "as is," and nothing should be removed or added prior to providing the copy. This is why it is important to maintain an accurate employment file. *See the Employee Incident and Discipline Documentation Form as well as the Employee Performance Review, and Time Sheet-Hourly Employees on the CD that accompanies this book.*

Employment Contracts and Employee Handbooks

One of the most common questions regarding employees is "Should I have an employment contract or employee handbook?" A formal employment contract is not required and in many cases is not necessary. This is particularly true of low-level positions within a business. Employers want to make sure they do not create additional or onerous requirements with a contract or employee handbook. For example, if an employer enters into an employment contract for five years and does not set forth early termination procedures, the employer can be held responsible for some or all of the salary due under the contract even if the employee no longer works for the employer. Keep in mind that verbal employment policies and employee handbooks or manuals are often considered a contract by the courts. Because employers are responsible for establishing such policies or handbooks, any ambiguities are often construed in favor of the employee. You will want to be careful to avoid restrictive language that may result in creating policies or procedures that you do not wish to follow. Generally, in small businesses with few employees, a handbook is not necessary; however, as a business grows to over ten employees, it may be advisable to put policies in writing. Given the complexities of creating an employee handbook, it is wise to use an attorney to review any handbook before it is provided to your employees. This will also help to ensure that your handbook complies with the laws in your state. *See the Offer of Employment and the Employment Contract in the Forms Section of this book. Also, see the Company Employee Handbook in this same section.*

Equal Opportunity Employer and Sexual Harassment

At a minimum employers should establish that they are equal opportunity employers, which means that an employee's age, race, color, national origin, sex, religion, and in some states sexual orientation will not be considered in decisions on hiring, promotions, pay, or benefits. Also, a sexual harassment policy should be put in place. This policy should state that the employer will not tolerate any form of sexual harassment connected with employment in or outside of the workplace. For both of these policies, the employer should set forth clear procedures for making a complaint or grievance pertaining to any alleged violation of the policy. The key is having a clear set of procedures identifying where an employee can make a complaint. Business owners and management should be educated in the procedures and how to handle a complaint in a sensitive and effective manner. Generally, employers will not be held responsible for the offensive behavior of their employees unless they knowingly encouraged or allowed such behavior to continue. However, employers can be held responsible if they do not have stated procedures for making a complaint and investigating the matter. *(See the Employee Grievance Form on the CD that accompanies this book.)*

For example, Good Food Restaurant had no stated sexual harassment policy. One of the cooks had patted one of the servers on her bottom. There was little doubt as to the truth of the claim, as the waitress had a floured handprint on her bottom when she made her complaint to one of the managers. The manager did not inform the business owner and just handled the situation by having a stern discussion with the cook, who promised not to do it again. With that, the manager made a few notes in the employment files and let the issue go. Unfortunately, the lack of communication with the waitress left her uncomfortable and she felt her complaint had not been addressed. She quit, claiming the sexual harassment had forced her to do so. In a settlement to avoid a wrongful termination or sexual harassment case, the employer was forced to pay the waitress $15,000. If both the waitress and the manager could have relied on written procedures for such a problem, the business may have been able to avoid legal action and the need to make a monetary settlement.

Be aware that an offending employee does not have to be fired, but efforts should be made to keep the parties involved separated during the investigation, and to inform the parties of any action taken. An employer may have a zero-tolerance policy for sexual harassment or may attempt to educate the offender on the issues. Keep in mind that often this is a "he said/she said" situation and it may be difficult to be sure of the events in question. The key issues are to state that sexual harassment will not be tolerated and to set forth the procedures for making a complaint (with whom the complaint should be made), investigating the matter, and taking action if necessary. These policies and procedures do not have to be set forth in a contract or employee handbook; in fact, they can be written independently and attached to your employees' first paycheck or W-4 Form, with a copy for their records and a copy to sign for their employment file.

Exempt vs. Nonexempt Employees

Most business owners have heard or will hear the terms *exempt* and *nonexempt* as it pertains to employees; however, few people really know what it means. The Fair Labor Standards Act (FLSA) requires employers to categorize jobs as either exempt or non-exempt. Generally, the distinction is whether the position is paid by an hourly wage (nonexempt) or salary (exempt).

Generally, salaried positions are exempt from minimum wage, overtime regulations, and other rights and protections afforded hourly wage positions.

Typically, only salaried positions such as management, executive, supervisory, professional, or outside sales positions are exempt positions. Employees who are paid an hourly wage are non-exempt and must be paid at least minimum wage and must be given time and a half for any hours worked in excess of 40 per week. Salaried positions are not entitled to overtime pay as they are paid to get the job done whether it takes 35 hours or 55 hours per week. Currently, the federal minimum wage is $5.15 per hour; however, states and sometimes local governments have been granted the power to set their own minimum wage rate. Today, there are 27 states that have a minimum wage rate higher than the federal rate, and one state (Kansas) has set its minimum wage rate lower than the federal rate. Tax issues are not impacted by the exempt versus nonexempt status. Generally, both exempt and non-exempt employees are entitled to a safe and healthful work environment, the right to equal opportunity employment, and rights provided by the Family and Medical Leave Act (applies to employers with 50 or more employees).

Part-Time vs. Full-Time Employees

Most states and federal law leave it up to an employer to define what constitutes part-time status within a company and to determine the specific schedule of hours. Most companies define full-time employees as those who are regularly scheduled for a set number of hours each week (40 hours or similar amount), and part-time status is for anyone who is regularly scheduled to work less than full time. The main reason for differentiating between part-time and full-time employees is to distinguish between the employees who receive company benefits and those who are not eligible for such benefits, or to provide a way of distinguishing between two sets of benefits for two classes of employees. It is legal to have one set of benefits, or none at all, for part-time employees, and another set of benefits for full-time employees. When it comes to benefits, an employer should treat each employee within a class of employees the same, to avoid claims of discrimination and to comply with the Employee Retirement Income Security Act of 1974 (ERISA). ERISA is a federal law that sets minimum standards for most voluntarily established pension and health plans in private industry to provide protection for individuals in these plans. Among other things, ERISA requires employers to provide participants in employee benefit plans information about the plan's features and funding, to establish grievance and appeals procedures, and to grant participants the right to sue for benefits and breaches of fiduciary duty. The employer is treated as a fiduciary of the plan, which means it must operate the plan in the interest of its participants. ERISA has a strict anti-discrimination provision, which requires the employer to treat each participant within a particular class of employees equally. Over the years, amendments have been made to ERISA, the most notable of which are in the area of health plans and include:

- *Consolidated Omnibus Budget Reconciliation Act (COBRA)*, which provides some workers and their families with the right to continue their health coverage for a limited time after certain events, such as the loss of a job.
- *Health Insurance Portability and Accountability Act (HIPAA)*, which provides important protections for workers and their families who have preexisting medical conditions or might otherwise suffer discrimination in health coverage based on factors that relate to an individual's health.
- *The Newborns' and Mothers' Health Protection Act (Newborns' Act)*, which includes protections for mothers and their newborn children with regard to the length of the hospital stay following childbirth. The Newborns' Act requires that group health plans that offer maternity coverage pay for at least a 48-hour hospital stay following childbirth (96-hour stay in the case of Cesarean section).

Employment Taxes

Employers have responsibilities with regard to taxes, including withholding, depositing, reporting, and paying employment taxes to the IRS. The Social Security Administration has additional reporting requirements (Forms W-2 and 1099). In addition, most states have their own requirements with regard to withholding, depositing, reporting, and paying income taxes withheld from employee paychecks. Finally some local city and county governments have what is called an *occupational tax*, which is a flat tax paid for each employee working for the employer. This tax is often called a *head tax* and may be paid by the employee or the employer, or both. You will need to check with your local government to determine if it imposes an occupational tax.

Federal employment taxes include the following:

- **Federal income tax.** Employer must generally withhold federal income taxes from an employee's gross wages. The amount withheld is determined by the amount of gross wages, employee filing status (single/married, etc.), the frequency of pay periods, and the number of employee withholding allowances claimed on the Form W-4. The employer remits the amount withheld to the IRS to cover the employee's federal income taxes on those wages. This is a trust fund tax, which means that the employer holds the tax in trust on behalf of the employee until remitting it to the IRS.

- **Social Security and Medicare Taxes (FICA).** Social Security (12.4 percent) and Medicare Taxes (2.9 percent) pay for benefits that workers and families receive under the Federal Insurance Contributions Act (FICA). Remember there is a wage limit for Social Security taxes of $97,500 (2007) and there is no wage limit for Medicare taxes. Employers are required to withhold part of these taxes from their employees' wages (7.65 percent) and the other half (7.65 percent) is required to be paid by the employer. Federal income taxes, Social Security taxes, and Medicare taxes, both employee and employer portions, must be paid semi-weekly, monthly, or quarterly depending on the amount due and the employer's wage history.

  If you are a new employer and have never paid wages before, you are a monthly schedule depositor for the first calendar year of your business, unless you are a special exception to the rule. Monthly achedule depositors should deposit taxes from all of their paydays in a month by the 15th day of the next month, even if they pay wages every week.

Employers with prior payrolls and taxes of $2,500 or more per quarter must determine if they make either monthly schedule deposits, or semi-weekly schedule deposits. This determination is based on the taxes due in the look-back period, which is the four calendar quarters preceding the prior July 1. If during the look-back period the total income tax withheld and the FICA taxes (both the employer and employee portions) totaled under $50,000, you will be required to deposit the taxes monthly. If the total taxes in the look-back period were over $50,000, you must deposit the taxes semi-weekly. *Again, monthly schedule depositors must deposit* each month's taxes by the 15th day of the following month (for example, taxes from paydays during July are deposited by August 15).

Semiweekly schedule depositors must follow the following schedule: for wages paid Saturday, Sunday, Monday, or Tuesday, deposit by the following Friday; and for wages paid Wednesday, Thursday, or Friday, deposit by the following Wednesday. There is an exception; if you accumulate a tax liability of $100,000 or more on any day during a deposit period, you must deposit the tax by the next banking day, whether you deposit monthly or semi-weekly.

Remember: deposit rules are based on when wages are paid, not earned, and if a scheduled deposit day falls on a Saturday, Sunday, or federal or state bank holiday the deposit is due on the next day that is not a Saturday, Sunday, or federal or state bank holiday. These taxes and deposits are required to be reported to the IRS quarterly on Form 941, Employer's Quarterly Federal Tax Return, which is due by the end of the month following the close of the calendar quarter (April 30, July 30, October 31, January 31).

- **Federal Unemployment Tax (FUTA).** This is the federal portion of the state programs that offer unemployment compensation to workers who lose their jobs. The federal FUTA rate is 6.5 percent, but the employer is given a significant credit for unemployment taxes paid to the state. FUTA is paid only on the first $7,000 of wages paid to each employee. FUTA tax is paid separately from withheld income tax and FICA. Employers pay the FUTA tax. It is not withheld from the employee's wages. FUTA is required to be paid and reported annually (the last day of the month following the close of the year—January 31 for a calendar year taxpayer) unless more than $500 in FUTA tax is due; then the employer should be depositing and reporting the tax on a quarterly basis. The FUTA tax is reported on Form 940, Employer's Annual Federal Unemployment (FUTA) Tax Return.

State and local employment taxes may include the following taxes:

- **State Wage Withholding Tax.** States that have an income tax require that state income taxes be withheld from an employee's gross wages. *See Appendix C for a state-by-state listing of income taxes.* Generally states will require businesses to report and pay withholding on a quarterly basis. You should check the rules for your state to be sure of the deposit and reporting requirements.

- **State Unemployment Tax (SUTA).** Each state operates its own unemployment compensation program that is funded largely by taxes on employers. These taxes are in addition to any FUTA you may owe. For the most part, state unemployment taxes are imposed directly on employers and are not withheld from the employees' wages. Today, only three states, Alaska, New Jersey, and Pennsylvania, impose additional unemployment taxes on the employee directly through withholding. New Jersey also includes a disability insurance tax as well. To calculate the amount of state unemployment taxes, multiply the taxable wages by the employer's unemployment rate. Each state assigns a rate to each employer every year. The fewer unemployment claims an employer has, the lower the rate. Every state limits the tax you must pay with respect to any one employee by specifying a maximum wage amount to which the tax applies. (For example, Colorado taxable wages are $10,000 per year.) If you are a new employer, you will pay tax at a new employer rate (usually higher) until you have established a history (generally one to three years) with your employees and unemployment claims. State rates generally vary from about a half of one percent to as high 11 percent. The state unemployment tax, like the FUTA tax, is an employer-paid tax. Most states require payment and reporting of the unemployment tax on a quarterly basis, but it is best to check with the department of labor for your state.

- **Employee Occupational Tax (or Head Tax).** Some local governments (cities or counties) impose a flat tax on employees and/or employers for each worker within their jurisdiction. For example, Denver has what it calls an occupational (and business) tax on every employer and employee providing services of at least $500 within the city limits. The tax is imposed on both the employer ($5.75 per month) and the employee ($5.75 per month). Usually the tax is paid and reported quarterly. Check your local government to find out if it imposes a head tax. This may help you choose one business location over another.

Failure to Pay Employment Taxes

As an employer, you must pay employment taxes. If you fail to pay, the IRS and often the state will come after you. This is particularly true with regard to taxes that have been withheld from an employee's wages. Because such taxes are actually the employee's money held in trust by the employer, the IRS and most states get particularly testy when an employer does not deposit trust fund taxes. The IRS penalty for failure to pay trust fund taxes is 100%. This is known as the *trust fund recovery penalty* and is assessed against the person responsible for paying the tax, rather than to the entity. Thus, the business owner may not have limited liability when it comes to the trust fund taxes and the trust fund recovery penalty. *In short, a business entity is not going to protect you from the wrath of the IRS. Also, these taxes may not be dischargeable in a personal bankruptcy.*

Penalties for late payment of employment taxes can run a business between 2 and 15 percent in addition to interest. If you must rob Peter to pay Paul, just make sure that employment taxes are always the top priority. More than 15 days in delay is going to push the penalty to 15 percent. If you delay this long, the IRS will be peppering you with penalty notices telling you where you stand. Because of the complexities of payroll and employment taxes, it is recommended that businesses with employees use a payroll service that not only cuts the checks but makes tax deposits and files employment tax returns too.

Workers' Compensation Insurance

Workers' compensation is an insurance that covers injuries and occupational diseases that occur while on the job. The system is generally a no-fault system, meaning employers are liable even if the employee may have contributed to the injury or illness. Workers' compensation insurance is mandatory in every state but Texas. (Texas has an optional program.) As usual, the rules and rates can vary from state to state. Some states exempt small employers (fewer than three to five employees) and in some states an employer may choose to self-insure. Workers' compensation is insurance; therefore, the employer pays a monthly insurance premium for the coverage. Rates are based on the type of work being performed by the worker. For example, for an office worker the premium would be lower, say $1 per $100 of wages, than for a plumber, for whom the premium might be $5 per $100 of wages. Often the rates are based on estimated payroll and are reconciled with actual payroll figures after the end of the year. Some programs will give a dividend (a refund of part of the premium) to employers with fewer or lower claims. The workers' compensation program in your state may be through private carriers or may be run by the state. North Dakota, Ohio, West Virginia, Washington, and Wyoming have state-run agencies that provide all the workers' compensation insurance.

Employee Incentive or Retirement Plans

As a business owner, you will want to consider whether to provide your employees with a retirement plan or perhaps some other type of incentive program. Generally, employers will offer such benefits as an incentive to attract and retain the best employees. There are many types of retirement and benefit plans available. Below is a discussion of the most common plans.

- **Cash Bonus.** Often, new businesses are not in a position to immediately start and maintain a retirement plan for their employees. In such cases, perhaps, a discretionary cash bonus program would serve as an adequate incentive program. This type of bonus program can be extremely flexible and it can be entirely discretionary for the employer. Any cash bonus paid to an employee should be included in the employee's gross wages and all employment taxes should be paid on any cash bonus paid to the employee. Any such bonus would be a business deduction to the employer.

- **Profit-Sharing Plan.** This plan allows an employer to share a percentage of profits with the plan participants by contributing a percentage of profits to each participating employee's account. As with any other retirement plan, the contributions must be invested in a prudent manner. These simple and straightforward plans do not require a contribution every year, but contributions must be regular. No plan participant can receive more than the lesser of 100 percent of their earnings for the year or $44,000 for the year. Employer contributions in excess of 25 percent of the total compensation paid to all plan participants in any given year are not tax deductible. In addition, there is a money purchase plan (Keogh) that requires an annual contribution but can provide a larger deduction for the employer. These plans are nice for the employer who does not wish to give an equity position to its employees.

- **401(k).** This is maybe the most common of employee retirement plans. This plan allows the employees to make tax-deferred contributions to their own retirement account from their wages. Employers can contribute to the employees' 401(k), but employer contributions are not required. These days it is common for an employer to match an employee's contribution. There are some complex rules in order for a 401(k) to remain in effect and to ensure the plan is fair to all participants. As a result, administration of these plans can be a bit expensive, but the employer contribution requirements can be adjusted to make up for administrative costs and can therefore make the 401(k) plan attractive to the employer. In addition, there is a self-employed 401(k) plan available to self-employed individuals and one-person entities that is inexpensive to administer.

- **Defined Benefit Plan.** This is one of the more complex of the employee retirement plans. This plan sets forth a formula that specifies the exact benefits a plan participant will receive if he or she works until retirement. All contributions are made by the employer and are based on the future defined benefits. There is no limit to the annual contribution made by the employer, but the maximum annual benefit paid to a participant is limited to $175,000 or 100 percent of the final average pay at retirement. This plan, while complex, may offer the highest tax benefit to the employer and the greatest benefits at retirement to business owners.

- **SIMPLE IRA.** This plan is a sophisticated version of an individual retirement plan that allows employees to defer up to $10,000 ($12,500 if over 50 years of age) of their annual compensation. Employers are required to match the employees' deferrals up to 3 percent of the employee's total wages or 2 percent of total wages regardless of whether the participant makes a deferral. SIMPLE plans are similar to 401(k) plans except they do not have all the testing rules. There are some drawbacks, however; employer contributions are immediately vested with the employer rather than over years as with most other plans. SIMPLE plans severely limit what an owner can contribute and they cannot be used with other retirement plans. Also SIMPLE plans cannot be used by employers with more than 100 employees.

- **Employee Stock Ownership Plans (ESOPs).** These are tax-qualified defined contribution retirement plans designed to provide employees with an ownership stake in the company. First, ESOPS have several advantages over other defined contribution retirement plan: ESOPs are intended to be invested primarily in company stock, rather than a diversified portfolio. Second, ESOPs can borrow money to purchase a large block of company stock. Third, there are substantial tax advantages, including corporate tax deductions for both principal and interest payments on ESOP loans. Fourth, there can be a deferral or total avoidance of capital gains for stock sold to an ESOP by owners of privately held companies. And fifth, there is a tax deduction for dividends paid on ESOP stock. The big question is, do you want to give your employees ownership in the business?

- **Qualified Employee Stock Purchase Plans (ESPPs).** These are also known as Section 423 plans and allow a company to make its stock available to its employees for purchase at up to a 15 percent discount from fair market value. To qualify, the opportunity to purchase stock must be made available to virtually all of the company's full-time employees who have been with the company at least two years. As with qualified stock option plans, employees will receive favorable capital gains tax treatment on the stock purchased through the ESPP if they hold the stock for at least two years after the purchase offer or one year after they actually purchase the stock. These plans are used primarily by public companies, because there are strict securities rules and high administrative costs and because privately held companies often have difficulty establishing a fair market value for their stocks. Employee participation in an ESPP is strictly voluntary.

The employee benefit plans described above are just some of the options available to employers today. Getting professional assistance in determining the appropriate plan or group of plans is essential. The rules are complex and easy to misinterpret, so get expert advise.

Terminating Employment

Any termination of employment should be well documented in the employee's file, regardless of whether the termination is voluntary or involuntary. The details of termination may be important for state unemployment claims or for claims of wrongful termination. Never fire an employee based on age, race, color, national origin, sex, religion, marital status, or in some states sexual orientation. In addition, if you need to terminate an employee based on a medical condition, make sure you have provided all appropriate accommodations (addressed any special needs) to help the employee succeed. If an employee's medical condition makes him or her unable to perform a particular job, it may be wise for the employer to offer the employee another position in the company that he or she can perform without being affected by the medical condition.

When firing an employee, it is wise to have a witness in the termination meeting. This should be a member of management or the head of personnel rather than a co-worker of the employee. If your business is small, you may want to have your attorney sit in on the meeting. This is purely a protective measure but may be particularly useful in case of a later wrongful termination action. The termination should be well documented and clear reason(s) for termination should be given to the employee. Ambiguity here can cause a problem with both unemployment claims and potential wrongful termination lawsuits. Employment records should be kept indefinitely, as they may be used in the future to prove adherence to employment policies and procedures. Any wages and unpaid sick or vacation pay should be given to the employee at the time of termination. Any keys should be returned to the employer and authorized personnel should escort the employee from the premises. Many employers follow a similar process when an employee voluntarily quits. In some cases, employers have paid an employee who has given two weeks' notice for the last two weeks without requiring the employee to continue working.

Severance Agreements

Often in lay-offs and in some other types of terminations, an employer will offer the employee a severance package. Often this is an agreement to continue to *pay compensation or benefits for a specific period of time or to pay a lump sum in exchange for a release by the employee of all claims related to employment.* All severance agreements should be set forth in writing. There is no standard amount of money that is generally offered, as each employer will determine the severance package they can afford. Often, the employer will pay a set amount for each year employed. The employer is generally required to give the employee at least 21 (sometimes 45) days to consider a severance package. Hourly workers are rarely offered a severance package. One of the major purposes in executing a severance agreement, even when the employee resigns, is to avoid a lawsuit that claims the employee quit because the employer created an unacceptable environment in the workplace, constituting "constructive termination" by the employer. Be careful to follow the rules when offering a severance package or get help from a professional.

W-2s and 1099s

After the close of each calendar year, each employer is required to report employee wages and all payments made to independent contractors to the worker, the IRS, and the Social Security Administration. Employee wages are reported on the W-2 Form and all independent contractor payments are reported on the 1099. The forms are not difficult to prepare, but must be printed on special forms. Forms and software are available from most office supplies stores for a fee. You can order blank forms from the IRS at 1(800) TAXFORM (829-3676), but be prepared to wait at least 10 to 14 days for the forms. W-2 forms are due on January 31 following the end of the tax year and 1099s must be filed and mailed by the 28th of February.

Additional Costs of Employment

Wages and employment taxes, including unemployment insurance and workers' compensation insurance, are not the only cost of employment. Don't forget any benefits you plan to provide your employees. In addition, employers should also consider the cost of providing the employee with office space, equipment and tools, vacation and sick pay, promotional materials, business cards, and anything else the employee may need to do the job. You should consider at least these additonal costs of employment.

Illegal Questions

When hiring, make sure that you have reviewed your employment application for illegal questions. Question about age, sex, race, national origin, religion, sexual orientation, marital status, and children should not be asked on an employment application or in an interview. While you may be curious, these questions may be answered (not asked) once you have hired the candidate.

Confirm Employment Records and Check References

It is wise to confirm employment records and to check references for any applicant you plan on hiring. Be aware some candidates will provide limited information, such as dates of employment and whether or not the employee is eligible for reemployment with the company. Still, much can be learned from such limited information, especially the honesty of your applicant. If you are fortunate, a former employer may be willing to provide additional information or answer more detailed questions. if so, go for it. Ask about the candidate's ability to be on time, the types of projects or tasks he or she performed, the reasons for leaving the company. Confirm employment dates and whether the former employer would recommend the candidate for the job in question and ask one final question. Ask the reference to verify the address of his or her business. This simple question may help to weed out any make-believe references.

Employees Come and Go, Equity Is More Permanent

As a business owner, you will need to think long and hard before giving your employees an equity position in your business. Often once equity is transferred, it cannot be returned, although, in some cases, you could provide that an employee who stops working for the business must sell the equity back to the business. However, this may or may not be an optimal situation for the business and its owners. Such a requirement could create a financial hardship on the business, as you may not have control over the timing of events. New businesses may want to stick with other types of incentive programs for their employees, such as a discretionary cash bonus, 401(k), and other types of benefits before they consider making equity an option. If you are going to give employees an equity position, it is wise to require that they be employed by the business for a significant period of time before receiving any equity.

Background Checks

Performing background checks on new employees is not required by law, but is a good idea for most employers. This relatively inexpensive precaution can protect you, your other employees and your customers. It can save you time and money, not to mention give you peace of mind regarding your new hires.

Review Questions

1. Will you need to hire people to help you operate your business?
2. Have you determined if those people will be independent contractors or employees?
3. If they are independent contractors, do you have an independent contractor agreement?
4. If they are employees, do you need an employment agreement?
5. Do you have an employee application?
6. Are you prepared to make a written offer to a potential employee, including wages, sick and vacation pay, job description, at-will hiring and termination policy, start date, uniform or dress requirements, and any other specifics necessary to do the job?
7. Have you checked references and previous employment for your job applicant?
8. Do you plan to use a payroll service?
9. Do you plan to use an employee handbook or manual?
10. Will you pay your employees by the hour or with a salary?
11. Will you provide your employees with benefits such as health insurance or a retirement plan?
12. Will your employees be part-time or full-time?
13. Have you done a background check on your candidates?

CHAPTER 11

Get It in Writing

In order to do business in today's marketplace, it is essential that you understand some basic aspects of a business relationship. Unless you are a practitioner of the law, it is unlikely that you will understand the entire spectrum of legal language. It is possible, however, for you to have a handle on many of the fundamentals. With this basic sense of the contract relationship, you should be able to develop a workable vocabulary. Without these basics, you are likely to find yourself vulnerable to those who are anxious to take advantage.

Basic Language

The first lesson to be learned is that there is nothing so complex that it must remain a well-kept secret to all but those few who are legally indoctrinated. If that were the case, many in the American business marketplace would be unable to cope and the marketplace would collapse. Such is, obviously, not the case. As with any difficult problem (or sentence), the idea is to break it down into its component parts, examine and understand the meaning of each part, and then reassemble the whole. The whole will invariably become more understandable.

There is nothing, conceptually, philosophically, or otherwise, that cannot be broken down into simple language. Anyone who suggests otherwise is being less than honest or has a problem with the basic concept of communication. Don't ever be embarrassed into believing that you can't understand. If your professional can't explain it adequately, get another professional. In fact, a good contract should be written in "plain language" so that it can be understood by all parties, not just the lawyers.

Oral Contracts

It is common to hear clients say, "We never put anything in writing, so therefore there is no contract. Right?" Generally, an oral contract is just as binding as a written agreement; it is just harder to prove. Each state has slightly different laws about many aspects of business. Most states have what is called a *statute of frauds* that establishes that certain contracts will be enforceable only if they are in writing. In some states, for example, an oral contract is not valid if it is for a value in excess of $500 or if the contract will take more than one year to complete. Also, in most jurisdictions, any contract involving real property (lease or sale) must be in writing in order to be valid. It is always appropriate to check with your local professional to examine the laws of your particular jurisdiction.

The most important thing to remember is that resolving issues with an oral contract invariably depends on the ability of the arbiter (the judge, the jury, the arbitrator) to discern which of the parties is telling the truth. Truth, therefore, is essentially based on credibility. The problem is that some people appear to be more credible than others, whether they're telling the truth or not. It is wise to depend on the written word carefully structured at the outset of a relationship, rather than trying to resolve differences in what people remember or because of language ambiguities.

Handling the Noncontract

If it is deemed inappropriate or unnecessary by one of the parties to document the business relationship, it would be wise for the other party to keep a running narrative. Although such a narrative would certainly be called self-serving by anyone who wanted to deny its validity, courts are very inclined to accept notes that are made contemporaneously to an event.

The more such notes that are kept, the more difficult it is for another party to contest them. It is interesting that such notes are often able to resurrect vague memories, especially when the failure to remember is really a question of bad memory and not bad faith. It is also a good idea to share these notes with the other party. If the other party fails to disagree with the notes in timely fashion, that failure often suggests to a finder of fact (judge, jury, or investigator) that the narrative was accepted by both parties. In some cases, when it is appropriate, some people even put the following language at the close of the narrative that they are communicating to another party: *"If I do not hear from you to the contrary, I will assume that the above is a fair representation of our discussions to date."* You can certainly see the import of such a statement and the effect on a court of the recipient's failure to respond.

Ambiguities vs. Clear Definition

It is easy enough to recognize the really problematical words, such as "may," which should usually be either "will" or "shall."

The client may respond within 30 days.
The client will respond within 30 days.
The client shall respond within 30 days.

Other words, such as "satisfactory," should be clarified by indicating whose satisfaction is necessary to have a job deemed "satisfactory."

When the job has been deemed finished in a satisfactory manner, the last payment will be made.

*When the job has been deemed finished in a satisfactory manner **by the architect**, the last payment will be made.*

The more difficult problem is involved with words that appear to be definitive but that, in the context of a sentence or paragraph, become unclear.

"If the job is done well, the client may pay a bonus."

Does the word "job" require any further definition?

What are the specific elements that constitute the job?

What about "done"?

Is the job "done" when the roof is on or not until the interior painting has been finished?

What about "well"?

Some people may consider that the job was done "well." Others may consider it to be quite shabby.

What about "bonus"?

What amount is to be paid … and when?

This should give you an idea as to the need for clarity of language at the outset of any business relationship.

What Is a Contract?

Aside from the legal definition of a contract, which is an offer, acceptance, and consideration (payment), it is fair to say, from a practical standpoint, that a contract is (1) an acknowledged relationship between two or more people, (2) with obligations, (3) and prerogatives, (4) to be exercised and enjoyed under particular terms and conditions. "Acknowledged" merely suggests that both parties have agreed to the elements of the contract. Generally, with a contract each party will contribute something—product, services, or money—in return for which that party will be receiving something—product, services, or money. It could be services for money or it could services for services. A contract should have a date at the beginning and should be signed at the end by each of the parties involved. The terms and conditions usually refer to time elements and the things that one party needs to be done before the other party is obliged to contribute his or her product, service, or money.

The real key to any contract is that each party understands what he or she is expected to do and what he or she is entitled to receive. If you enter a contract and anything is unclear, go back and start again, until you understand all of your obligations and prerogatives. Even the most carefully designed language may be subject to ambiguities, especially as a business relationship matures and changes in time. The best protection is to be reasonably careful at the outset to avoid using misleading language and to address any unresolved questions.

Amendments

Although there are simple contracts that require no changes during the course of a contract period, many will. Each party to a contract has expectations that are built into the language of the contract. These expectations may change. Circumstances may cause changes to be made. Anticipated time schedules may have to be aborted. Prices for materials increase. It is true that proper language can anticipate many of these things and assess a cost to each change, depending on circumstance, but the language is often generic to cover a variety of exigencies rather than well defined to cover a specific change. A good example is the contract to build a house. How many things will cause changes—an increase in the price of raw materials, the absence of a subcontractor, inclement weather, or just the client's preference for a different size, shape, or color?

As a result, a contract should include language that allows for the contract to be altered or amended. Any amendment to a written agreement should be done in writing and should be signed by the parties. If you are not using a written contract, it would be wise to acknowledge any changes from the original understanding by an agreement in writing (a letter would probably suffice), so that such changes are well documented and understood by the parties involved.

Mediation and Arbitration

If two parties have a problem resolving an ambiguity or defending a "cost for change" situation in a contract, the results could be disastrous. Not only might the contract never be completed, but the ensuing litigation would certainly have a long-term negative effect on the relationship of the parties. In addition, their respective reputations in the community would likely never be the same. A good way to anticipate such problems is to have a clause in the contract that allows an objective third party to resolve any disagreement. Since such a person, who is friend to both parties, is rarely waiting for the opportunity to serve in this role, the parties may agree that any disagreement be taken to an independent or unrelated arbitrator or mediator instead of the alternative of seeking redress in a court of law. Because of the extensive length of time and the high cost of retaining attorneys and going to court, mediation or arbitration has become a very satisfactory method for resolving to these problems in a timely and cost-effective fashion. The difference between an arbitrator and a mediator is that the former will actually make a binding decision after hearing the facts, while the latter will act as a conduit through whom the parties will examine the differences and, hopefully, arrive at a negotiated settlement or compromise.

What Is a Lease?

Clearly, a purchase is a simple case of paying for a product or service and receiving it. Sometimes payment is made in cash, sometimes in the form of services, or in kind (by another product), or by a promissory note (which will be discussed later in this chapter), but the sale is made and each party is finished with all aspects of the sale.

With a lease, one party has the right to use a particular product or property for a specified period of time during which the other party receives money for extending this privilege. At the end of the lease, the lessor (who owns the property) can take it back. There are also leases with options to buy the product or property at the end of the leasing period. This means that the lessee (who used the product) has the right to buy it at a particular price (a residual value) or based on a specified formula such as a percentage of the value. Make sure you understand the terms and conditions under which you, as the lessee, would have an option to purchase at the end of the lease.

During the lease term, of course, you as the lessee have the obligation to insure and protect the product or property in anticipation of returning it to the lessor at the end of the lease in the same condition it was when you started using it. The usual language that follows this protection language is "reasonable wear and tear excepted." In other words, it is expected that normal use could affect the product. It is the lessee's obligation to protect against "unreasonable or extraordinary" wear and tear. Think of an automobile lease as an example.

The Hidden Danger of the Option

It is always difficult to think in terms of options available at the end of a lease when you are in the process of negotiating the basic terms at the beginning. Unfortunately, this is the only chance you get to do so. You will certainly want to know if the lease will terminate or expire without any options at all. If it does, you will have to return the equipment or property leased, and you will have to consider replacing it, if necessary. The real questions come up when you do have options.

If you have a buyout clause at the end of the lease, you will need to know the price is the buyout price, $1.00. This is sometimes the case when the price has been entirely covered by the lease payments. Is the buyout is based on a specific residual value? (This is often the case with automobiles or heavy equipment when the residual value depends in great part on the mileage or usage put on the equipment during the lease term. The value will remain as quoted provided that the usage has not exceeded the specified use. Is the buyout based on market value at the time the option to purchase is exercised? (This buyout clause requires an additional caution, since some companies consider the replacement value, some use depreciated value, and still others may predicate the value on the condition of the equipment at the time the option is exercised.)

And Don't Forget the Maintenance Contract

Some companies will continue a maintenance contract after you've purchased the equipment. Some will not. This should cause you to wonder about the balance of the equipment's anticipated life and the cost of replacement parts as well as the availability of competent repair personnel. Some companies will continue your maintenance contracts, but you should watch out for an increase in cost or changes in the contract details. The original maintenance contract may have included all parts and labor. The new maintenance contract may be without labor or without parts or only if the equipment is shipped to the lessor's repair facility. Some may agree to give you a loaner during the period needed to repair the equipment. Others may just leave you without the use of the equipment for an indefinite period of time.

Then, there are the additional costs of purchasing the equipment when you exercise your option. There may be hundreds or even thousands of dollars to which you might have agreed when you signed the original documents years before. It is usually in the small print on the reverse side of the contract.

If you intend to operate your business for some time, you must actually separate your thinking into two parts at the time you negotiate the lease contract. One part should be to negotiate the best deal you can for the term of the lease. The other should be to carefully examine the options that you will have at the end of the lease contract.

Then, you must factor the options into the lease to see what it is you will really be paying in the long term as opposed to the cost if you would merely finance the purchase of the equipment at the outset. The only problem with this is that many lending institutions might not be interested in loaning you the purchase price based on your particular financial condition at the time you apply for the loan. The manufacturers are, obviously, a little more liberal in their approach to this situation, since their primary goal is to sell product.

Also, carefully examine the horizon in terms of the level of sophistication of the equipment you are obtaining and the likelihood of a gigantic jump in the level of sophistication throughout the term of your lease. One good example is the computer and its software, which changes so dramatically over relatively short periods of time.

A Promissory Note

If you do not have enough cash to buy a product or service, the provider or vendor may accept, for some or even all of the price, your promise to pay. You might also borrow the money from a third party, like a bank. Then you would have an obligation to repay the money to the lender.

In either case, this promise to pay will be evidenced by a paper that you signed by which you agree to pay a certain amount at a particular time or during a particular period, usually with some interest for the privilege of paying later instead of immediately. This paper is called a *promissory note*. It is also a contract of sorts, so it should have a date at the top and the terms and conditions of repayment, and it should be signed by the party to be charged, that is, the borrower.

This promissory note, as in any other contract that is clearly defined, is enforceable in a court of law. If the signing is witnessed by an independent third party who can testify to the validity of the signature, the note is even more secure because the party signing the note is less likely to deny the signature. The strength of this witness is evidenced by the fact that a witnessed promissory note in some jurisdictions is enforceable for a longer period of years. Most notes would be enforceable for a much shorter period of time, normally, four to six years unless the note specifies otherwise.

Be careful, however, to seek the appropriate professional advice before making your own legal judgments. For example, the length of time for potential enforcement of the note might be from the date of the last payment, not from the date the note was negotiated or signed. Also, ibe careful of language that would destroy the negotiability of the note—the ability of the note holder, the payee, to sell it to a third party at a discounted rate.

The Statute of Limitations

If one party wants to sue on a contract, the party must recognize that this privilege has certain limitations. Generally speaking, an action can be brought in court within a set number of years from the date of a contract unless the contract states otehrwise. (Also, remember the witnessed promissory note.) This general rule, however, has many variations, such as the date of last payment (as noted above), the waiver by one party not acting in timely fashion, and a variety of other exceptions, all of which depend on the nature of the agreement and the relationship of the parties. Always seek professional advice whenever these questions arise. Each jurisdiction may have very diverse answers. It is a good idea to examine many of these questions with your professional at the time the document is prepared, rather than have to look for the answer after a problem has arisen.

The Intimidation Factor

Insisting on a written contract for each and every business relationship is not necessarily the best approach to business relationships on a practical level, especially those with a shorter time frame or those involving less money. Sometimes, it is better to assess your risk and decide that the best approach is an informal one. Sometimes, setting out goals in a memorandum simply initialed by the parties to create an acceptable priority list may be the best way document an agreement to ensure that it will survive the memories of the parties. Remember: it is usually not the malintentioned that you are trying to protect against. It is the failing memory of the parties and the ambiguous language that is more often the core of a problem.

The need for a written contract and the nature of that contract should be dictated by the scope of the activity involved, the length of time for the performance and payment, the intricacies of the terms and conditions, and the amount of money or value involved. You would certainly have a different approach to get the lawn mowed than you would to have a house built. If you consider these factors on a practical level, you will probably pick the best approach to use in most cases.

The Small Print

Some people are intimidated by a contract or a lease that has many pages. Although the salesperson would like you to believe that the transaction is a simple one between friends, the number of pages seems to belie this casual approach. The fact is that each party seeks to protect those interests that he or she considers important. In a lease, which, by its very nature is a long-term relationship, it is certainly necessary that a variety of contingencies be included and defined primarily for the benefit of the lessor, whose property is going to be at risk.

What is interesting is that most of these contracts, because of concerns that the average person would likely feel intimidated by their length and be more likely to take them to an attorney, are written in type so small that many people can't read it. Sometimes this small print is even put on the reverse side of the signature page, making it appear to be a secondary aspect of the contract. The use of smaller font and the reverse of pages seems to work to the benefit of the lessor or seller. Most people are told (and they seem to accept it) that the language is "standard" and "there only because it's required by law." *Don't be deceived!*

The two pages might contain the same language as would fill 12 regular-size pages. Yes, much of the language is required by law. But don't lose sight of the purpose of the law. The lazws are intended to protect you and require that you be made aware of certain information. If you don't read it and understand it, woe be unto you. Don't let the small print fool you. Take it to your professional. Have him or her explain it to you. If necessary, make some notes in your own language so you will understand and remember the terms and conditions of the contract that you are signing. Don't let anyone tell you that it's not really important. If those words are really not important, why are they there?

Although many states now have laws that will allow you to walk away from a contract within a certain period of time (such as three business days), it is unfortunate that the reasons normally leading to a change of heart often don't surface until this cancellation period has passed.

Warranties

Many contracts contain warranties by which the purveyor of goods or services guarantees the work or the product for a certain period of time and under a certain set of circumstances. Be careful that you understand the parameters: exactly what is covered under the warranty and the conditions under which the coverage is in effect. The roof on a house may be guaranteed—but only for one year. It may include all labor—but not the materials. An automobile can be warranted for five years or 50,000 miles, but with exclusions that in some cases may be so extensive as to essentially provide no protection at all. Read the language carefully and go over it with your professional if there is anything you don't completely understand or if there appear to be ambiguities that need clarification.

You ought never to be obliged to sign a contract as it is printed. There is no such thing as a standard contract allowing no change. You may normally negotiate whatever elements are unsatisfactory to you. If you don't ask—the answer is no. *For an interesting exception to this, see the Chapter 15, Franchise or Otherwise: Why Reinvent the Wheel?*

Some Common Language

Below are some common provisions you will find in many contracts. They are often stated in a "general provisions" section at the end of the contract:

- **Governing Law.** This Agreement shall be governed by and construed in accordance with the laws of the State of _____.
- **Modification.** This Agreement cannot be changed orally, but only by instrument in writing, signed by both parties.
- **Waiver.** No course of dealing between the parties, and no delay on the part of any party hereto in exercising any rights hereunder shall operate as a waiver of such rights. No covenant or other provision herein may be waived otherwise than by an instrument signed by the parties waiving such covenant or other provision.
- **Legal Fees.** The prevailing party in any dispute between the parties shall be entitled to be paid, by the non-prevailing party, for all legal fees and out-of-pocket expenses incurred in connection with such dispute.
- **Entire Agreement.** This Agreement constitutes the entire understanding and agreement of the parties as to the matters set forth in this Agreement.

- **Assignment.** Neither party may assign its obligations under this Agreement or any document executed by it in connection herewith without the prior written consent of the other party.
- **Severability.** Whenever possible, each provision of this Agreement will be interpreted in such manner as to be effective and valid under applicable law, but if any provision of this Agreement is held to be prohibited by or invalid under applicable law, such provision will be ineffective only to the extent of such prohibition or invalidity, without invalidating the remainder of this Agreement.
- **Counterparts.** This Agreement may be executed simultaneously in two or more counterparts, any one of which need not contain the signatures of more than one party, but all such counterparts taken together will constitute one and the same Agreement.

A Refresher on Corporate Signatures

Remember: if you have created a corporation or an LLC and intend to use its protection, you must sign any contract as an officer of the corporation or a manager of the LLC, not with just your personal signature. *Be sure to review the chapters on legal entities to be sure you understand the difference.*

Customer Agreements

It is wise to use a written customer agreement whenever possible. However, if you use a customer contract, keep it simple and to the point. If you give customers or clients a ten-page contract, in most cases you will scare them away. One to two pages should cover the basic terms of your agreement. Things like key dates, fees and costs, description of the product or services, payment terms, return policies, and interest or late fee. This agreement should not necessarily cover all things but should serve to help make sure the parties at a minimum start out on the same page. This will likely protect you against a loss of memory and give you some proof of the basic agreement between the parties.

Interim Rent

When leasing equipment, your lease may provide that the lessor may charge an interim rent for the time period between the funding of the lease and the actual delivery of the equipment. Make sure you understand when the leasing company or lender will be making the money available to purchase the equipment and how soon thereafter the equipment will be delivered or available to the business that is leasing the equipment. This can increase the cost of the lease significantly, particularly with equipment that is located far away or that is being customized in some way.

One-Sided Contracts

If you draft a contract, be careful to make it fair, since a one-sided contract may be construed against the person who wrote it by a judge or arbitrator. In some cases, a contract may be null and void if it is too one-sided. For example, if a large soup manufacturer makes a contract with carrot farmers and most of the contract provisions are in favor of the soup company with very limited rights for the farmers, a court could find that the bargaining position between the parties is so inherently unfair as to be against public policy. The one exception to this would be the lease, which tends to be one-sided in favor of the property owner, landlord, or lessor.

The Penalty Clause

A penalty clause is a clause in a contract that is void or is not enforceable. The most common example of this is a clause in someone's last will and testament that states "If anyone contests the provisions of this Will, they will not have the right to take under the Will." Because many states give certain heirs the right to contest a will, this provision is likely void or unenforceable. The provision, however, is not illegal to put in the document. In fact, people who read the provision may very well not contest the will because they believe the clause to be valid.

Businesses have been known to use penalty clauses in their agreements, such as a non-compete clause that is likely to be found too broad in length and geographical area, in an attempt to make a party take a certain action. Just be careful that any contract you sign is not full of penalty clauses, particularly any contract that you write. Clauses of this nature calling for money damages, if drafted properly, can be designated as liquidated damages, providing the amounts involved are commensurate with the actual loss and not over the top. ("Liquidated damages" are an amount required to satisfy a loss resulting from a breach of contract.)

Read It before You Sign ItB

Many attorneys will tell you to have the contracts you sign reviewed by an attorney. But, the better advice is that *you read* any contract you sign. Believe it or not if, after reading it, you do not understand something, that is the time to get an attorney to help you understand or, better yet, if you are unsure of anything, have an attorney review it. The more complex an agreement, the more likely it should be reviewed by an attorney.

Review Questions

1. What is the best way to protect yourself if your contract is oral?
2. What is the difference between a contract and a lease?
3. What does the statute of limitations mean?
4. What should you look for under a warranty?
5. How do you document changes in a contract?
6. Have you read the contract or lease before you signed it?
7. Do you need assistance in understanding a contract or a lease?

CHAPTER 12

Getting the Money

Whether you are starting a lemonade stand at age eight or starting a consulting practice based on a lifetime of experience at age 80, you will need start-up capital: the money necessary to fund the business, enabling it to buy raw materials, build an office capability, rent premises, or acquire inventory. It may be as simple as a dozen lemons, a cup of sugar, a pitcher, some paper cups, a box to use as a stand, and a sign to attract customers. On the other hand, it may be as complex as a computer, computer software, a telephone, a fax machine, a telephone answering machine, a photocopier, paper, stationery, business cards, and dedicated telephone lines for the modem and the fax, and the all-important cell phone. Instead of a sign to get the attention of passing traffic, you may also need a brochure or other method of advertising your services as well as, in many cases, Internet positioning.

Whatever the Business . . .

If you start a retail business, you'll need a place of business and an inventory. If you start a service business, you'll need equipment and possibly transportation. Whatever the venture may be, you will need working capital, the money necessary to convert the business idea into a functioning business. One of the biggest reasons for failure in the start-up of a new business or the takeover of an existing business is the lack of adequate working capital. This is good enough reason to build a business plan that shows just what dollars are going to allow the business to achieve certain plateaus during its growth period. The business plan is an essential element to remind the entrepreneur of the road ahead and to allow the investor to envision the expectations of business success.

Look in Your Pocket

Since most people will not have the same vision as you do for the success of your business, it will be difficult to get them to loan you money or invest in your business. The first place to look for money will be your own pocket. If you have enough of your own money to start the business, you will not have to share the profits with anyone. If you don't have enough of your own money and you need to borrow some, you will at least be showing people that you have enough confidence in your business idea to put your own money at risk. After all, why would anyone want to risk his or her money on your idea if you are not willing to risk your own?

The Joint Venture

Every new business venture needs start-up capital. Every existing business that is purchased requires working capital. Sometimes, the money is used to buy equipment or raw materials. Sometimes the money is used to hire the people you need to help build the business, including yourself. Apart from finding it in your own bank account, there are really two basic ways to get money for a business venture. You can *borrow* it with the intention of paying it back some day with interest for the period of time you've used it. Or you can *sell a part of your business* in return for the money that a person invests. This is called giving an *equity position* to the investor. There are, of course, combinations of these two concepts, a little borrowing and a little equity selling.

Variations on the Theme

There are many variations on these concepts. As the business becomes more sophisticated, a lender may have *options* to take an equity position (an opportunity to acquire an interest) in the business at a later time, when the company has proven itself successful. Sometimes, this opportunity is built into the concept of the company going public. This happens when the company sells part of its stock to outsiders in the public marketplace, such as on the stock exchanges.

But these positions are for a later time, when the business goes beyond simple concepts. On the simple side, it is fair to remain with the two basics; either borrowing from a lender or sharing your profit with a third party who has invested on the basis of taking an equity position in your business.

Borrowing

The problem with borrowing is that you have to pay it back with additional payments for interest. You can borrow it for a period of time, say one year. Your agreement can be that you'll pay it all back plus interest at the end of the year. You can also pay interest only on the note during the year and pay the entire principal (the entire borrowed amount) at the end of the year. Or you can agree to pay portions of it back on a monthly basis with the accrued (earned) interest each month, so that, at the end of the year, the borrowed money and the interest is all paid. This is called *amortizing* the loan. And, of course, there are many variations on these basic approaches.

Security for the loan

When people loan money to other people, they usually want some assurance that the money will be paid back. However, just in case they would like to know that they can depend on another method to ensure the return of their money. They will usually ask for some security (collateral), which will serve as compensation in the event the borrower cannot repay the loan. If that happens, they will keep the security, which could be a car, a house, or other personal property or real estate that has a substantial market value and that they can, relatively easily, convert to dollars. Of course, for some businesses a personal guarantee may be sufficient.

Investing

The aspect of sharing your ownership position with someone who has money to invest has some positives and negatives, just as borrowing does. The positive side is that you won't have to return the money to the investor, because it's an investment, not a loan. The negative side is that the investor will have the right to look over your shoulder as you operate the business. After all, the investor wants to make sure that his or her investment is being used properly and not going down the drain because of bad business decisions. As you can see, by taking money from an investor for an equity position in the company, you will have to give up some degree of control. Sometimes, it's better to borrow the money and pay it back with interest, because you can completely control the company without any interference from someone who may know very little about the business but who will want to make business decisions in order to protect his or her investment. This may often be opposite to what is best for the growth of the company and its long-term goals as you envision them.

At other times, it is better to have an investor helping to make the decisions because it causes your creativity to be balanced by an objective caution to protect your working capital. Oftentimes, this gives a better focus to the business. This, in fact, is one of the reasons why internal managements will often turn to an outside board of directors to help guide the management team in making long-term decisions. Which approach would you rather take?

Return of Investment (Return on Investment)

Every person putting money into a business that someone else owns is going to be interested in getting the money back (return of investment) and in earning money while it is being used (return on investment). After all, if the person put the money in a public company or in a mutual fund that invests in public companies, he or she would expect a return of the investment and a bonus for the use of the money. Often the bonus is the fact that the investment has grown during its tenure and is worth more than when the dollars were originally invested.

If the money is being loaned, then the lenders will know just how much interest they will collect for the use of their money. If the money is being invested, the investor wants to know the conditions under which the investment will be returned and the method by which the investor can expect a bonus for investing in the business.

How Does the Investor's Money Get Returned?

The reason that fewer people are interested in investing than in loaning is because there are basically three methods by which the investment could be returned and the bonus earned.

1. If the company is successful in its initial program and decides to accelerate its growth by going into the public marketplace (this is called an *initial public offering*), then the stockholders (investors holding equity positions) may get a multiple of dollars for each dollar invested. This is not the usual occurrence.

2. If the company is very unsuccessful and is forced into liquidation or bankruptcy, the owners or investors may get their investment back. Unfortunately, this is only after all the debts of the company are paid. It is unlikely that investors will recover all of their investment. And it is quite certain that they will receive no bonus for the money.

3. If the company is very successful and is acquired by a larger company, their equity position will probably be worth more than the money they invested in the smaller company. If the acquiring company is already in the public marketplace investors may be able to sell the new stock that they received in exchange for their stock in the smaller company for more than they invested.

Again, there are many variations on this theme, but it should give you an idea as to how the investor views the investment and what the alternative exit strategies may be. That is, how the investor expects to get his or her investment and any bonus out of the company. Sometimes, the investment may be purchased by other parties, either inside or outside the company. This is often done by a second wave of investors when the company has gotten on its feet but needs additional working capital for continued growth.

These methods are basically for the investor's return *of* investment. If the company is successful, the investor may receive dividends (a share of the distributable profit). This, of course represents the investor's return *on* investment, the bonus earned for the use of the investment. Most investors, however, are sophisticated enough to recognize that, even if the business generates an early success, it is quite likely that management will use this profit to reinvest in the business, rather than distribute the profits to shareholders (investors). After all, most businesses need to buy inventory, acquire equipment, add personnel, move to larger facilities, or use the money for other things that will enable the company to grow—all, by the way, to the ultimate advantage of the investor in the long term.

Getting the money is sometimes the only thing on your mind when the start-up or continuity of your business is at stake. This is a good time, however positive or optimistic you may be about the venture, to get some good professional advice on the risks involved. In other words, what will happen and where will you (and your family) be in the event that your labor and creativity do not pay off. An objective perspective should not necessarily deter you from your goals, but it may suggest some alternative directions that may be less problematical or more likely to succeed. Although investors usually understand the risk inherent in a new business venture, lenders, who are not involved in the ultimate success of the business, will usually have the business owner guarantee the loan personally. This means that the business owner will be obliged to repay the loan, whether the business is successful or not. Would this change your thinking about lenders and investors?

The Business Plan (Developing a Road Map)

Most business plans are prepared with a singular purpose in mind: to generate an interest in the business that will cause people to either lend money or invest. There is, however, a much better reason to create a business plan: to give management a clear picture of the short-term and long-term goals of the company. A periodic rewriting of the plan will cause you to recognize the shortcomings of the previous plan and adjust your thinking for the future. This is the reason for constantly revisiting and restating your business plan.

Short-Term vs. Long-Term Goals

In the case of a lemonade stand, the entrepreneur may have the short-term goal of making enough money to buy a bicycle. On the other hand, he or she may have a much greater, long-term goal of growing the business to the point where it can handle additional product lines, such as cookies, sandwiches, and coffee, or it can generate enough activity to open on another street corner (which would entail hiring someone to operate the second location), or even to create a franchise, if the entrepreneur's lemonade recipe is distinctively good enough that other kids could use it successfully. Certainly, these may be grandiose ideas for the lemonade vendor, but you must understand that *long-term goals can be achieved only when they've been conceived.*

Creating the Road Map to Success

In order to convert a business idea into a business structure, it is important to have a plan that will establish the basic parameters of a successful start-up; design the alternatives to meet the contingencies that will invariably arise (in other words, prepare for the problems and the pitfalls), and create the discipline among the participants to follow the plan. The business plan, properly prepared, will give you this road map to success. It will examine alternative roads that may prove to be quicker but more dangerous or slower, but with a higher degree of certainty.

You should prepare a plan consistent with the size of your business and with your goals. You have also heard that a business plan has got to cover everything. But the larger the plan, the longer the reading, the less likely people will read it completely. And the purpose is defeated before it has a chance to succeed. Be careful that you don't use trade or industry language that the readers will likely not understand. This will clearly defeat your purpose—whatever it may be, whether to entice people to join the company or to intrigue people to invest. Use language that anyone can understand and don't use the excuse that industry jargon is necessary to explain the project.

Stick to the Basics

The basic business plan should include about tne fundamental components. And, keep in mind, that there is no magic required to create it. Therefore, there is no given priority schedule necessary in its preparation. Think logically about what the readers may be looking for and design the plan to meet their expectations. This may require that you have more than one business plan. Some purposes require different explanations.

1. *Look at the trade or industry* of which your business is or will become a part. Describe how it started, how it has developed, and where it is likely to go. This should obviously be designed to show your competitive position in the marketplace.

2. *Describe the company*—in part, as it relates to the entire industry but, more particularly, how the idea has (or will) become a reality. Discuss its potential, indicating both the dollars needed and the timeline required for its growth. And don't forget to indicate why your product or service will be able to compete in the industry. A competitive matrix is a good idea.

3. *Discuss the management*—the people, including yourself, who are going to be able to achieve the short- and long-term goals. This will involve disclosing the education, background, and prior experience of each person necessary to operate the business. Describe what each person brings to the table to contribute to the success of the company. Be careful to examine any negative aspects of any participant before you decide

whether or not to include it. It might be better, for example, to include a bankruptcy—and explain it as not being relevant to this business, rather than excluding it and being guilty of misrepresentation. Such an omission can lead to problems later—and possibly substantial liability. At the very least, it will keep your presentation from achieving your purpose. See your professional before you decide on matters that have such potential negative consequences. Most investors are more concerned about management than any other single element. There is an axiom in investor circles: "It is better to have a mediocre product and good management than mediocre management and a good product." This portion of the business plan will also show what other people are willing to risk—whether it is money, reputation, or both. It gives the investors some comfort in knowing that their investment is not the only risk being taken.

4. *Examine the competition*—in order to better understand why your company will have a competitive edge in the marketplace. If you sell hamburgers, you are clearly in competition with everyone else who sells hamburgers. But, keep in mind, even if you have developed a new and unique toy that no one else carries, you are still in competition with everyone else who is selling toys. You will need to understand your competition in order to compete appropriately and effectively in the marketplace.

5. *Analyze your target market*—make sure you can recognize your potential customer. Then, discuss the methods by which you expect to target this customer. You should include any reference materials that will give credibility to your analysis.

6. *Discuss carefully your working capital situation.* You will need to know, and any potential investor will want to know, just how judiciously you will spend your dollars to achieve the different plateaus you expect to reach on the way to your short-term and long-term goals. How long will your present finances last? Will they be enough to satisfy the requirements of the company's strategies?

7. *Future finances.* Future growth will probably require a second round of financial investment. Discuss the purpose of the additional dollars, the

goals you intend to serve, and the rationale by which you expect to achieve those goals. The time within which you expect to do these things will be an important element of your analysis.

8. *Look at projections.* Design a format that will show just how much money is required at different stages during the anticipated timeline. How many people will you need in six months? How much inventory will you need in the first year? What kind of replacement equipment will be required in the first 24 months? *Be realistic. Investors are not interested in the* possible. *They are interested in the* probable.

9. *Management of operations.* Discuss the job category of each person necessary to operate the business. Will he or she be an employee or will the job be outsourced? Will the products be completely manufactured or merely assembled? Do you need to own real estate or can you rent premises?

10. *Show your investors (or yourself) how you intend to create a payback* for the money invested, the time parameters for making these payments and the source of the payments. This is often referred to as the exit strategy, the method by which the investors can anticipate leaving the business with their original investment intact and any anticipated bonus or interest.

Examine the Concept in Action

Tony, age 11, needed money to buy a bicycle. He decided that going into business was his best opportunity to earn the money. He needed to borrow the start-up capital necessary for the business. He developed a business plan and presented it to his father. It was an oral presentation and not a formal written business plan, but the same basic requirements prevailed.

He needed to buy straw baskets, three kinds of fruit, colored paper to be shredded as stuffing for the baskets, ribbon, and plastic wrap. He bought these items, packaged them attractively, and offered them for sale in the neighborhood for Christmas presents. He generated enough money to pay back the loan (his father did not ask for interest), buy his bicycle, give five of his creations to members of the family for the holidays, and had enough money left over for two tickets to the ball game.

The following approach was responsive to the questions his father asked before committing to investing in Tony's business.

He went to the market to price his raw materials.

He went to the specialty stores to price other similar products (and to check on the best design and packaging).

He decided how much time he would need to build an appropriate inventory.

He sought advance orders (or at least promises for some advance orders) from some of his potential customers.

He understood the necessity of timing his product properly for the holidays, keeping in mind the shelf life of the product and the time most people would be interested in buying this or an equivalent product.

As you can see, this is not an academic exercise. It is the necessary beginning to any business venture. Selling fruit baskets may be a little simplistic as a business, but it contains the basic elements of manufacturing, retailing, and obtaining the capital necessary to start the business. The basics are always the same.

In some cases, the plan may include advertising materials, charts on the history of the industry, projections on the anticipated growth of the company, and other drawings, concepts, articles, or pictures of that nature.

More on Investors and Partners

The concept of giving up control was examined briefly earlier in this chapter. The problems, however, are so deeply rooted and are potentially so devastating that a second, more careful scrutiny is clearly in order. The primary goal of the average entrepreneur is to be captain of his or her ship and master of his or her destiny. This certainly suggests that he or she expects to set the goals, chart the course, and maintain continuity until the goal has been achieved.

Everybody Answers to Somebody

The problem is that everybody answers to somebody: the worker answers to the boss, the V.P. answers to the president, the CEO answers to the board of directors, and the entrepreneur must ultimately answer to the customer. The question is, apart from the customer, who else will the entrepreneur need to examine business decisions with before being able to implement them? The answer will normally be "to an investor or a partner." The term "partner" has been used here in a generic manner, as opposed to meaning a specific entity.

What Tools Are in the Toolbox?

A well-worn business axiom that the business owner would do well to remember is: "Diamonds are forever, but partnerships are not." On the other hand, not only can a partnership be a positive structure through which to initiate a business but, in some cases, it is the only way that a business can move from the starting blocks. Each person comes to the table with certain basic skills and with some experience. It would be unusual for anyone to have acquired all the tools necessary to properly operate a business in almost any trade or industry. The exception might be the person who has, early on, decided on a life's work and who has studied and worked toward this singular goal starting early in life. One example might be the surgeon. Another example might be the son or daughter who has been brought up in the business and trained by the mother or father for ultimate family succession.

For the most part, however, this will not be the case. And the average entrepreneur will find that the business's toolbox is missing a number of important items. It is then necessary, in one way or another, to acquire these tools. Such an acquisition can be made by affiliating with someone who has the tools.

Joint Ventures

In the business world, you have undoubtedly heard the words "joint venture" many times. Many beginners are put off because it really sounds like something special. It isn't. A joint venture is exactly what it sounds like. It is a team of two or more people or businesses embarking on a business venture. It can take the form of a partnership, a corporation, or any of the other legal entities covered in more detail in the chapters on types of entities. Each person can put in the same dollar investment or the investment can vary from joint venture to joint venture. Sometimes, two or more mature companies can participate in a joint venture. Sometimes, the joint venture can be horizontal, that is, companies on the same level doing the same thing, such as two retail stores. Sometimes, it can be a vertical joint venture; that is, companies on different levels doing different things, such as a manufacturer and a retailer. Each will presumably have something of value to contribute, in return for which each will expect a reward of some kind, usually in the form of money or discounts that will ultimately convert to dollars.

Partnership Synergy

The partnership is probably the most prevalent of the joint venture concepts. A partnership can be composed of two or more people or entities. Remember: the term "partnership" is being used loosely here to describe a relationship rather than a legal entity. In some cases, the partners will contribute equal dollars to initiate or buy a business. But this does not have to be the case. In some cases, an individual with technical or mechanical expertise will partner with an individual with marketing or financial abilities. It is the synergy of two different backgrounds that will, in most cases, be the predicate for a successful partnership. In still other cases, the partnership may be made up of one individual with the expertise in the particular business and another with the money to fund the business and allow the first partner to function in the business marketplace.

Active or Passive

A combination of partners may not necessarily have both working in the business. One may be an active participant; the other, who may have contributed the money, may be passive, that is, not actually work in the business. In fact, in many cases, in the early days of a business, one partner (this may also be a husband or a wife) will continue to work outside the business until the business can afford to meet the salary requirements of both partners. This concept of a passive partner begins to mirror the concept of investors. But, before examining that aspect, take a look at the negative side of the partnership.

Diamonds Are Forever

It is certainly difficult enough for even husbands and wives, which is the highest aspect of the partnership concept, to agree on all things all the time. Consider, then, two individuals, spending most of their waking hours working on the singular goal of creating a business success. Would you expect them to agree on all things all the time? Clearly not. How then are these conflicts, these failures to agree on the concept, direction, or specifics of the business, to be resolved? Most of the time, the conflicts are relative to a minor problem and will usually be answered by virtue of one partner having more expertise in that area than the other. Sometimes, resolution comes from one partner not considering the problem significant enough to warrant creating a problem in the personal relationship between the two. Sometimes, the conflict may require the use of an arbitrator, and, sometimes, the conflict may, unfortunately, have a long-term, negative impact on the partnership relationship.

The fact is that the worst of these problems could conceivably cause a serious breach in the partnership, resulting in both parties recognizing that they can no longer work together. In some cases, loss of one partner can actually cause the business to falter or fail. This contingency must be anticipated and adequate preparation must be made, at the beginning of the relationship, to handle this potential problem between the partners without the business being destroyed as a side effect of the conflict.

Other contingencies must also be anticipated. Very often, at the beginning of a partnership, an insurance policy might be taken on both partners to accommodate the untimely death of either, allowing the business to survive. The idea of conflict must be approached from this same perspective. After all, the goal (at least in part) is for the partners to protect and grow their investment, whether of time, energy, creativity, or dollars. The destruction of the business will deny all partners any possible equity that might have been earned during the life of the partnership.

The Buyout Concept

To avoid any such permanent damage, the original agreement or contract should contain a method by which one or the other of the partners can exit the company without destroying the business. This can be done in a variety of ways, one of which would be to agree to a formula for a buyout, which can be applied at any time either partner desires to leave. Arrangements must be made, of course, to replace the missing partner and his or her expertise in order to ensure continuity of the business. In the case of a passive partner, arrangements must be made for a return of dollars and possibly distribution of profits based on the earned equity existing at the time of the breakup. The agreement should be careful to ensure that the money taken from the business does not leave the company with insufficient working capital to maintain its operation. You will find that, even though it may never be necessary to use any such contingency language, it will at least serve to alleviate any pressures caused by conflict during the course of the relationship.

The Investor or Lender

The investor or lender gives a different cast to the problem. The day-to-day conflict resulting from working closely together may create conflict, but it could be worse. The working partners may differ with respect to any aspect of the day-to-day business approach, but it is likely that their goals will be the same because they both understood the initial dream. The investor or lender, on the other hand, may understand the long-term goal but might be much more conservative relative to how that goal is achieved, watching the dollars much more closely in the short term. This kind of attitude can be devastating to the entrepreneur who recognizes that, very often, the biggest dollars have to be spent in the earliest days. The second-guessing of the investor or lender can be harmful not only to the entrepreneur but, ultimately, to the lenders or investors as well.

All of this must be considered at the outset of the relationship and taken into account when the decision is made as to who will be responsible for what kinds of judgments or expenditures relative to actual operation of the business.

With a clear understanding at the outset, minor as well as major problems and conflicts can be avoided. Do not take for granted that everything will probably work out. If it is not specifically delineated, the odds are that it probably will not!

Value for Money

The real question you must ask, in any situation where your decision making may be subject to someone else's thinking, is whether the introduction of a third party, for any reason, is going to be worth it. More money will certainly allow for accelerated growth, but just enough money will allow you to get started without anticipating any interference. Technical or marketing expertise might give you great comfort in the decisions you need to make in order to move the business forward, but there are negatives to consider as well.

A partner can service this need, but the same expertise is probably available at a price outside the business. Your question should be, which is the best way to achieve short-term and long-term goals? If you don't have the money, the partner will be ideal in the short term. Remember, however, the partner will have an interest in the long-term rewards as well. Which direction would you prefer to take in your business?

The Board of Directors

There is, of course, another side to this issue. It is fair to say that, however expert you may be with respect to the business you own, it is impossible to anticipate the myriad of problems that will arise on any given day or in any given period of time. There could be shortages in available inventory, precipitous price changes, dynamic changes in competition, or new equipment becoming available, any one or more of which would be impossible to anticipate and any one of which could dramatically affect your business, either in the short term or in the long term. Without the years of experience in facing changes of this nature, you can often be left in a position where a wrong decision could entirely alter your business's prospects for continuity or success.

By having partners, lenders, or investors at your shoulder, you have people with experience other than your own who can contribute to your decision making and help to step over these unexpected hurdles, allowing the business to maintain itself. Certainly, you could solicit advice from any number of professionals. You could even put together, as many companies do, an outside board of directors, which, by its varied experience, can be helpful in making appropriate business judgments. However, people who already have a vested interest in your future, and in their own as well, will likely spend more quality time helping you to make a valued decision than the outsiders whose help is really momentary until they get into a car or onto a plane to go home. The other side of that argument, however, is that, since they don't have a personal involvement, their thinking may prove to be more objective. Which would you think is the better advice? Would you think that the kind of problem to be solved might play a big part in your answer?

It is this kind of alternative that you must factor into the positives and negatives of partners, investors, and lenders. Whatever your decision, make sure that the parameters of the relationship are clearly set out in language that is careful and unambiguous. It will put you on a much clearer road to the goals you've chosen. *See also Chapter 17, Exit Strategies and How to Value a Business.*

Owners As Creditors

As an owner of a business, you can loan money to the business. Such a loan should be documented by a promissory note and interest should be charged. Be aware that a business owner who is also a creditor will always be the last creditor to be paid if the business is closed or liquidated. The up side is that a business owner who is a creditor may be paid back before the any remaining assets are distributed to all the owners in accordance with their ownership interest (return of investment).

It Takes Money to Make Money

Generally, to borrow money from a bank, one needs to have money or assets. Sounds a bit like the age-old question: which comes first, the chicken or the egg? Banks are conservative and usually do not want to take risks. It is important that you understand this before applying for a bank loan. The use of the personal guarantee or collateral will often be enough to satisfy a lender, but it still requires that you have money or assets.

Where You Fall on the Food Chain

Creditors are higher on the food chain above business owners, partners, shareholders, or members. That is, all unrelated creditors will be paid before owners if the business is closes. This could be important when talking with friends and family about investing in your business. If they are creditors as opposed to equity owners, they may take a slightly higher position if the business is liquidated.

The Business Plan Is a Useful Tool for All

Many people think that you need a business plan only if you will be borrowing money or seeking investors. While it is true you will need a business plan for those purposes, the business plan is an excellent exercise for all business owners. It can serve as a feasibility study for your business and it may force you to address issues you would not have otherwise thought about. A business plan does not have to be formal or lengthy. Who will be reading your plan will dictate its length and formality. Even if no one but you sees the plan, it can be a valuable tool in the formation of your business.

Summaries in the Business Plan Can Help the Readers

The use of summaries can be very effective in a business plan, especially if a particular section is lengthy or contains industry-specific complexities. Use an appendix if necessary so that you do not slow your readers down. If they like what the summary says, they will read further.

Are You a Control Freak?

Know that if you take investors into your business, you will invariably lose some control. Make sure the partnership synergy is valuable enough to warrant sharing the equity. Determine the degree of control you will be giving up for the investor's participation. Discuss early on the working parameters involved in each person's part of the business. Put in writing agreements to ensure continuity of the business in the event of conflict.

Your Board of Directors

Remember that if you name people outside your company to your board of directors, you may lose some control. For a small business or closely held business, it may be wise to put only those involved in the business on your board, or even just owners. If you want help in the running of the business, the use of an *advisory board* may be more appropriate. An advisory board is group of professionals or experienced individuals who are interested in your success and can help guide you in making business decisions. The advisory board can be any size and can be casual or formal. As an owner you are not obligated to follow the advice of an advisory board; however, if you were to routinely disregard your advisors, you may find yourself without an advisory board.

Review Questions

1. What is the difference between a loan to your business and the purchase of an equity position?
2. What kinds of things can be used as security for a loan?
3. What is the difference between return *of* investment and return *on* investment?
4. What additional security are you prepared to put at risk to borrow money?
5. What is the value of taking in a partner?
6. Have you establish a formula to value the business in the event of a conflict?
7. What purpose can investors serve in addition to their financial support?
8. Have you identified who will be reading your business plan?

CHAPTER 13

Business Ethics or Just Good Business

In any contemplation of business, it would be a mistake to speak only of the technical aspects: those things like deciding which business entity to use, applying for the various licenses to do business, and the differences among employees, independent contractors, and other outsourcing capabilities. Yes, these things are essential. It is also essential to recognize that how you do business is a serious and substantial predicate for success. It goes beyond the technical. It supercedes the technical. And, yet, it is mandatory that you consider just how you will address these basics.

The two sides of business today are perhaps best represented by the words "responsibilities" and "prerogatives." The responsibilities or obligations are the elements to which the business owner must pay attention if the business is to have any hope of survival. Prerogatives include the care and feeding of the people on whose shoulders rests the responsibility for implementing the business concepts. Other aspects of these prerogatives are the highest levels of image, service, and quality that represent the business and its products or services. And the last prerogative is the obligation of the business owner to the community and to the other people with whom he or she does business. The prerogatives are those things that the entrepreneur controls, including the all-important decision making and, hopefully, the profit.

How you do business will, in large part, determine if you will stay in business. It would be wise to decide ahead of time how you will handle certain types of situations. It is relatively easy to know how to handle those situations that are good or going well. Giving some thought to how you will handle an unhappy customer, employee, or vendor may prevent you from overreacting or getting angry when the time comes. Treating others the way you would like to be treated is a good place to start. Below are some of the issues you may face as a business owner. It would be wise to give them some thought before you start your business.

Building Your Business Model on Trust

Building your customer base and, terribly important, retaining your customers are the results of your attitude toward the marketplace. Most small businesses survive by delivering to the customer the fulfillment of advertising promises about its product or service. The successful business is based on its reputation for fulfilling those promises consistently. The quality and the price must be consistent with the customers' expectations. Failure to maintain consistent quality and price can lead to failure of the business. The bait-and-switch tactic of some businesses leads to, at best, a short-term success.

If you have an unhappy customer or client, fix the problem—offer a refund, replace the product, or perform the service over again. There are two reasons for doing this. One is that if we like what someone does for us, we tell two people, and if we don't like what someone has done, we tell ten people. You really do not want customers out there bad-mouthing your business. The other reason is that the only person who can pierce your corporate veil is a judge. Customers do not sue businesses that have made a refund or solved a problem. If you never find yourself before a judge, you will never have your corporate veil pierced. Remember that, in most cases, it is not the initial problem (mistakes happen) that is the issue, but how the business addresses the problem.

The Business Depends on People

However small the business may be, very few entrepreneurs can handle all aspects of operation. Although outsourcing to independent contractors may be a partial alternative to hiring employees, internal working relationships must be created for the long term. Dependability becomes one of the bywords, "Will you be as available to me in the bad days as you were in the good days?" And this goes both ways: from the employer to the employees and from the employees to the employer. It's easy to share some of the profit with your employees when things are going well. What happens when there is a downturn in business? What will your relationships be with your employees in that situation? The answer lies in your attitude toward the future. If you discharge people to maintain your profit position, will you be able to find them when the business rebounds? Do you think they will wait for that to happen? Or, will you structure some sort of a plan that will enable them to survive even at the expense of a new car for the owner? There are many ways to phrase such a business moment, but that analogy is clear enough for everyone to understand.

In dealing with your employees and your independent contractors, you would do well to always treat them with respect and to always do what you say you are going to do. As you should do with your customers, do not promise what you cannot deliver.

Dealing with the Business Community

In some industries, raw material or component parts necessary to survive in business may become scarce. Those businesses that have shown loyalty during times when supplies were plentiful will likely be the businesses that continue to receive these necessary supplies when inventory gets tight. You're right. It doesn't necessarily happen all the time but adopting that attitude will often ensure success later on. It's something to think about.

For example, printing requires paper. Remember the days when paper was plentiful? Can you also remember the days when paper was precious and difficult to obtain? When the printer was overly aggressive in the time of the plentiful period and negotiated strenuously for a price that precluded profit for the paper purveyor, what happened when paper became precious? Those stingy paper negotiators couldn't get paper. Or, the price of paper—for them—was extraordinarily high. It is said that the one hand washes the other; that thesis represents a fairness to be considered at all times. It allows each of the players to survive the game. You may call it ethics in business or you may call it a survival plan. In either case, it is this stature that builds your business's reputation and allows for continuity in the marketplace. There are, indeed, other approaches to business and, in many cases, one business will survive and another may fail. That's just the nature of the business community. But, there is an attitude that each business owner must choose to adopt in this fight for survival and success. What will your attitude be?

Never Coming Back

It is interesting that, in the retail business community, the counter person is often the lowest paid and the least respected member of the team. This seems to fly in the face of perfect logic, since these are the people who have the closest ties to your customers, the people with whom the customers have their closest contact. In some communities, unhappy customers will discuss their problems with the counter person, and the answer, or the attitude assumed by the employee, may determine whether these customers return. Unfortunately, this is not always the case. In some communities, the customers do not often choose to have this confrontation and will merely refuse to return to the business. As noted earlier, building a customer base is important, but perhaps even more important is the ability of the business to retain the customers. Without this ability, a business does not survive, let alone succeed. And you, the owner, may never know why because the contact with the customers was not yours; it was with your employees.

A good example is the restaurant that adopts a policy of giving its wait staff permission (with supervision to avoid abuses) to remove an item from a bill if a customer is unhappy rather than offering a discount on his or her next visit. This allows the wait staff to not only assess the situation, but to immediately make the customer feel better about the problem and allows the customer to leave the restaurant feeling that his or her complaint was addressed. That customer will be more likely to return and give the restaurant another try.

Borrowing Without Permission

Business ethics is not a question of doing things. It is a question of adopting an attitude. It is an attitude that involves cooperation. It is, indeed, the golden rule of business: "Do unto others as you would have others do unto you." It is a question of one hand washing the other. And there are many aspects to this concept. When business gets a little slow and cash flow becomes a problem, you will pay some of your bills later than usual. What you are actually doing is borrowing from your vendors without getting permission first. In some cases, you may pay a premium for this privilege. In other cases, it may cost you nothing—except your reputation. The other side of that coin is that others may borrow from you in the same fashion. So long as you can survive this borrowing, you can be flexible—up to a point. You must be careful to ensure that you don't overreach or, conversely, that others are not overreaching. The attitude that extraordinary times require extraordinary measures must be acknowledged as part of the flexibility of the business marketplace. Be careful that you don't permanently hurt your business, but also be careful that you don't destroy important business relationships that allow your business success in the long term.

The Bait-and-Switch Approach

There is no question that the long-term success of any business depends, in great part, on the company's reputation in the community. Although some businesses survive by getting a customer once, and only once, most businesses depend for their success either on retaining customers or at least on inspiring customers to recommend the business to others, who will then try the business for the first time.

The "loss leader" is a business concept used more often than you might think. It is, essentially, an advertising ploy that brings customers into a store by offering a product or service at an extraordinarily low price. Instead of having sufficient supply on hand to satisfy customer demand, the store may have just enough to legitimate the advertising and then offer a comparable, albeit more expensive, item to customers who cannot buy the product that drew them to the store. Sometimes, it's difficult to tell whether the business merely ran out of product because the owners or managers didn't anticipate the customer demand or whether the advertising was designed to sell the more expensive product. One way to be sure about the company and its long term philosophy of business is to remember that old adage: "Fool me once, shame on you—fool me twice, shame on me." And, of course, remember the basic theme of all deceptions, "You can fool some of the people all the time and all of the people some of the time, but you can't fool all of the people all of the time."

Trust and Credibility

There is legitimacy to all business. This is represented by the customer's ability to trust the vendor in his or her local marketplace.

It is unfortunate when the curtain of trust is broken: the roofer who says you need a new roof when you don't, the car repair shop that says you need new brakes when you don't, the inspector who says you have termites, when you don't. These are examples of the trust curtain broken. These are examples of companies that only need to get you once. The price is high enough for the occasional purchase rather than the consistent customer. These are often the purveyors of fraud and mistrust.

And you may never know that you've been taken. The best approach to this problem is to get at least one second opinion. After all, if one doctor said you needed surgery, wouldn't you get another doctor's opinion before proceeding to the operating table? The high expense of a roof, a brake job, or tenting your home mandates a modicum of caution.

Most businesses, however, need to keep their customer returning in order to succeed. In those instances, you have some control over that business's future. You can return—or not. You can recommend—or not. And it will certainly depend on the trust and credibility that the business has developed with you. Is this an ethical position? Or is it just good business? Or is it both?

Deception and Misrepresentation

In some cases, the description will indicate the utility of the product. In other cases, the description will compare this product with competing products. Whatever the situation, provide information that will help potential customers decide whether or not to buy. Don't try to interest them with information they don't need or want. This can be time-consuming and deceptive. Tell the customer about the utility of the product and be honest. Is it as good as you say or is there a minor glitch in your description? A product should be able to perform and serve the purpose for which it was designed and advertised. And, although planned obsolescence appears to the attitude of many manufacturers, the product or service ought to be able to function for a reasonable period of time. *Always be legitimate in your advertising.*

Guarantees and Warranties

Although some businesses depend on single sales to survive, most businesses succeed because of repeat sales over time. Part of retaining customers and growing a reputation growth is certainly guaranteeing the products or services sold. Guarantees create a comfort zone for the customers, assuring them that they will be able to use the product or service for a reasonable period of time. This assurance shows customers which companies will stand behind their products and services. One of the best advertising approaches is to say, "We have been serving the community since 1925." Longevity certainly suggests legitimacy. If you are going to offer a warranty or guarantee, make sure you stand behind it and honor it.

Buying or Selling a Business

Perhaps the most significant exercise of ethics is in buying or selling a business. Although there are certain legal protections inherent in every sale document, such as an agreement that the seller will not compete with the buyer after the sale, there are many elements that are up to the people involved.

An important element is the disclosure of information. Information can be disclosed various ways—completely, selectively, even deceptively. In some cases, for example, it might not be the information disclosed that is deceptive; the deception may be in the absence of complete information. Often, the lack of a complete story can be more devastating than any deception or misrepresentation could be.

Here's an example. A buyer is interested in the key employees operating the business. The seller may be aware that a key employee intends to leave within a certain period of time. Without this key employee, the buyer will be less secure about maintaining continuity of the business. The seller's failure to disclose this information could hurt the buyer's chances for success. And, worse yet, what if the key employee is leaving to go to work for a competitor? And what if this is why the seller wants to sell the business? Of course, there are other implications to such a deception. In the case of the sale of most small businesses, the purchase price is not paid in cash. It is often paid by a down payment, with the balance paid over a period of time. If this is the case and the buyer is unable to meet the payments because of misrepresentations by the seller, the sale is not likely to fulfill the seller's expectations in terms of the negotiated price. Even when the sale is a cash deal, some portion of the purchase price is often held in an escrow for a long enough time to determine if the seller is guilty of any misrepresentations or deceptions. The ultimate answer is for all parties to be candid and honest in their representations. You can't really protect against everything. And, if someone "with larceny in his heart" wants to get you, he probably will.

If the seller fails to disclose industry innovations that would be detrimental to the buyer's future activities, would you consider this a deception? Shouldn't the buyer be expected or obliged to ascertain such information during his or her industry due diligence? Where does the obligation to be candid and forthcoming begin and end during negotiations for the sale of a business? There are ways to protect against even the more subtle deceptions, but even the most complete legal agreement will usually leave much of the information disclosure to the ethics of the parties.

The Loyalty Factor

Treating people well and with respect also applies internally. The people who work for you are, to a large extent, responsible for the success of your business. If your highest priority proves to be the business instead of the people, don't be surprised that when the tough times roll around, the highest priority of the people is to themselves and not your business. Be careful of this dichotomy. It's well to consider it in advance. If your best salesperson is not happy with the attitude you've assumed regarding your employees, he or she might just go across the street to work for your competitor. And remember: the loyalty of your customers is quite likely to be with your salesperson, not with your company. Treat your team members with respect and they will likely do the same for you.

Training Your Staff and Reporting Complaints

It's wise to train your employees, especially those who interact with the public, on how to handle complaints. You can do this through role-playing and developing clear policies and guidelines on what the employees should do if they are faced with a complaint. Taking the time to properly train your staff on these matters can strengthen your team. Role-playing at staff meetings can provide your staff with an opportunity to bond and possibly a few laughs. As a business owner, you should require that all complaints be reported to you or a manager. If nothing else, having your employees report any complaints will allow you to assess the number of complaints and determine how your staff is handling them.

The Unreasonable Customer

When talking about customer service, the question often asked is "What if a customer is being unreasonable?" The answer to that remains the same: if you can fix the problem easily with a replacement or refund, do it. It is the unreasonable customer that will probably make the most trouble for you if his or her complaint is not addressed. Of course, a replacement or refund may not solve every problem, but think about what you would pay to have the complaining customer go away. If you are not sure how to address a complaint, you may want to ask the customer what you can do to make them feel better. Some times an apology or simply an acknowledgement of the problem is a customer wants.

Setting Your Price

Often, business owners do not spend enough time determining fees or prices. Of course, an analysis of the cost of raw materials, inventory, labor, and overhead will play a large role in setting your price. It is well worth the time to look closely at this issue. All too often, business owners do not objectively analyze pricing; they just set their prices based on the competition. Make sure you are covering costs and that you can make a profit; otherwise, why go into business? This is particularly important for the service provider who has less numerical data to use in setting fees. Do not just assume that undercutting your competition will be enough. As the saying goes, you get what you pay for. Once you have decided on your fee or hourly rate, practice saying the rate and then closing your mouth: "My rate is $100 per hour." Period. In the beginning, you will probably feel the need to justify or defend your rates. A little practice will make you more comfortable and make you appear more confident to your potential clients.

Review Questions

1. Have you determined how complaints will be handled?
2. Have you clearly communicated to your staff that you want all complaints reported to you or a manager?
3. Are you aware of the refund policies of your vendors or manufacturers?
4. Have you made certain that any advertising you are using is truthful?
5. Have you done the appropriate analysis to properly set your prices or fees?

CHAPTER 14

Starting a Business
or Buying One

It appears to be a general perception that the more money you invest in buying a business, the bigger the business you will be able to buy. It also follows, if you subscribe to this conventional wisdom, that you will also enjoy a larger personal income from operating the larger business. It is very interesting that neither of these perceptions is valid.

What is more interesting is the fact that for starting a business as opposed to buying a business there's much less conventional wisdom available, and there is good reason for this. If you are buying a new franchise, the franchise sales person is likely to tell you the reasons why starting a new business is a better idea than buying one. On the other hand, a business broker will likely suggest that an existing business will afford you a better opportunity for success. Do you wonder why the advice is different?

Doing a Comparative Analysis

The fact is that a good comparison is almost impossible to make. For an existing business, its position in the marketplace can be examined from a variety of perspectives. All equipment being used for production can be compared with similar equipment in use by the competition. All sales elements and the cost factors that support the sales will have a history. Good and bad periods, customer variations, and seasonal fluctuations can all be carefully monitored. In other words, a potential buyer can get a pretty fair reading of the business by comparing its current profit picture with years, or at least months, of operations.

The new business is not the same. The entrepreneur can probably anticipate the business growth and the capital that will be necessary to get the business to its break-even point. This can be done by comparing the business with others of similar size and activity in that industry. However, there are many elements that cannot be compared with any serious degree of reliability. After all, the city in which the business is situated may not have sufficient similar businesses to make the comparison valid. Location, especially for a retail operation, is often a defining cause of success, and one location may not be equivalent to another for a variety of reasons. The effect of competition, although clearly defined in relation to the existing business, may be very unclear until the new business actually enters the marketplace.

If the new business sounds like an outright gamble to you, as opposed to the more calculated risk of an existing business, you would not be far from wrong. It is an historically sound axiom that buying a business will usually cost no more and, in many cases, will cost less than starting an equivalent business from scratch. The simplest reason is that the existing operation has a known cost-to-sales ratio. That is, the cost of generating the sales will likely have been maintained within acceptable limits or else the business is probably not viable. In a new venture, the cost of doing business will be a day-to-day drain on working capital before the reservoir of working capital can be replenished by sufficient sales to cover the cost. The time it takes to achieve this equilibrium requires cash.

But the Trade-offs Are Significant

The positive side of starting a new business is that you can start on the proverbial shoestring, even beginning, in some cases, as a home-based business. Rent can be eliminated from the initial costs of doing business. Also, equipment can be rented for the periods required, as opposed to a purchases or leased with a long-term commitment. Renting may be a little more costly in the short term, but it allows for more flexibility and a more judicious use of the limited working capital.

Many business functions can be outsourced as needed, rather than hiring employees, which would entail a constant cost, including the concurrent benefits that might be standard features of employment in the industry. And the entrepreneur can handle many business functions, early on, that will later be allocated to outside sources or inside personnel at an additional cost as profits become available for these purposes. There are, therefore, as always, tradeoffs that must be considered.

Looking More Carefully at the Components

In Chapter 15, on franchises, you will be able to compare the comfort zone of franchising with learning on your own. The differentials in this chapter are not much different. If you choose to start a business from scratch, you will have many of the same questions as you might if you bought a business. The difference is, as you've seen, that in a new venture, you will have fewer answers.

Location

If you are contemplating a retail business, whether you will be selling products or services, you will need to examine and compare locations. You will need to examine space and cost to determine whether your anticipated sales revenue can be produced in that space and whether that sales revenue can afford that space. In an existing business, the ratio of cost to sales is already established.

Personnel

In a new venture, you will have to analyze your personnel requirements, such as sales people, equipment operators, and so on. You will also have to examine those functions that can be outsourced, such as bookkeeping, legal, accounting, and, perhaps, outside sales. In an ongoing business, these functions and related costs are already part of the picture that you can examine.

However, think about whether current employees are likely to stay after you purchase and take over a business. If the business is dependent on key people, you will need some assurance that these people will remain with the business. The loss of such people could be disastrous to the continuity of the business. And, what if a key person were involved in sales, having a direct relationship with one or more important customers? What if this person decided not only to leave the business but join competitor What effect is this likely to have on your business? Are there any ways to protect against such a defection?

Tom and Shelley in Chicago certainly faced this problem in dramatic fashion. Over a period of 11 years, they lost three salespeople, each of whom went to work for the competition. In each case, the defector took 10 to 20 percent of the business to the competitor. Each time, the loss of business caused a cash flow problem. It is fortunate that this business was successful enough and the cash reservoir was big enough to handle this problem. Not every business has additional dollars to cope with such an emergency. In many instances, such an event could easily destroy the business.

After getting some professional advice, Tom and Shelly decided to establish a tax-deferred compensation plan with each of their salespeople. The agreement provided for putting a portion of their income and a contribution by the company into an escrow (holding) account. When an employee leaves the job, he or she will receive this money over a period of time, providing that the former employee does not go to work for a competitor in the area during that designated period. There are various ways to arrange an incentive like this, but this is the concept. And it works.

Many companies use a covenant not to compete in their employment contract. A covenant not to compete is designed to prevent such a disaster. It is an agreement by which the employee promises not to compete with the business after leaving the job. Be aware that these covenants not to compete generally must be reasonable in time and geography, meaning that preventing your employee from competing with you forever anywhere in the world would not be enforceable. Each state will have different views on the issue, but an agreement not to compete for two to three years within a ten-mile radius would most likely survive court scrutiny. Also, employers generally will not be allowed to impose a covenant not to compete on low-level employees. Do you think that having employees sign a covenant not to compete is a good idea? Do you think that this is enforceable in court in your particular state? Do you think a deferred compensation agreement is a better idea? Would you think that discussing this with the appropriate professional is smart?

Understanding Your Capital Requirements

The most important element, aside from the validity of the concept and the competitive position of the product or service in the marketplace, is money. In a new business venture, you will need to make preliminary judgments relative to the amount of capital you will need for rent, for personnel, for equipment, for inventory, for advertising, for legal, for accounting, and for your own living expenses, to name just a few of the business needs that will require working capital.

Even in an established business, you will need to assess your working capital requirements. The simplest reason for this is the concept of the receivable turnover period. If a successful company wants to buy your product or service but pays its bill 90 days after delivery, you will likely do the job. However, you will need to have cash in the bank during this waiting period. You will have to buy raw materials, pay your rent, personnel, and other administrative expenses during this period before your receivable turns over into cash.

Handling the Growth Problem

This preliminary assessment will be to take you to your first plateau, survival. It is interesting that business success, usually evidenced by growth, will require additional capital. The growth will often exceed your capacity to produce. Growth might cause you to consider a larger location, more equipment, additional or more specialized personnel, a wider range of inventory, and advertising over a larger geographical territory. Dynamic growth might even cause you to contemplate an entirely different delivery system, such as additional locations or franchising. This kind of growth will demand even more capital.

The best way to anticipate this kind of problem and, make no mistake, it is exactly the kind of problem that most entrepreneurs dream of having, is to do a periodic appraisal of your business goals. This means that you must have a plan, a road map, to see where you've been, where you are, and where you're going. *You might want to look again at Chapter 12, Getting the Money,* which includes information on developing a business plan, the road map of your business, as well as additional information on lenders and investors.

The Advantage to Buying

The advantage to buying a business is that you will be able to assess the costs, the competition, and other elements of the sales picture as it exists at the time of purchase. You will have an idea of where the business can go based on where the business has been. You will have fewer questions unanswered and you will probably have a pretty good idea what the activities and profit should be over a given period of time.

How Much Money Will You Need?

Buying a business should hold fewer surprises. The cash flow of the business you buy should be able to take care of you and should be able to pay the balance of the purchase price. In other words, *the business should be able to buy itself.* You should be sure to completely understand this concept. Remember: very few businesses are purchased for cash. Most businesses are bought with a down payment; say 20 percent of the purchase price, with the balance of the price being paid over five to ten years. Since most people use most of their available capital to buy the business, it is essential that the cash flow of the business itself be available to take care of the buyer's family as well as to meet the payment obligations on the balance of the purchase price. *For more on this concept, you will want to read Chapter 17, Exit Strategies and How to Value a Business.*

Starting a New Venture

When you start a new venture, whether it is an independent or a franchise, you will need to get the operation to its break-even point as your first objective. In fact, this becomes the first plateau you need to reach, and achieving this goal will take capital. The amount of money needed to get to breakeven will, of course, differ according to the business. To start a lemonade stand does not require the kind of investment necessary to start a software manufacturing company. The equipment is different, the approach to the customer is different, and the profits are certainly more conjectural in the one than in the other.

Setting Your Own Style

Many businesses can be developed along a variety of different lines. A food business can serve various kinds of food, or it can devote its menu to a singular palate. Some Mexican restaurants serve only Mexican food. Some also serve Italian food. Some restaurants noted for hamburgers also serve tacos. Some clothing stores carry a line only for women, some only for children, some only in petite sizes. By buying a business, you are buying its position in the marketplace. Yes, you can change its direction but don't forget the basics. If you buy an existing business, you are doing so because it has already established its niche, its position in the marketplace. If you disturb this strength, you may weaken its position. You might even destroy it. Then, what purpose was served? What you should do is capitalize on its strength. If your intention is to divert its direction to a different product line, then perhaps you ought to reconsider the acquisition. You might be better advised to start a business from scratch. Be careful about understanding the goal you need to pursue.

Other Reasons for Acquisition

There are, as always, exceptions to this rule. Sometimes a business is purchased, not to maintain its continuity but to acquire its geographical location. In other instances, the business may be bought because it is synergistic to another business, already owned by the buyer. In yet other cases, the business may be an exciting proposition because the buyer is acquiring a particularly good staff, or a specially trained or knowledgeable person, or even the owner, who may have excellent contacts in the industry the buyer wants to enter.

In today's technological business environment, creativity is a valuable asset. The computer has created a plethora of categories in which software development is a never-ending source of new ideas on which businesses are predicated and built. However, buying a business to acquire the genius, either the idea or the individual who created it, might not end up being a bed of roses. Creators think their ideas are their own. Businesses that pay the creator's salary think the idea created while he or she is on salary belongs to the business. Legal cases on this problem go both ways. Do not think that a contract defining this problem is the answer. Contract language is ambiguous and subject to interpretation. The conception of the idea is quite subjective and difficult to position in time. "Was the idea developed during the week or on the week-end?" is a question that will give you some idea as to the magnitude and the complexity of this problem. Litigation to resolve this dilemma is time-consuming and costly even when successful. Another part of the answer is, "You can make the basketball player get on the court, but can you make him play well?" The answer to this question should raise many of the questions inherent in the acquisition of a creative person. The answer lies in a fairness doctrine that will be incentive for both the creator and his or her relationship with the company. See your professional before you embark on such an acquisition.

There are two ways to purchase a business (other than a franchise): an asset purchase or a stock or entity purchase. Generally, the asset purchase entails purchasing all or substantially all of the assets of a business—the furniture, fixtures, equipment, and inventory, as well as the goodwill of the business, which may include customer lists, existing advertising, trade names, and other intangible property, such as the name. Under this approach, the purchaser will generally form a new entity to house the assets. More often than not, this type of sale will not include liabilities, with the exception of ongoing services such as Yellow Pages advertising or security agreements. In the stock or entity purchase, the purchaser buys a share of the the outstanding stock or membership interest in the business. This type of sale will leave the original business entity in place, and often the purchaser is taking on the existing liabilities of the business. It is probably no surprise to you that most people who buy a small business do an asset purchase.

Get professional advice when you are purchasing a business, whether it is an asset purchase or stock purchase. There are many hidden dangers for the purchaser and many aspects of the sale of an existing business that will be unknown to the new business owner. A formal written agreement is a must, and professional advice can save you a lot of time, money, and heartache. Also, make sure that you understand the tax ramifications of selling a business.

In general, the seller will have capital gain equal to the sales price less the adjusted basis (or cost) of the business. Also be aware that many states will want to collect sales tax on the sale of some of the business assets (usually the furniture, fixtures, and equipment).

Landlord Approval

Many leases require the tenant to get approval from the landlord when selling their business or making a substantial change in ownership of their business. It is important to address this issue well in advance of a sale or transfer of ownership, because it can take time and documents will likely need to be drawn up. The landlord may not release the seller from obligations under the lease. Sometimes a landlord will be willing to cancel the previous lease and grant the buyer a new lease. A landlord can potentially block a sale or transfer of ownership. It is better to know the landlord's position on this issue well in advance. Also, many landlords will charge a transfer fee for preparing paperwork and reviewing the financials of the purchaser.

Physical Counts and Inspections

When purchasing a business, it is wise to make the time to do a physical count of inventory, supplies, and raw materials, particularly if the value of such items is significant. Inspect all equipment to make sure everything is working properly prior to closing. In addition, if you are going to be paying any or transferring a security deposit, it may be wise to have the landlord physically inspect the premises for unusual wear and tear or damage that would jeopardize the security deposit.

Verify Taxes, Liens and Liabilities

When purchasing a business, you will want to get proof that all taxes (i.e., sales tax, franchise tax, personal property tax, income taxes, and employment taxes) have been paid through the date of closing. This could be important as government agencies may hold the purchaser responsible for such taxes if they cannot collect from the seller. You can often get written verification from the IRS or taxing authorities, but keep in mind, this takes time. Also, you will want to check for any liens that may have been placed on the business or its owner for business debts or obligations. Often this can be done by checking with the secretary of state's office (often referred to as a "UCC" check, and with the clerk and recorder's office of the county where the business is located.

Training and Familiarization

When purchasing a business, it is common to have a provision requiring the seller to train or help familiarize the purchaser with the business. This training or familiarization period should not be too lengthy, as it is difficult for a former owner to watch a new owner run the business. Perhaps a short period of training with the ability to ask questions later via phone or e-mail is the best compromise. Remember: sellers tend to be better at answering questions if there is still money on the table, such as escrow funds or seller financing.

Phone Numbers and Web sites

When purchasing a business, you will want all phone numbers, fax numbers, domain names, and Web sites to be specifically included in the asset purchase agreement or contract. Get the seller to formally transfer the rights to these important assets of the business at or prior to closing.

The Right of Set-off

In an asset purchase, it is wise to provide for the right of set-off to cover any unexpected costs that should have been paid by the seller, that is, the right to reduce future payments to the seller to cover such costs or expenses. If the full purchase price is being paid in cash, escrowing certain funds for such unexpected issues is a good idea. An alternative is to put an indemnification clause in the stock purchase agreement.

Review Questions

1. Once you have determined what kind of business you want, have you done a comparative analysis to determine whether you should start from scratch or purchase a business?
2. Have you researched whether a franchise is available or a wise option?
3. If you are going to purchase a business, are you clear on the difference between an asset purchase and a stock purchase?
4. Do you understand the due diligence (inspections, verifications of tax payments, and checks for liens) that you should perform prior to the purchase?
5. Do you realize and understand that a lien holder or government agency may hold you, the purchaser, responsible for unpaid obligations of the business?

CHAPTER 15

Franchise or Otherwise: Why Reinvent the Wheel?

Just Make Sure the Wheel Doesn't Cost You More Than You Can Handle

In today's competitive marketplace, getting involved in business requires a good deal more than just a wing and a prayer. An entrepreneur must have a complete view of the business undertaking. This includes a history of the industry, the current competitive environment, and the future as it relates to innovations on the horizon. But, even more than this, the businessperson must understand the basic elements of the local marketplace, including adequacy of location, availability of competent personnel, advertising and marketing demographics, and the many aspects of competition.

The Necessary Knowledge

All of this information is available to those who choose to seek it out. It is a complex search requiring at least the following: reading trade publications, discussing the industry with manufacturers and vendors, and, perhaps the most significant examination of all, discussions with those already in the business. People love to talk about their children, their pets, and their businesses. When seeking information from those already in business, it is probably best to do so from those with whom you will not compete directly. Without having this information under your belt, your business adventure can become seriously problematic.

Aside from the fundamental industry knowledge already noted, you will certainly need to understand the basics of operating a business. Your knowledge of accounting and law, however sparse, should serve as a starting point, suggesting when it would be necessary to seek the appropriate professional advice. And, in addition to these aspects of business operations, you will certainly want to have a minimum depth of knowledge with respect to the particular business on which your future will likely depend, whether the business is manufacturing, food service, or printing. If you do not have experience in a particular field or industry, you may want to consider working for someone else before you start your own business. This type of on-the-job training may be invaluable to you as a business owner and might very well be worth the time commitment.

Another Way to Go

There is another way to acquire this necessary knowledge. You can affiliate yourself with someone who has already acquired it. You could, as suggested above, work for a company in the field or industry. This would at least give you the practical knowledge from a front-line perspective. You could buy into a business as a partner, giving you a jump-start in the industry. You would, of course, have to hope that your partner has the knowledge you expect him or her to contribute. There is another very practical approach to solve this problem. You can buy a franchise.

When a company sells you a franchise, they essentially grant you a permission. They will permit you to enjoy the knowledge and experience that they have developed during their time in the industry. They will permit you to enjoy their reputation in the industry, normally acquired through advertising dollars spent in building their name, their trademarks, their logos—their recognition in the marketplace. They will permit you to take advantage of their quantity discounts with vendors. The purchase of a franchise will eliminate most of the time that you would otherwise normally invest in searching for the above-mentioned information. In addition, many of the elemental operational aspects of the business will be taught to you, reducing the mistakes normally made during on-your-own learning. Yes, there is a cost to all of this. But, keep in mind that the question should not be "How much?" so much as it should be "What is the equivalent value to you in terms of the savings of time, energy, and potential error?" It requires a careful analysis.

The Franchise Method

Franchise companies are not normally interested in how much you, as a franchise candidate, know about the particular industry of which the franchise is a part. With the knowledge and experience that they bring to the table, they feel that they can give you a broad perspective on those aspects of the business. They also have the experience to teach you how to operate the shop, whether it is a service business, a retail location, or a manufacturing or distribution operation. For the most part, this will usually be the case.

There are some special characteristics that the franchise companies are looking for—people who can sell (and who enjoy selling) and people who can pay attention to detail. Although both of these qualities can be taught, each requires a trait that must be inherent in the individual. Selling requires an inclination to risk rejection. Attention to detail requires a discipline and willingness, to one degree or another, to conform to rules and regulations.

Franchising depends for its success, in great part, on the willingness of all franchisees (franchise owners) to conform to a game plan, to a pattern, to a method and (some say), to a look. It is through this sameness that the franchise is able to meet the expectations of its customers. Wherever customers finds the franchise name or logo, they can expect similar surroundings, similar pricing and quality, and consistent products or services. Although every entrepreneur should be expected to exercise some degree of personal preference, the undisciplined franchisee who chooses not to conform can represent a clear danger to the continuity of the franchise. Nonconformity can destroy the concept.

The Costs: Today and Tomorrow

The franchise company will have a franchise fee payable when you join the franchise. This will normally include your training, the company's help in finding an appropriate location in the marketplace of your choice, as well as a initial period during which franchise personnel will hold your hand while you begin operations. In most franchises, this fee will also grant you some exclusivity with respect to a particular geography within which the franchise agrees it will not operate a similar franchise business or authorize others to do so.

There will then be an ongoing payment called a royalty or a service fee, usually payable in monthly increments and usually based on a percentage of your gross sales during the balance of the franchise contract. This payment is for ongoing support and education and is usually augmented by a secondary dollar contribution (often called a marketing royalty or fee), also calculated on a percentage of gross sales in most cases. These secondary dollars are allocated to an advertising budget, either local or national, or both.

Analyzing the Dollars

You must determine if the fee will result in value commensurate with the expenditure. You must decide if the reputation of the franchise will help you grow the business. You must analyze the savings you will enjoy as the result of being a franchisee in terms of inventory or equipment purchasing power. You must evaluate the services you expect to receive on an ongoing basis in relation to what those services would cost if you obtained them from outside sources. You must essentially create a comparative analysis equation that will help you decide if the costs, initial and ongoing, are consistent with your needs and expectations. The conservative position would certainly suggest that the franchise is a good partner if you've little knowledge about the industry or little experience in the operation of a similar business. Much, however, will depend on the franchise itself. *Be sure to see Chapter 14, Starting a Business or Buying One.*

Disclosure

Every company offering to sell a franchise, anywhere in the United States, must first, by law, give you a disclosure document. In some states, it is called a Uniform Franchise Offering Circular (UFOC). In other states, it is known as a Federal Disclosure Document. Beware of any company that discusses selling you a franchise without first offering you this document! This disclosure will tell you a great deal about the company as well as give you information or sources of information from which you can obtain material relative to the industry. It will also disclose the history of the company, background on the people involved in operating the company, the financial status of the company, a copy of the agreement you will be expected to sign (the franchise agreement), and a list of current franchisees.

As you examine the franchise disclosure, you will note that all significant lawsuits will be discussed. An analysis of this litigation will suggest the kinds of problems that the franchise company has dealt with. It will also disclose any problems that were substantial enough to have caused a break in the franchisor-franchisee relationship. This relationship, aside from the specific services you will be offered, is an important element to consider. Remember: you will be expected to live up to the terms and conditions of the franchise contract and any conflict will have to be resolved on the basis of mutual cooperation or end up in the courtroom. The disclosure document will give you plenty of things to think about and suggest additional sources (especially franchisees) from whom you might obtain important information. To ensure that you totally understand both the financial and the legal aspects of the disclosure, it is recommended that you meet with your respective professionals to discuss its content.

Keep in mind that you must receive a disclosure document about the franchise before any franchisor can have you sign agreements or take money from you. Note the language involved:

This offering circular summarizes certain provisions of the franchise agreement and other information in plain language. Read this offering circular and all agreements carefully.

If [franchise corporation] offers you a franchise, [franchise corporation] must provide this offering circular to you by the earliest of: 1. the first personal meeting to discuss [the] franchise; or 2. ten business days before the signing of a binding agreement; or 3. ten business days before any payment to [franchise corporation].

You must also receive a franchise agreement containing all material terms at least five business days before you sign any franchise agreement.

If [franchise corporation] does not deliver this offering circular on time or if it contains a false or misleading statement, or a material omission, a violation of federal and state law may have occurred and should be reported to the Federal Trade Commission, Washington, DC 20580 and the appropriate state regulating agency listed in exhibit G.

I have received a Uniform Franchise Offering Circular dated June 5, 2006. This offering circular included the following exhibits:

- Franchise Agreement and Its Exhibits
- Non-Competition–Non-Disclosure Agreement
- Required Purchases from Franchisor
- Financial Statements
- List of Agencies/Agents for Service of Process
- List of Affiliate-Owned Stores
- List of State Agencies Responsible for Franchise Disclosure and Registration Laws
- Landlord's Consent to Assignment
- Table of Contents for Policies and Procedures Manual
- List of Franchises
- Receipt

This is the law. Also keep in mind that, at the back of these disclosure documents, there is a list of current franchisees together with their telephone numbers. The best advice anyone can get relative to acquiring a franchise is to talk with a person who owns one.

Different Things for Different People

Each franchise offers different things to different people. Some will offer a complete accounting or inventory control system that eliminates the need for this tedious aspect of an inventory-heavy business. Some will offer relationships with manufacturers or vendors, which will create advantages for your business that otherwise only many years on your own would gain. Some will offer constant training and keep you up to date on innovations in your industry. Some will give you immediate credibility or recognition in the marketplace that otherwise would take years to achieve. Some will offer secret formulas for the product you will be expected to offer. Each must be examined in the context of your personal needs and expectations.

Franchising is not for everyone. Some entrepreneurs need a great deal of help in initiating their business programs. Some need constant supervision in order to maintain success continuity. Some like to have someone looking over their shoulder or on whom they can rely in times of emergency. Some need to know they can rely on marketing and advertising savvy that they don't bring to the table.

The Ice Cream Franchisor's Dilemma

A franchisor of ice cream parlors was facing a serious problem with its franchisees. Sales had stopped growing; in fact, sales were dropping nationwide after the company had enjoyed decades of success and growth. Management hadn't paid much attention to changes in the marketplace, because revenues had maintained a fairly steady growth due to new franchise openings. When they finally recognized that revenues from normal ice cream sales were stagnant, they realized that they had missed something. They brought in some professionals to do an analysis of the marketplace. They were shocked at some of the results.

Four things had been happening in their industry to which they had not paid enough attention.

1. The high-calorie ice cream was suffering under the constant pressure of the new diet syndrome that suggested healthy people should not be gaining weight.
2. Exotic flavors had been brought into the marketplace by a competitor that was doing a fantastic sales job on those for whom the diet syndrome played no part.
3. Yogurt had started to generate a much greater market than in previous years.
4. The supermarket chains had gotten much more aggressive in terms of the kinds of the flavors, sizes, and nonfat, and low-calorie alternatives they offered.

Recognizing the problem is one thing. Doing something about it is always another. In this case, the franchisor wasted no time. They improved their assortment by including low-calorie ice cream, a new range of flavors, and yogurt, including low-fat and nonfat. It was something that needed to be done expeditiously on behalf of their franchisees—and it was done.

The individual operator, whether a franchisee or an independent, might not have the personnel, the money, or the awareness to make so many changes in such a short time. The difference is that the franchisor had the money to advertise this new approach to customers nationwide. The individual operator would always find it difficult to allocate such substantial dollars to so large an advertising campaign.

There are all kinds of franchise services to accommodate the different needs of the entrepreneur. *The best advice is to carefully go over Chapter 1, Looking in the Mirror,* and decide what kind of support you feel is necessary to best ensure your success. Then, examine the franchises in the industry that attracts your attention and do a comparative analysis of the franchise companies available. Next, ask franchisees and independent operators in the industry for their best judgment. Finally, ask yourself again what is the equivalent value to you in terms of the savings in time, energy, and potential error. You will be much closer to deciding if the cost of the franchise relationship has an equivalent in terms of your potential success.

Franchises—Past and Present

If a franchise chain is relatively new, it is possible that as the number of franchisees is low, you might get more personal attention. On the other hand, this advantage must be weighed against the franchisor's lack of significant experience in the marketplace. A franchisor that has been in the business for many years may be the better choice. A large franchise company may be better known nationally, whereas a smaller franchise may have tighter integrity and a closer relationship with its franchise owners.

You might also check the length of the franchise contract, during which you will be expected to commit to the following terms and conditions of the relationship. *Be careful to note the conditions that will prevail after the contract expires.* Will you be permitted to stay in business without operating under the franchise banner? Will you be permitted to keep your location? Will you be obligated to turn over the telephone number? How important do you consider these things to be?

As with any contractual relationship, you will want to completely understand your obligations while under contract and after expiration of the contract. Since most legal language is subject to interpretation, and since many contracts are loaded with ambiguities in language, whether intentional or inadvertent, it is absolutely necessary that you seek professional advice before making any final decision on which your future and the future of your family may depend.

Changing the Contract

You may, as with any potential contract relationship, discuss with your counsel those items that you find onerous or that might suggest the possibility of future problems.

Elements of most contracts are usually subject to negotiation. Keep in mind, however, that consistency is the very essence of franchising. In order to maintain and preserve any system where many people are part of a group where each is presumably equal to all others, there needs to be a basic contract relationship that is relatively the same in all cases. As each contract change is made, the equality among owners begins to wear thin. Each owner then begins to wonder if he or she got as good a deal as the other owners. These disparities will ultimately lead to bad feelings and a loss of the camaraderie so important to build the integrity of the group.

Don't be surprised if it is a difficult one to make changes in the franchise contract. The consistency of the contract is part of the uniformity of the franchise relationship throughout the group. If you feel that you cannot live without certain changes, you should move on to a different franchise company. But keep one last thing in mind. If the franchise company is easily convinced to make changes in your contract, you must then wonder what changes, significant or otherwise, might have been made in other contracts? And where do you stand in the line of preferential treatment?!

The Franchise Fee and Royalties

Many franchisors will charge an initial franchise fee at the time a franchise agreement is signed. Training represents a big portion of the franchise fee, which is generally the franchisor's first dip into the franchisee's pocket. This fee is usually for the initial set-up and paperwork prepared by the franchisor. The amount is often predicated on the size and scope of the anticipated business. And sometimes, this up-front franchise fee is entirely arbitrary. This initial fee is often considered fair by franchisees because of the training, advice, and cautions given by the franchisor. It is more often than not the ongoing royalty that usually creates the problem in the relationship.

The Franchisor's Extra Margin of Profit?

You may also want to note that that many franchisors make a profit on any goods that they have manufactured for the benefit of the franchise system for delivery to the franchisees. There have been situations where the product developed by the franchisor and sold by the franchisees was so proprietary nature that its protection was of an extremely high priority. The pancake batter used by a national chain of restaurants, or the formula for a cola drink produced by an international manufacturer as examples. Unfortunately, the concept has been developed beyond all logic. The protection is now guaranteed by virtue of the language in a franchise contract and prohibits the franchisee from examining other sources of components or finished products without the specific permission of the franchisor. And it makes no difference whether or not the product or service has any unique or special qualities for which it would deserve any protection. It's merely another method by which the franchisor can enjoy a profit without worrying about whether the individual franchise operation shows a profit or not.

Exit Strategies

One of the problems with a franchise is that, in the event that the franchisee and the franchisor have a disagreement of any kind, there is virtually no exit strategy for the franchisee. The franchisor may terminate the contract and the relationship if the franchisee defaults on any of his or her obligations. The franchisee has no such option, since the franchisor is essentially under no obligation to perform any specific activity. In the early days of franchising, the franchisor was under obligation to help the franchisee in a myriad of ways. As time showed litigation to be the only viable strategy for franchisees to exit the relationship, the franchise documents appeared with fewer and fewer obligations on the part of the franchisor. Now, in current documents, there are virtually no obligations at all.

Franchises and the Covenant Not to Compete

Many franchise agreements have a covenant not to compete with language similar to that set forth below:

> Upon termination or expiration of this Franchise Agreement for any reason ... for a period of three years ... neither you, nor your family, nor any of your members, owners, partners, managers, officers, or directors ... shall directly or indirectly participate as an owner, operator, shareholder, director, partner, consultant, agent, employee, advisor, officer, lessor, lessee, or franchisee or serve in any other capacity whatsoever or have any interest in or assist any person or entity in any business, firm, entity, partnership, or company engaged in the sale or offering of products or services or using a business format which is the same as or similar to ours or the system within the territory allocated or within ten miles of the territory of any other franchisee's or company owned store's territory or business operation.

Make sure you understand this language and are prepared to live with it. In many cases franchisors have even anticipated the possibility that a court might find a particular non-compete clause to be unenforceable, since it precludes the franchisee from pursuing perhaps the only business with which he or she may be familiar. So, just in case, they might included the following language: "In the event these post-term restrictions are found to be unenforceable, the franchisee shall be obliged for a period of no less than three years, to pay a fee of one-half of the royalties and advertising fees which would be payable if the business operated by the former franchisee was still a franchise."

Buyer Beware

When looking at whether to purchase a franchise it would be wise to do a comparative analysis of franchise services versus outside sources. The franchise relationship is a long-term relationship that may be difficult to terminate. This is one area where you do not want buyer's remorse.

Review Questions

1. What kinds of services are offered by a franchise?
2. Do you know the source or sources of the franchisor's income?
3. What does the franchisee get in return for the initial franchise fee?
4. How does the franchisor decide on the amount of the initial franchise fee?
5. What is the purpose of the UFOC or disclosure document?
6. What will the litigation section of the disclosure document reveal?
7. What does the franchisee receive for its ongoing royalty payments?
8. What other options does the franchisor have for generating income?
9. What kind of post-termination, post-expiration noncompete language is in the franchise agreement?

CHAPTER 16

Preparing to Turn Over Your Family Business

Preparation is the key to the success of the transition and the ultimate survival of a family business.

In some cases, the two generations have been working together in the business before time comes to consider transition. This is not always the case, however. In the current business environment, a business, started by a parent offers a unique job opportunity to a son or daughter as well as a potential for the future. With job opportunities decreasing and the competitive element being as strong a market force as it is, many young people are looking at the family business with a new perspective.

Another aspect to this is that, in many cases, the parents are trying to perpetuate the business for their own benefit—their retirement. Leaving the business in the hands of family might be a more secure transition than taking a chance by selling the business to a stranger, even with a smaller or even no down payment.

The Relationship Before the Takeover

There are many variables in terms of the relationship that exists just prior to a family takeover. In some cases, the son or daughter may have been working in the business for such a long period of time that he or she has actually become an integral part of the operation. In other cases (and acknowledging this is sometimes difficult), the son or daughter may never have become an integral or necessary part of the operation, regardless of how long he or she may have been associated with the business.

With respect to the current working relationship, some parents never think the children are capable, regardless of how hard the children may try and how effective they might appear to their peers. There are other parents who give their children credit for total competence without ever having done a really objective analysis of their value to the company if they were responsible for managing it. In other situations, there may be a good general manager who is not a member of the family and who is perfectly competent to maintain the continuity of the business. The relationship between the manager and the son or daughter appears to be working well when the parent is present. but is the manager capable of getting along with the son or daughter in the parent's absence? On the other hand, if the general manager and the parent give the operating responsibility to the son or daughter, will the parent lose the general manager and thus jeopardize the continuity of the business, particularly as the parent will no longer be available for day-to-day consultation?

In one situation, the owner of a business had both his son and daughter working in the business with him when he succumbed to a heart attack. Neither of his children had any intention of making the business a permanent part of their future. The business, however, represented so large a portion of the father's estate that both children agreed to maintain the continuity of the business for the sake of their mother. The problem of holding the pieces together during the takeover period (for which no preparation had been made) caused tremendous pressures between the children.

The daughter finally left. The son was not capable of handling a lot of the paperwork by himself. He was not trained for this responsibility and he did not have the inclination to handle the myriad details that his sister had handled. The business eventually got into trouble. It survives today but its business tempo will never be as dynamic as it was during the father's tenure. Adequate preparation could have avoided many, if not most, of the problems that arose after the father's death.

Facing a Harsh Reality—Obligations That Live on

The extent to which you will want to maintain a relationship with the business after takeover depends on a variety of things. To what extent is the continuity of the business essential to your retirement? To what extent are you still responsible for certain contractual obligations, like the lease, even though you will no longer be connected with the operation of the business? Keep in mind that when you signed the lease, it may have been for five years or it may have been a five-year lease with successive five-year options. If the latter, you may still be responsible for payment even after leaving the business. You wouldn't be the first person to whom this harsh reality came as a surprise after leaving the business.

Day-to-Day Consultation After Takeover

Are you ready to give up the business and its equity by telling your son and daughter that it is a sink-or-swim situation? To what extent are you obliged to make working capital available in the event the business enters a slow period or the industry takes a downturn? In other words, just how quickly are you prepared to cut the cord?

There are a number of things to keep in mind. Primarily, there is the question of the business concept. You have undoubtedly formed the business and maintained it with a certain philosophy and with the idea in mind that it take a certain position or niche in its field or industry of which it is a part. It is very easy for someone to quickly and dynamically superimpose a whole new set of principles on the business in your absence. Some of these may be only subtle changes with little long-term effect; others may well impact the very nature of the business.

Cost-to-Sales Ratios

It is a good idea to monitor the business by maintaining a certain cost-to-sales ratio. You can mandate, for example, that until you, the seller, have been paid in full, the buyer shall not allow the labor factor (including his or her income) to exceed a certain percentage of sales. With this restriction, it would be difficult for the new owner to dramatically change the business concept without seeking some agreement from you. Another protective device is to require your approval on any business purchase in excess of a certain dollar amount. After all, you must protect yourself against the possibility of the buyer using the cash flow to pay everything and everybody but you. In fact, this approach may be wise regardless of whether you are selling the business to family or to a stranger.

Staying in Touch vs. Staying in Control

But here is a place to take care. On the one hand, staying the course and maintaining continuity are important. On the other hand, you must never forget the importance of the creative juices of new blood and new energy and recognize that the business environment is constantly changing. It requires creativity and change. The competitive element can be quickly lost by not taking advantage of change when change is necessary or appropriate. It is for this reason that you should stay in touch. This does not mean stay in *charge*. It means stay in *touch*. Make sure that you can monitor the changes and recognize the impact that each change will likely have on your position in the marketplace, before it is too late to correct. After all, larger companies do this by having a board of directors.

In one particular situation, the son took over the business after spending many years as an apprentice under the supervision of his father. Immediately after takeover, in an attempt to ensure a good competitive position, he leased some new state-of-the-art equipment.

The increase in his productivity was minimal. The increase in his client base was also small. But the increase in monthly obligations was substantial. He had not generated the advertising necessary to fill the time of the new equipment and make the lease, and the monthly payment worthwhile. The father would have taken a much more conservative position. He would have carefully examined the market potential before making the investment. The father was devastated, but the paperwork was already signed. The modest retirement income that the father had hoped for turned into a Chapter 7 bankruptcy. Instead of retirement, the father got a new job. Staying in touch after the takeover would, undoubtedly, have netted a different result.

Vulnerability of Assets After Takeover

Unfortunately, when you start a business, you might sign a long-term lease for the premises, a franchise agreement for ten or 20 years, leases or contracts for the use or purchase of equipment, and you might very well sign a promissory note for money borrowed from a bank or other lending institution, or from the seller from whom you purchased the business. These people might be very encouraging and personal when you tell them that you are turning the business over to your son or daughter. They will normally, however, not be inclined to release you from your obligation, since you are probably more stable in the community and likely have more assets than your son or daughter. In other words, your assets and your dollars will remain at risk even though you may no longer be personally involved in the business.

Remember: even though you may have a corporation that is responsible for most of those obligations, you have probably signed all the paperwork as an individual as well. Most banks, landlords, and purveyors of expensive equipment will not allow the corporate signature without either a co-signer or a guarantor. In either case, you will remain responsible until the entire debt is paid. The reason for this is that most closely held corporations, particularly new ones, are not substantially funded. Having access to a limited reservoir of dollars is no comfort to the purveyor of expensive equipment or to the lessor of a long-term lease when the amount at risk is usually quite substantial.

In one situation, a son, who was particularly knowledgeable in a particular business, took over from his mother and father. He operated the business very well for a number of years. In fact, he grew the business quite dramatically. Then, he hit a downturn and the business verged on the edge of disaster. The franchise company, the landlord, and the equipment companies all came after the mother and father, neither of whom was capable any longer of operating the business. They weren't even aware of the business's' day-to-day activity; but their assets were still vulnerable. This business has made all kinds of arrangements for readjusting its debts and will probably survive. In this case, of a permanent takeover, arrangements should have been made to close out certain obligations after a given time period and let the parents off the hook, providing the business showed proper stability in the early stages, which it did.

Moving your business into the hands of the next generation is a dream held by many parents. The children recognize the great opportunity that such a transition provides. It is unfortunate that, in the face of this joy, there are pitfalls to which little or no serious consideration is given until it is too late. If you are involved in such a situation, make sure that your successor completely understands the very nature of the business, its position in the marketplace, and its future in the competitive field. Plan for the future and make sure patterns for potential growth.

Make sure that certain investments, particularly in the early days, are discussed, analyzed, and agreed upon rather than allowing individual, inexperienced judgments to prevail. *It is in the nature of youth to reach out creatively toward the future. It is in the nature of parents to reflect on the past to ensure a conservative approach for the future. Neither is wrong. It is, in fact, in the combination of these things that you will find the most successful transitions.* It is worthwhile to take the time for this exercise.

Uncle Sam as Your New Partner—After the Sale

Because of the tax implications of every sale transaction, it would be careless of you not to consider the methods by which you can eliminate or, at least, minimize the taxes that might be payable upon the transfer of your business to family members. The tax structure in this country allows for a variety of ways to approach this problem. These alternatives range from creating a legal entity that will allow incremental increase of ownership over a period of time to giving participation to the family member on a gift basis, being sure not to incur a gift tax in the process, to creating a trust or the use of a family limited partnership to hold the stock. A purchase over time, while it will not necessarily eliminate tax, may defer the tax over several years. And, along with most of these alternatives, it will be critical to create an insurance program that will handle the tax problem by making dollars available to acquire stock without diluting its value or the participation of ownership. Failure to do so will often defeat the intention of the original owner.

A brief analysis of some of these alternatives suggests that gifts, like irrevocable trusts, can be inappropriate because they may cause the owner to lose active control of the business while continuing to operate. This is not usually the goal that the owner seeks to achieve. The limited partnership, on the contrary, allows the owner, as general partner, to maintain control while putting portions of the equity ownership in the hands of limited partners. However, you will want to remember that the limited partners are neither obliged nor permitted to participate in the day-to-day activities of the business. If they do participate, it may cost them their status as limited partners and their limited liability protection. What this can mean is that, instead of merely losing their investment, they may find themselves responsible for all the business debts. See the chapters on legal entities for a more extensive examination of this question.

Resolving Ambiguities

In a somewhat unique situation, an owner of two separate businesses had his son operating one of them and his daughter operating the other. As good fortune would have it, both locations were dynamically successful. It is true that the owner had not only initiated both businesses, he had also been responsible for training his children and, indeed, training them well. For the first ten years, he had been a hands-on operator. In more recent times, he had kept a particularly watchful eye on the businesses and scrutinized the purchase of equipment and the hiring of personnel.

In one case, his daughter owned 25 percent of the operation. This paperwork had been initiated early on at the daughter's request. In the other case, however, the owner's son did not have the same foresight. He had not made arrangements for a legal transfer of any kind and, as a result, had no equity participation at all.

Although it is accepted practice that business agreements be memorialized in writing, this same philosophy oftentimes seems not to prevail in the family environment. In this case of father and son, the father had been sharing 25 percent of the profits of the business with his son for the ten years that the son had operated the business, even to the extent that he legally did it in gift form, which allowed the son to avoid the payment of taxes on these dollars.

When the time came for the son to buy the business, he expected to pay only 75 percent of the purchase price (as did his sister) because he felt that he already owned 25 percent. In fact, he didn't *own* 25 percent—there was no agreement in writing. Resolving this ambiguity almost led to a family feud and a failure of the ownership transition.

Interestingly, the matter was resolved by a third party's intervention. Both parties were asked to adjust their expectations in favor of maintaining the family relationship and avoiding a family disaster. The son agreed to buy the 25 percent he felt he owned. In turn, the father agreed to base the price for the 25 percent on the value of the business as of the time the son took over, some ten years earlier, rather than at the current value, which was much greater and which was, in great part, attributable to the energy and work of the son during that period. The middle road solution saved everybody's pride and allowed the family to remain intact.

Don't let the family relationship create ambiguities. They can be devastating. Treat the family business as a true business relationship and keep such ambiguities from undermining the family.

Letting Go of the Controls and Protecting the Future

The last critical element that ought to be factored in is the fact that both children had been involved in their respective operations for ten years and both were in their early 40s. They wanted autonomy and ownership, both of which had been promised but not delivered. They were now threatening, subtly or otherwise, that, without a buyout they might both leave their positions. The owner's problem was his inability to completely turn over the responsibility of each operation. He still felt that neither was mature enough to make the hard choices in terms of purchasing equipment and selecting the most appropriate road for the future of the business. This is not an atypical situation between parents and their children. Certainly, it is true that each operation might change to some degree without the original owner's ongoing supervision, but this would likely be the case whoever bought the business. In this case, however, the father's choices were becoming clear and time was becoming critical.

Each business had a fair market value of about $500,000 if the businesses were sold to a third party. Without the son and daughter at the helm of each business, however, it was conjectural whether the successes would be maintained, since personal service is a key in this particular industry. In addition, in the event of an unsuccessful takeover by a stranger, it would not be possible for the original owner to return to active participation in the businesses. And, unless a sale in each case was orchestrated with present operating personnel intact, the positive selling values of the businesses could be undermined.

What would your decision be? Selling a business at the right time is often critical. The risk of turning total responsibility over to another person is part of the selling—and part of the risk. A simple assessment of the above situation would lead to a single conclusion. The failure to sell could destroy the retirement income that had been the owner's dream for years. And remember, putting some protective devices in the agreement between the parties, such as maintaining ratios, is perfectly normal in any sale, family involvement notwithstanding. *See Chapter 17, Exit Strategies and How to Value a Business.*

This brief examination should make it clear that any approach to the tax questions and the owner's ability to maintain control after leaving, as well as all the peculiar aspects of transfer and turnover, will require advice from the experts. The team of your attorney, your accountant, your business consultant, and your insurance planner should be consulted before any definitive move is contemplated.

Compare the Alternatives

Parents need to be sure that transferring or selling their business to their children is a good choice for all involved: the parents, the children, and the business. A comparative analysis should be made of any transaction involving family with a potential transaction involving a complete stranger. While money is an important factor, other factors may be relative (pun intended).

Define the Parental Involvement

Remember: staying in touch is not the same thing as staying in charge. Make sure the issue of involvement for the outgoing parent is clear. This is true whether the parent is to have little interaction or a great deal of continued involvement. Surprise issues in this regard could be devastating to both the business and the family. Perhaps, monthly or quarterly financials provided to the parents would suffice, while others may need or want weekly or even daily information.

An Estate Plan Is Essential

The transfer of your business to your children should be discussed with your business advisors as well as any professional who is assisting you with your estate plan. If you don't have an estate plan, get one—it is essential. Make sure you understand the effects transferring your business to a child may have to any estate plan you already have in place.

Insurance May Make You Feel Better

One way to protect yourself when transferring your business is through insurance. Obtaining a life policy on the person purchasing the business to be used to pay off business obligations, including payments not yet received by the parent, may give you additional peace of mind. Remember: this would protect the parent only if a child were to die.

A Handshake Won't Do

Maintaining control during the transition years must be carefully orchestrated. Planning is key. Make sure you have been thorough in your planning and communication. Even if the transaction involves family, the details should be written up as if the transaction were with an unrelated party. This may save you problems down the road and in some cases may save your family relationships.

Review Questions

1. Would selling your business to a stranger be better financially than selling to a family member?
2. What makes maintaining ratios a good method for avoiding precipitous changes in the direction of a business during takeover?
3. Make sure you are clear about any obligations that may remain with the original owner or parent.
4. Why is it a good idea to consult a financial or estate planner when thinking about family succession?
5. Have you reviewed or updated your estate plan so it will work well with the transfer of your business to one or more of your children?

CHAPTER 17

Exit Strategies and How to Value a Business

Any plan for a business—new or established—should also include a plan for how the owner will exit from the business or get their money out of the business. The exit strategy should be considered and developed from the beginning. A great place to start is to look at the long- and short-term goals and objectives of the owners, both from a business perspective and on a personal level. Knowing what a business owner or investor expects can help make the strategy more successful. Exit strategies can be as simple as liquidation, buying out a partner, or selling the business to family or to another entrepreneur. Or it can be as grand as an acquisition by a large corporation or, very rarely, an initial public offering (IPO). As was mentioned in *Chapter 12, Getting the Money*, if your business will have investors, you will need to be developed so that your investors understand how and when they can expect a return of their investment.

If You Have No Plan—Liquidation

More often than not, a business that has not developed a reasonable exit strategy may be forced to liquidate. Liquidation is not so much of a plan as it is just the shutting down of a business. Few owners plan to just shut their doors and auction off any assets, but it happens all the time. In its simplest form, liquidations require that assets be sold, creditors be paid, and anything left over be divided among the owners. This approach may leave a great deal of money on the table, as it does not account for goodwill, customer lists, and the good name or reputation of the business. You will likely only get pennies on the dollars for your physical assets in liquidation. This is just one of the reasons to figure out how you plan to exit. Another reason is that if you know your goals and exit strategy, the business can be created, maintained, and managed in a manner that will help make your exit strategy successful.

Common Strategies

Below is a brief description of some of the exit strategies that business owners may want to consider.

- **The lifestyle company.** Some business owners simply have no real plan in place except to build a business and take all of the money out of the business as it comes in. In this scenario, the business owner takes large salaries or draws and reinvests in the business in a minimal. This may be appropriate for certain types of businesses and certain kinds of business owners. Common lifestyle businesses include consulting firms, service businesses, franchises, and local retail operations. You may or may not become rich from operating a lifestyle business, but for many, it may not be the money so much as the lifestyle that is important. For example, they want to maintain control of their business, do what they love, have a relatively positive and constant cash flow, report only to themselves (and their customers), have flexibility, and enjoy a better quality of life. Taking the money as it is earned may seem the better choice for some business owners and will likely leave little to be sold when the owner wants to retire. This approach is often used by the business owner who is the business, such as an architect, attorney, or consultant.

- **Sell to a friendly buyer.** A plan to sell your business to an employee, customer, family member, or other entrepreneur is very common. The business owner will want to make sure that his or her business is, in fact, marketable. Knowing that you plan to sell the business in the future will undoubtedly affect business decisions you make today. Many business owners plan to retire on the proceeds from the sale of their business. The sale can be done in a number of ways to help minimize taxes and to provide outright wealth or an income stream to the business owner or his or her family. For some business owners, the continuation of their business is just as important as the money.

- **Acquisition and merger.** An acquisition is generally the purchase of one business by another business (usually larger). The acquisition is a very common exit strategy. Basically, you find another business that wants to buy yours and you sell it. In an acquisition, the seller often can get a higher price (within reason, of course) because the purchaser wants the seller's business, for very specific reasons, such as products or services, a particular market or niche, or other aspect of the business. Also, because the acquiring company often has plans for growth, they may perceive a higher price to be worth the investment. Finally, more often than not, the person making the acquisition decision is an employee of the acquiring company and therefore is less likely to feel the pain of a higher price. When looking for a company to buy your business, look for a strategic fit, such as a company that may want to expand into a new market, or offer your product or service to their existing customers. If acquisition is your exit strategy, you will want to make your business attractive to acquisition candidates. Acquisitions and mergers can be very complex and can have varied tax effects. Make sure you know what you are getting into.

- **IPO.** The initial public offering is flashy and it gets all the press. In addition, it is extremely rare. Out of the millions of companies in the U.S., only about 7,800 are traded on a public exchange. Getting funding from professional investors with a track record of taking companies public will most likely be necessary. Keep in mind, the professional investor will usually dilute your ownership to a small fraction. If you are a boot-strapping entrepreneur, believing in an IPO may be a bit naïve, not to mention the incredible costs of going public: capital requirements, costs of reorganization, underwriting fees, and risk of reduced value due to lock-out (or stock sale) restrictions.

Remember: there are many ways to get value out of your company. Think ahead, but be reasonable. Business owners who find themselves planning for their IPO in 18 months will not only be disappointed, but oftentimes out of business.

The Buy-Sell Arrangement

A more immediate issue all business owners should consider is what would happen to the business if they could no longer run it. For a small business with more than one owner, it would be wise, at the very least, to draw up a simple agreement that can provide the detailed procedures in case of the death, disability, or retirement of an owner. This can be done in a partnership agreement, operating agreement of an LLC, or in a shareholder agreement (sometimes called a *buy-sell agreement*) for corporations.

The buy-sell exit strategy should set forth the procedures and the process by which remaining owners will purchase the exiting owner's interest in the business. It should include how the business will be valued and who can purchase what (e.g., the remaining owners can purchase in proportion to their ownership interests immediately before the event causing the exit). This document is like a prenuptial agreement between or among business partners and should be developed well before it is needed. The agreement should specifically state whether a spouse, child, or heir *must* sell the ownership he or she inherits to the remaining owner(s) or if it is optional. In some cases, businesses will state that an heir to any ownership interest may remain an owner for as long as he or she works full time for the business. Non-owner spouses should sign your buy-sell agreement or the document setting forth these exit strategies to make sure they understand the arrangement and to avoid problems in the future.

The agreement can set a specific price for each share of stock or for each percentage of ownership interest (usually for LLCs and partnerships), such as $10 per share or $100 for each 1 percent of ownership. If a set price is used, it should be updated periodically or valid only until a specific date. More often than not, the price is set according to a formula based on the fair market value of the business at the time of transfer. The agreement often requires that the business be professionally valued by an expert. Because this can be expensive, several thousands of dollars or more, it is a good idea to include in the buy-sell agreement language that, if the parties can agree to a price without a formal valuation, they may do so. Remember: under some circumstances, when using the buy-sell type exit strategy, the parties will not always be in an adversarial position to one another. For new businesses, it may be wise to provide that if an owner leaves before a specific date (e.g., within two years of the start of the business), the exiting owner will receive nothing for his or her ownership interest; this can save a lot of trouble for remaining owners when the business is new and has relatively little value. In general, a buy-sell arrangement should always treat the owners fairly and equally to avoid problems later.

At the Very Least

Multi-owner businesses, at the very least, should have some kind of restrictive covenant in their governing document that prevents any owner from selling or transferring their interest in the business without first offering such interest to the remaining owners. Remember: this could prevent you from waking up one day and discovering that your business associate has a gambling problem and someone in Las Vegas is now your new partner. This covenant can be put into the partnership agreement, the operating agreement, or the bylaws of a corporation. Generally, this type of restrictive covenant would not apply to a business owner who dies and leaves his or her stock to family members. But it would keep an unhappy owner from giving his or her ownership interest away just to irritate the remaining owners, which, believe it or not, has been known to happen, particularly in new businesses that have little or no value.

Your professional should review exit strategies and buy-sell agreements or similar language in a document. These types of agreements can have long-term and lasting effects on you and your family. And when they are used, there will likely be no opportunity to amend the agreement between the owners.

How Do I Value My Business?

You may have noticed that when determining your exit strategies, whether you plan to have investors, sell your business, or buy out another owner, the value of the business will be an important part of the equation. A common question is, "How do I value my business?" A business owner should at a minimum understand the basic factors that go into valuing a business. The financial statements of a business—the balance sheet, profit and loss statement (income statement), and statement of cash flow—and tax returns are not the only factors to be considered.

There are many ways to value a business and just as many formulas for doing so. When valuing a business, many items should be taken into consideration, such as risk, unusual inventory or raw materials levels, interest rates, and the amount of money put down versus the amount financed. It is reasonable, if not necessary, for the buyer of a business to expect the business to pay for the financed portion of the purchase and the personal needs of the buyer. If the purchase price does not accommodate those two expectations, then the business is probably valued at too high a price.

The approach to valuing a business that follows may be used by both the seller and the buyer. It has been used to value and negotiate hundreds of business deals where both the buyer and seller were satisfied with the numbers, but also understood the numbers and the rationale for the numbers better than more complicated formulas. Every business is different and every sale is different; this approach takes that into consideration and is naturally customized to the sale at hand.

The Necessary Assumptions

In order to value a business properly, you must make two basic assumptions, both of which are normally true. The first is that the buyer, after the purchase, has probably exhausted all or most of his or her available financial resources. This is usually true because most buyers of small businesses follow the philosophy that the greater the investment, the greater the return. As a result, they will normally invest the most they can. Whether this philosophy is wise may be subject to examination. But the fact remains that most buyers invest in this way.

The second assumption is that the buyer has made a substantial down payment rather than pay all cash for the business. This means that the balance of the purchase price will be paid to the seller in incremental payments over an extended period of time. It is very unusual in today's business marketplace for a business to be sold for all cash. There are disadvantages to both buyer and seller, as will be further examined in this chapter.

What the Buyer Needs for the Sale to Make Sense

If you accept the above two assumptions, you are left in a situation where the buyer must depend on the cash flow of the acquired business to handle the two problems the buyer needs to address: taking care of the family needs of the buyer and making the periodic (normally monthly) payments to the seller. Although there are a variety of elements that must also be taken into consideration, not the least of which are the tax implications of the purchase, you now have the basic assumptions of business valuation in hand.

Discretionary Cash Flow

The discretionary cash flow (DCF) is the money left over after paying all the expenses necessary to properly operate the business. You must first decide how much money you, the buyer, needs in order to take care of your family. When you deduct this from the discretionary cash flow of the business, the balance remaining is the amount that can be used to pay the balance of the purchase price to the seller.

The Following Example May Be Helpful

The business has annual revenue of $200,000 and operating expenses (before paying the owner) of $110,000. Thus the discretionary cash flow (DCF) of the business is $90,000 per year.

The salary necessary for the buyer to handle the needs of the family is $40,000 per year.

The remaining $50,000 can be used to pay the seller the balance of the financed portion of the purchase price.

If the $50,000 is paid to the seller each year for 10 years, the value of the business is probably in the area of approximately $300,000. The reason for this is that to fully amortize (i.e., pay the principal sum and the interest at 10 percent over ten years) the purchase price of $300,000 would require an annual payment of $47,900 per year. Since the amount available from the discretionary cash flow is $50,000 per year, it would appear that there is enough money to make the annual payments based on the purchase price of $300,000 and still have sufficient money available to satisfy the salary requirements of the buyer. In other words, it works!

Finding the DCF and Converting Your P&L for Selling Purposes

You should be looking basically at your profit and loss statement (P&L) in order to find your discretionary cash flow (DCF). You may also need to refer to your balance sheet to clarify some questions on your P&L. One such problem, resolved by the balance sheet, is that a substantial investment or loan is often capitalized with the interest payments noted on the P&L, but with the principal payments reflected only on the balance sheet. The P&L should be refigured to adjust for large capital expenditures and unusual or non-recurring expenses. Also, the P&L is usually prepared for the purposes of substantiating the business's tax position to the Internal Revenue Service. Therefore the P&L usually takes full advantage of the deductions allowed by the government. In this way, a business will be creating as small a profit (DCF) as possible in order to minimize the income taxes. Presenting this minimal profit picture to a potential buyer would allow only a minimal selling price and would be unfair to the seller. Accordingly, you should make additional adjustment to the P&L on your way to determining the DCF.

Common Adjustments

The reason for this strange dichotomy is that there are three basic cost factors allowed by the government as legitimate business deductions, which will not be inherited by the buyer as necessary costs of operating the business. These include the following:

1. **Depreciation and amortization (Section 179 deductions).** Although these are allowable as expenses against sales, thereby lowering the profit on which taxes are assessed, they are noncash items. That is, the business will not have to pay this amount in cash during the course of the year. However, be careful that you know when new assets or equipment will be needed in the future.

2. **Non-recurring expenses.** The seller is entitled to deduct expenses of the sale, including lawyer, accountant, and broker fees. In addition, the seller may have purchased supplies that the buyer will not have to duplicate after the sale. These are deductions for tax purposes that the buyer will not have to pay for, after the sale, as operating expenses of the business.

3. **Personal expenses.** The seller may have taken a helpful educational trip, under IRS guidelines, to Europe, during which he or she visited competitive operations. The visitations might qualify the expenses of the trip as a deductible business expense even though the seller's primary purpose might have been to take a holiday. The buyer will not be obliged to duplicate this trip as a *necessary* business operating expense.

4. **Meals and entertainmentand vehicle expenses.** You should also review, as this is another area where some business owners tend to get a little aggressive. Also you should adjust to compensate for disallowed or limited deductions. For example, only 50 percent of meals and entertainment expenses are deductible and there are some limitations on the vehicle expenses that are deductible.

These items should be removed from or added to the P&L, to either increase or decrease the DCF, depending on whether they are a cash requirement of the business or not. In turn, this will represent a much more realistic picture of DCF and what the business can really afford to pay in terms of salary to the buyer and payments to the seller.

Selling for Cash

Although it is certainly possible to sell or buy a business for all cash, there are good reasons for both buyer and seller to consider carefully the negative aspects involved in an all-cash deal. From the seller's perspective, there are three disadvantages to consider.

1. The capital gains tax will be payable in total during the year of the sale if the seller received all of the money in that year.
2. The buyer, if paying all cash, will certainly expect, and be entitled, to pay much less than the asking price of the business. Although this is not always true and depends on the relative negotiating positions of buyer and seller, there is a certain rationale for this expectation.
3. The current interest percentage that this cash payment will generate as a passive investment in the open market is quite likely to be considerably less than the seller might expect from financing the sale after taking only a down payment. After all, carrying the balance of the purchase price over a period of time involves some degree of risk. This risk usually converts to a higher interest rate than a more secure passive investment might generate.

The advantage for the seller, of course, is that he or she will not be accepting the risk of collecting the balance if it is an all cash sale. The seller can consider the sale consummated and go on without looking back.

For the buyer, there is a singular disadvantage to paying cash. The buyer who pays all cash loses any leverage he or she might otherwise have had to protect against any misrepresentations by the seller, intentional or otherwise. In addition, the seller having received complete payment, loses all incentive to allow a long transition period or to help the buyer during those early takeover stages when experience can save many dollars and help ensure the continuity of the business. If, on the other hand, the seller receives only a down payment and is collecting the balance of the purchase price over time, he or she is likely to be a lot more careful about transitioning the business to the buyer in every way that can help to ensure a successful takeover. So long as the buyer follows the philosophy that *the business should pay for itself,* that is, the DCF should support the buyer's needs as well as the payment schedule to the seller, there is little advantage to paying all cash and many disadvantages.

The Down Payment

Although the value of a business should theoretically have little to do with the down payment, as a practical matter, it does. There is certainly a minimum down payment that each seller will demand, for two reasons.

1. It is often necessary for the seller to meet certain closing expenses in addition to other financial obligations. The seller will often depend on a certain minimum down payment to accommodate these expenses, as well as the all-important tax implications.
2. Most sellers feel that they should require a minimum down payment should be required for giving up the prerogatives of ownership and accepting the risk of collecting the balance of the purchase price.

From the buyer's perspective, a minimum down payment is likely to be in the vicinity of about 20%. If the buyer is willing to make a greater down payment, it is likely that he or she will expect something in return, normally a lower purchase price or a lower interest rate.

The most significant aspect of the down payment, however, is that, if the value has been determined and the length of time for the balance to be paid has been agreed, then ...

the larger the down payment, the smaller the balance,

the lower the payments, the more salary available to the buyer out of the DCF.

Remember: during all of these calculations, the DCF remains the same. The following example might be helpful.

	Case 1	Case 2
Purchase Price	$300,000 10-year note @ 10%	$300,000 10-year note @ 10%
Down Payment	20%: $60,000	40%: $120,000
Balance of Note	$240,000	$180,000
DCF	$50,000	$50,000
Annual Note Payments	$38,000	$28,500
Annual Salary to Buyer After Sale	$42,000 ($30,000 plus the additional $12,000)	$51,500 ($30,000 plus the additional $21,500)

Working Capital

Any examination of business valuation must include a discussion of working capital. Usually when small businesses are sold, the seller retains both the obligation to pay the payables and the prerogative of collecting the receivables for work already done or product already sold. This is not always the case, but it's normal. Some businesses will require a working capital reservoir in order to handle the expenses for work done while waiting for pyament for that work.

In the printing business, for example, IBM may place an order for a substantial amount of money. They will expect the order to be produced and delivered in two weeks. They may not actually make payment for a period of six weeks. During this time, the printer will have to buy paper and ink, pay its employees, pay the rent, make the lease payments on equipment, pay for all electricity, and so on while waiting for the bill (the receivable) to be paid. This is often called the receivable turnover period or sales cycle. This is perfectly normal for any business that bills its customers, that is not an all-cash business that receives payment at the time of the sale.

A cash business will not necessarily need this reservoir but may require available cash reserves for other reasons: purchasing equipment, replacing inventory, and the like. Be careful that you know if your acquisition will require working capital and, if so, how much.

The Balloon Note

Although payment arrangements for the purchase price of a business should not directly affect the valuation, in some cases, they do. Following the assumption that the business must be able to pay for itself, that the DCF must be able to pay the buyer's salary and fully amortize the balance of the seller's purchase price, consider the following.

If the balance of the purchase price is $300,000 and it is agreed that $100,000 will be paid at the end of a period, say ten years, then the monthly payments will only be amortizing only $200,000, instead of $300,000. Naturally, these payments will be lower than the payments necessary to amortize $300,000. This would allow the seller to increase the price of the business and the buyer would still have the money available from the DCF to meet the monthly payments. This would allow a purchase price higher than the valuation concept allows. Essentially, it means a payment schedule exceeding a ten-year period.

The question is what happens when the $100,000 comes due at the end of the ten years. The buyer will have to do one of three things: pay the $100,000, get a loan of $100,000 from seller or another lender (which extends the payment schedule beyond the original ten years), or return the business to the seller after paying $200,000 and failing to pay the balance of the purchase price.

Robert, a buyer, faced this problem when he decided to sell the business he had purchased before the end of the payment schedule. He had owned it only eight years. The problem was that he needed to have a new payment schedule for the balance of the purchase price to pay off the balance on the promissory note as well as the balloon note of $100,000, which would come due in two years. He needed this in order to make a presentation to potential buyers, explaining what their payments would be after the down payment. The seller wouldn't adjust the schedule in anticipation of a buyer until after a Robert found a buyer. But buyers were not interested in acquiring the business when the payment schedule was still up in the air. The balloon note situation created an unsolvable problem. Robert did not sell the business.

A business should be valued once and the DCF must be sufficient to meet a schedule of payments on the purchase price after a down payment. Using a balloon note to increase the purchase price allows the seller to get more than the value of the business. *Buyer beware this type of presentation!*

[Publisher's Note: For a much more definitive analysis of this question, both from the standpoint of the buyer as well as the seller, be sure to read the book, *Entrepreneur's Ultimate Guide to Buying or Selling a Business*, by Ira Nottonson.]

The Buy-Sell Agreement (or Shareholder Agreement) and Your Will

Some states require that a buy-sell agreement or shareholder agreement must be expressly mentioned in an owner's last will and testament to be valid. The good news is that this can be done by a codicil, which is an addendum or brief amendment to a will. The codicil will be less time-consuming and probably cheaper than revising the will.

Reading Financial Statements

Financial statements generally have the same information, but they can vary considerably in appearance considerably. Your accountant should be able to determine unusual items by reviewing the balance sheet, the profit and loss (income) statement, and tax returns. Any unusual items should be investigated to determine what effect, if any, the item has on valuing the business.

The Larger the Down Payment

When setting the purchase price for a business, a larger down payment should work to the benefit of the buyer. It can reduce the purchase price, lower the interest rate on the financed portion of the transaction, or shorten the payment period.

Always File a Lien

In general, the sale of a business when seller financing is involved will include a promissory note that is secured by the business. This means that if the buyer does not honor the note, the seller can take back the business. Often this security is evidenced by the filing of a lien on the business, either with the state department or the county where the business is located. If a lien is not filed, the buyer could sell the business to a third party and leave the original seller with no recourse against the third party purchaser. *Always file a lien.*

Review Questions

1. Have you considered your exact retirement goals and what it will take to reach them?
2. Can your business operate without you?
3. Who would inherit your interest in the business?
4. Would your family have financial security if something happens to you?
5. At what age do you plan to retire?
6. Do you know how much money you would need to retire, comfortably?
7. Have you discussed exit strategies with the other owners or investors in your business?
8. Do you have a restrictive covenant preventing owners from selling their interest without first offering to sell to the other owners?
9. Do you plan to sell your business at some point?
10. Do you understand how to value your business?
11. What is the discretionary cash flow of a business?
12. Why is the P&L prepared for the IRS different than for valuation purposes?

50-State Review of Sales and Use Tax

Alabama

Alabama requires an annual sales and use tax license of retailers, for which there is no annual fee. The state imposes a sales tax on retailers of tangible personal property and selected services; operators of places of amusement and entertainment; persons selling new and used automotive vehicles, truck trailers, or semi-trailers; food products sold through vending machines; and sales of farm equipment. *Alabama's sales tax rate for general items is 4%*, but there are a few exceptions to this 4% rate: vehicles and mobile homes are taxed at 2%; farm machinery and equipment are taxed at 1.5%; and 3% for food sales through vending machines (excluding beverages other than coffee, milk, and milk products) are taxed at 3%. Finally, there is a 5% tax on all persons in the business of contracting to construct, reconstruct, or build any public highway, road, bridge, or street. In addition, the state has a 4% tax on all leasing or renting fees involving tangible personal property, except that the rental of vehicles and house trailers is taxed at 1.5% and the rental of linens and garments are taxed at 2%. Lease-to-purchase contracts are treated as sales rather than rentals. *The consumer pays the tax, but the retailer collects and remits the tax to the state and local authorities.* Use tax is due on all taxable sales on which no sales tax was paid at the time of purchase. The use tax liability remains the responsibility of the purchaser unless the purchaser has a receipt showing payment of the tax to the retailer. Retailers in Alabama are required to give purchasers a receipt that includes: name and place of the business, name and address of the purchaser, a description of property sold, date of sale, sale price, amount of tax collected, and seller's license or authority number.

Alaska

Alaska does not levy a statewide sales and use tax. However, various boroughs (similar to counties) and municipalities are authorized and do levy sales and use taxes. The local rates can vary and can be as high as 7%. There is a similarity in the local ordinances levying sales tax in these cities and boroughs, but they are not uniform. Local rules differ as to the tax rate, return due dates, discounts, and late payment or filing penalties. The rules also differ as to what is considered a taxable sale and what is exempt from the sales tax. Each business in Alaska will need to contact the local sales tax collector or administrator to determine how the rules apply to that business. Boroughs may collect a sales tax on sales, rents, and services provided within their borders and they may also levy and collect a use tax on the storage, use, or consumption of tangible personal property in the borough. Generally, cities within boroughs that impose sales and use taxes must do so in the same manner as provided by the borough where the city is located.

Arizona

Arizona imposes what it calls a *transaction privilege tax*, which is essentially a sales and use tax. A transaction privilege tax license is required by the Arizona Department of Revenue for a one-time fee of $12. The tax is based on the volume of taxable sales transacted and is imposed on the retailer, not the purchaser. *Generally the state sales tax rate is 5.6%* on all retail sales of the following activities: amusement, job printing, membership camping, mining, owner-builder sales, personal property rentals, pipeline, prime contracting, private car lines, publications, restaurant sales, telecommunications, transient lodging, transporting, and utilities. Activities that are taxed at different rates are mining (3.125%) and transient lodging (5.5%). Tax-exempt sales include prescription medications and food sold for home consumption. This transaction privilege tax is the responsibility of the retailer regardless of whether it is passed on to the purchaser. Arizona imposes a use tax on all tangible personal property not previously taxed. Taxable sales include the lease or rental of personal property in Arizona and there is a surcharge for the rental of vehicles for less than 180 days. Real estate rentals are not subject to the sales or use tax in Arizona.

Arkansas

Arkansas has what it calls a *gross receipts tax*, which is also essentially a sales tax based on the gross receipts of a retailer or certain service businesses. The gross receipts tax permit is required by the state for a fee of $50. *The state tax rate is 6% on all sales* of tangible personal property or services to contractors and the following services: wrecker and towing, collection and disposal of solid wastes, cleaning parking lots and gutters, dry cleaning and laundry, industrial laundry, mini-warehouse and self-storage rental, body piercing, tattooing and electrolysis, pest control, security and alarm monitoring, boat storage and docking fees, furnishing camping spaces or trailer spaces at public or privately owned campgrounds (except federal campgrounds), on less than a month-to-month basis, locksmith, and pet grooming and kennel services. *The gross receipts tax is the responsibility of the retailer or service provider regardless of whether the tax is passed on to the purchaser.* Use tax is imposed on sales and services on which no gross receipts tax was collected. In addition, Arkansas has a similar tax on all tangible personal property purchased by public transportation carriers, railroads, public pipeline carriers, airline carriers, telephone and telegraph companies, gas, water, and electric power companies, and financial institutions. Under Arkansas law, many sales are tax-exempt, including newspapers and gasoline. Arkansas does include rental payments on tangible personal property in its definition of taxable sales However, a rental vehicle tax is imposed on vehicles rented for less than 30 days, instead of the gross receipts tax. The rental vehicle tax, however, has several exceptions, such as a diesel truck rented for commercial shipping, farm machinery and equipment rented for commercial purposes, and trucks rented for residential moving or shipping.

California

California assesses a sales tax on all retail sales of tangible personal property. The state tax rate is set at a minimum of 6%. *The sales tax is the responsibility of the retailer, who may or may not collect the tax from the consumer.* California also imposes a use tax on any sales of tangible personal property purchased from another state. Generally, services are not taxed in California and any property or equipment provided as a result of the services may also be excluded, provided that the services provided are the main purpose of the transaction and any property acquired by the consumer is merely incidental to the services provided. For example, if a doctor provides her patient with an X-ray and a cast for a broken arm, the patient is clearly paying for the doctor's services and the X-ray and cast are incidental to those services. On the other hand, if a customer at a hair salon receives a haircut and purchases several different hair products to take home, then the customer should pay sales tax on the hair products. To help clear up any confusion, the state applies what it calls the "true objects test," which looks at the main purpose of the transaction to determine if any sales or use tax is required. In California, all leased and rented property will be subject to the sales tax. However, the leasing or rental of the following types of tangible personal property will not be treated as a sale or purchase: motion pictures, including television, films, and tapes (except videocassettes rented for private use); linen supplies and similar articles by professional cleaners; household furnishings included in a lease of living quarters; mobile transportation equipment; and property for which sales or use tax has been paid by the person leasing the property.

Colorado

Colorado imposes a sales tax on all gross receipts from the following activities: all retail sales of tangible personal property, retail sales involving exchange of property, intrastate telephone and telegraph services, gas and electric service to consumers, sales of steam, meals and cover charges furnished at any place where meals are regularly served to the public, and charges for rooms or accommodations. A sales tax license must be obtained for an initial fee of $16, with a recurring fee of $16 every two years. In addition, Colorado requires a one-time deposit of $50, which will be returned once the business has collected and remitted $50 worth of sale tax to the Colorado Department of Revenue. The Colorado sales tax rate is 2.9%. Services are not taxed under the Colorado sales tax rules. The sales tax is imposed on and paid by the purchaser; however, the retailer has the responsibility of collecting and remitting the sales tax to the proper governmental authorities. Colorado imposes a use tax when no sales tax has been paid. The use tax is generally the responsibility of the purchaser. *In addition, Colorado exempts from sales tax the rental of tangible personal property for a period of less than three years unless the person renting the property agrees to collect sales tax on all lease payments. For all leases over three years or for the collection of the sales tax on a monthly basis, the tax rate is 3%.*

Connecticut

The state imposes a general sales and use tax rate of 6%, local municipalities and governments cannot assess a local sales tax. The 6% sales tax applies to the gross receipts from all of the following long list of services:

- advertising or public relations services
- business analysis, management, management consulting, and public relations services
- community antenna television services

- credit information and reporting services
- employment and personnel agency services
- exterminating services
- flight instruction and chartering services by a certificated air carrier
- hospital charges for patient care
- janitorial services
- landscaping and horticultural services, except those provided by a licensed landscape architect
- lobbying or political special interest group consulting services
- locksmith services
- maintenance services
- motor vehicle repairs, parking, and car washing services
- painting and lettering services
- certain personal services (other than specific massage services)
- photographic studio services
- private investigation, protection, patrol work, security, and armored car services
- renovation and repair services to noncommercial real property
- repair or maintenance services to tangible personal property
- services in connection with the sale of tangible personal property
- services providing piped-in music
- services to industrial, commercial, or income-producing real property
- stenographic services
- storage or mooring of noncommercial vessels
- swimming pool cleaning and maintenance services
- telecommunications services
- telephone answering services
- window cleaning services
- furniture reupholstering and repair services

Also note that hotel accommodations for 30 days or less are charged a sales tax of 12% and repairs and replacement parts for use in machinery involved directly in the manufacturing or agricultural production process are taxed at

5.5%. The license required has a one-time application fee of $20 and must be renewed every two years for no additional fee. The lease or rental of tangible personal property is considered a taxable sale in Connecticut. *The sales tax is the responsibility of the retailer or the person renting property; however, he or she is entitled to collect the reimbursement of the tax from the purchaser.* Connecticut exempts many items from the sales tax, such as food products and prescription medication. Use tax is also imposed by the state on taxable property or services on which no sales tax has been paid. The use tax appears to be the responsibility of the consumer.

Delaware

Delaware does not have a general sales tax. However, the state imposes a tax called a *manufacturers' and merchants' license tax*, which is similar to a sales tax as it is assessed against gross sales. This tax applies to the following types of businesses: contractors, manufacturers, wholesalers, food processors, commercial feed dealers, retailers, restaurant retailers, grocery supermarkets, and farm machinery dealers. *This tax is the responsibility of the merchant or manufacturer and is not passed on directly to the consumer.* The tax is based on gross receipts and varies greatly depending on the industry. If your business is located in Delaware, you should look into this tax carefully when deciding what type of business you will be doing. The rates are currently as follows:

- contractors: $75 plus 0.624% of aggregate gross receipts, less a monthly deduction of $50,000
- manufacturers: $75 plus 0.18% of aggregate gross receipts, less a monthly deduction of $1 million
- wholesalers: $75 plus 0.384% of aggregate gross receipts, less a $50,000 monthly deduction
- food processors: $75 plus 0.192% of aggregate gross receipts, less a monthly deduction of $50,000
- commercial feed dealers: $75 plus 0.096% of aggregate gross receipts, less a monthly deduction of $50,000
- retailers: $75 plus $25 per business location, plus 0.72% of aggregate

gross receipts from goods sold or services rendered, less a monthly deduction of $50,000

- transient retailers: $25 plus 0.72% of aggregate gross receipts over $3,000
- restaurant retailers: $75 plus $25 per business location, plus 0.624% of aggregate gross receipts, less monthly deduction of $50,000
- farm machinery, supplies, or materials retailers: $75 plus 0.096% of aggregate gross receipts, less a monthly deduction of $50,000
- grocery supermarkets: $75 plus $25 per branch plus 0.384% of the first $2 million per month and 0.72% thereafter, less a monthly deduction of $50,000

District of Columbia

The District of Columbia assesses a sales tax on the retail sales of tangible personal property and the following services: admissions, lodging for less than 90 days; repairs, alterations, mending or fitting personal property, or applying or installing personal property as a repair or replacement; copying, photocopying, addressing, and mailing services; laundering, dry cleaning or pressing; parking, storing, or keeping motor vehicles; telecommunications; deliveries within the District when separately stated; employment services; real property maintenance services (including cleaning, maintenance, and repairs); landscaping services (including landscaping design and architectural services); data processing services (including entering, processing, and maintaining data and information by a third party);, and information services (including the furnishing of general or specialized news or current information by printed, mimeographed, or electronic means). *The state sales tax rate is 5.75% on all taxable sales and is the responsibility of the seller.* However, the District requires the retailer to collect the tax from the customer and has reserved the right to go after the customer if the tax is not correctly paid or remitted. A use tax is also assessed by the District against all persons who use, store, or otherwise consume property in the District of Columbia that was purchased outside the District. Generally, if the retailer is registered in the District of Columbia, the use tax should be paid to the retailer or service provider; if not, the use tax should be paid directly to the District. Leased property will also incur the sales tax, with the exception of the rental or lease of films and sound equipment to theaters and radio and television stations.

Florida

Florida assesses a sales tax on the following sales and services: retail sales; rentals, use, consumption, distribution, or storage for use or consumption in Florida of tangible personal property; and rental or furnishing of taxable things or services; renting or granting of a license to use living quarters, sleeping, or housekeeping accommodations for six months or less; leasing or renting motor vehicle parking, boat docking, or storage spaces for either renting or leasing real property, unless the property is used for agricultural purposes or used exclusively as dwelling units; admissions, including membership fees and dues, any facility or device used primarily for the control of pollution or contaminants from manufacturing or industrial plants, charges for telegraph; long-distance telephone calls, telecommunications service, television system program service, installation of telecommunication and telegraphic equipment; and charges for electrical power or energy detective; burglar protection, and other protection services, nonresidential cleaning and pest control services.

The sales and use tax rate is generally 6%. However, the following exceptions apply: self-propelled or power-drawn farm equipment is taxed at 2.5%; coin-operated amusement machines are taxed at 4%; and telecommunication services and electrical power or energy are taxed at 7%. Florida does exempts many specific items, such as food and drink for human consumption and certain prescription medications. In Florida, *the seller pays the sales tax and use tax, but the seller is required to collect the tax from the purchaser.* The retailer, service provider, or a party leasing personal property must register with the state for a permit. Fees for the permits are based on revenues and the number of locations. Rental or leased tangible personal property is considered a taxable sale in Florida.

Georgia

Georgia assesses a sales tax on the retail sales price of tangible personal property. *The sales and use tax rate in Georgia is 4%.* Also, the following services are taxed: admissions to places of amusement, coin-operated musical or amusement devices, transportation, local telephone service, and lodgings. As with many other states, Georgia assesses a sales tax on sellers for the privilege of doing business in Georgia and requires them to collect and remit the tax to the state, but the state requires the retailer or service provider to collect the tax from the customer, so the state could go directly to the consumer to collect any tax not properly collected. The same general rules apply to the use tax.

Hawaii

No matter what you do in Hawaii, you will pay either a sales tax or a use tax. All gross proceeds of sales and services are taxed in Hawaii. *The general tax is 4% for sales of tangible personal property; services are taxed at the rate of 5%.* Manufacturers and wholesalers pay 0.5% and insurance agencies pay .15%. *The sales tax is assessed against the seller or service provider; the use tax is assessed against the purchaser, although it may be paid to sellers who are registered in Hawaii.* In addition, Hawaii taxes the leasing or rental of personal property or real estate at 4%.

Idaho

Idaho imposes a 5% sales and use tax on the sale of tangible personal property. A permit is required by Idaho. The sales tax applies to the following services only: producing property to the special order of the customer; producing property for consumers who furnish the materials used; food, meals, and drinks for a consideration; admission charges and charges to use property or facilities for recreational purposes, providing hotel and trailer court accommodations; leasing or renting tangible personal property, and intrastate transportation for hire by air of freight or passengers except as part of a flight by a certified air carrier or an air ambulance service. There is no application or permit fee; however, if the business is the sale or rental of amusement devices, an annual permit fee of $35 may be paid instead of the sales tax. Use tax applies when property is purchased from out of state or when the seller is not required to collect the sales tax. *Both the sales and use tax are the responsibility of the consumer but are collected by the retailer.* Idaho exempts many items, such as certain prescription medications. All leasing or rental of tangible personal property is taxable in Idaho on the date the property is delivered.

Illinois

Illinois levies a sales tax on all sales of tangible personal property at the rate of 6.25%; however, certain foods, drugs, and medical appliances are taxed at 1%. The sales tax is the responsibility of the seller, but the state requires the seller to be reimbursed by the consumer, thus retaining the right to collect the tax directly from the consumer. *Services are generally not taxable in Illinois.* Any tangible personal property transferred along with services is taxable unless sales tax has already been paid on the property when it was purchased by the retailer from its vendor before transferring to the consumer. The use tax is assessed against the consumer, but may be collected by the seller if the seller is a registered retailer in Illinois. Generally, leased and rented property won't be subject to sales or use tax. However, Illinois will examine the leasing arrangement and classify it as a sale if it appears that ownership will transfer to the consumer for a nominal amount once the lease term has ended. *For example, if you lease a refrigerator for three years and, at the end of the lease, you are able to purchase the refrigerator for $30, Illinois would likely treat the transaction as a sale because the ending price is such a nominal amount.*

Indiana

The state charges a sales tax of 6% on the sale of all tangible personal property. The following types of services do incur the sales tax: the softening and conditioning of water, the renting or furnishing of certain rooms, lodgings, or other accommodations for a period of less than 30 days, and the renting or leasing of tangible personal property to another person. Nontaxable services will be subject to the tax if tangible property is transferred with the service, except if the price of the tangible personal property being transferred is separately stated from the charge for services and the cost of the property in relationship to the total bill does not exceed 10%. Also, the person providing the service must be in an occupation that primarily furnishes and sells services. In addition, the tangible personal property purchased must be used or consumed as a necessary incident to the service and the person providing the service must pay the sales and use tax on the tangible personal property at the time of acquisition. *Sales tax is the responsibility of the seller, but the seller is required to obtain reimbursement of the tax from the purchaser.* Thus, the state retains the right to collect from the consumer. The lease or rental of tangible personal property is taxed, with the exception of motion picture film, videotape, and audiotape.

Iowa

Iowa assesses a 5% sales or use tax on the gross receipts from the following sales or services: tangible personal property sold at retail in Iowa to consumers or users; utility and communication services; tickets or admission fees; amusement devices and games of skill or chance; rentals of hotels, motels, inns, etc.; optional service or warranty contracts, engraving, photography, and printing services; and solid waste collection and disposal services. A retailer is required to obtain a permit for each place of business and there is no fee. Temporary and occasional businesses do not need a permit but must pay all sales tax due. *Use tax is the responsibility of the consumer and is due on any taxable sales that take place out of state if the goods or services are used in Iowa.* If a consumer pays tax in another state, Iowa allows a credit for that tax. If a person using taxable goods or services in Iowa pays tax in another state that is higher than the Iowa 5% use tax, no use tax will be payable to Iowa. The rental of tangible personal property is subject to retail sales tax in Iowa. Gross taxable services from rentals include rents, royalties, and copyright and license fees and are payable within the tax period received.

Kansas

In Kansas a sales tax is levied upon the gross receipts from the following retail sales and services:

- retail sales of tangible personal property
- telephone or telegraph services
- furnishing gas, water, electricity, and heat
- sale of meals or drinks at private or public businesses
- sale of admissions to any place providing amusement
- coin-operating devices dispensing tangible personal property, amusement, or services (except laundry services)
- rentals of rooms by hotels
- renting or leasing of tangible personal property
- dry cleaning, pressing, dyeing, and laundry services (except laundry services rendered through coin-operated devices)
- washing and waxing vehicles
- subscriber radio and television services
- sales to contractors, subcontractors, or repairmen of materials and supplies for use in building, improving, altering, or repairing property for others
- fees and charges by private and public clubs, organizations, businesses, and political subdivisions of Kansas for participation in recreational activities
- isolated or occasional sales of motor vehicles or trailers
- installing or applying tangible personal property that is not held for sale in the regular course of business
- repairing, servicing, altering, or maintaining tangible personal property associated with realty and not held for sale in the regular course of business
- fees or charges made under service or maintenance agreement contracts
- sales of canned computer software and services or modifying, altering, updating, or maintaining computer software
- telephone answering services
- sales of electricity, gas, and water that is essential to or used in a qualified production process
- sales from the service of renting rooms by an accommodations broker

The sales tax rate in Kansas is currently 5%. In Kansas the sales tax is the responsibility of the purchaser and is collected by the seller. The sales tax debt is a debt owed to the retailer until such time as it is paid by the purchaser and the tax must be separately stated on the invoice or billing statement or the statement "All applicable tax is included" must be stated on such invoice or statement. If neither requirement is fulfilled, the state will presume that the sales tax has not been collected by the retailer. All retailers and service providers of taxable goods or services must obtain a certificate of registration from the Kansas Director of Taxation. The use tax in Kansas is paid only if sales or use tax is not paid to another state on taxable goods or services. It is the responsibility of the consumer and is considered a debt owed to the retailer. Leases of tangible personal property that are treated as a sale for federal income tax purposes will be treated as a taxable sale in Kansas.

Kentucky

Kentucky imposes a sales tax on the gross receipts from retail sales of tangible personal property or on its lease or rental. Kentucky also charges sales tax on the following services: the rental of transient accommodations, the furnishing of sewer services and intrastate telephone and telegraph services, and the sale of events admissions. *The Kentucky sales and use tax rate is 6%.* In Kentucky, a permit is required of retailers for each separate location and can be obtained from the Kentucky Revenue Cabinet. The sales tax is imposed upon the gross receipts of the retailer, but is a debt of the purchaser or consumer. The sales tax is required to be separately stated on the invoice, billing statement, or receipt. As with many other states, Kentucky has exempt items such as certain prescription medications, so you should get a list of the exemptions. *Use tax is paid only if sales tax was not paid on the taxable sales of goods or services and it's the responsibility of the consumer or purchaser to pay the tax unless collected by the retailer.* Leases and rentals of all kinds of tangible personal property (except motor vehicles and property qualifying for exemptions) are subject to the Kentucky sales and use tax.

Louisiana

Louisiana sales tax is a general tax on the retail sales of tangible personal property or on its lease or rental and on the furnishing of the following services: lodging and associated storage and parking, admissions, printing, cleaning, cold storage, and repairs of tangible personal property, and telecommunications. *The Louisiana tax rate is 4%.* Sales and use tax in Louisiana is different than other states because sales tax is collected on both retail and wholesale transactions. However, the retailer (referred to as "dealer") will be able to deduct advanced sales tax paid to a wholesaler when the retailer collects the tax from the consumer. In Louisiana, dealers must register for sales and use tax purposes with the state. However, vendor registration is informal and dealers are asked to contact the Application Central Registration Unit of the Department of Revenue and Taxation for the necessary forms and details. Review a list of exempt items such as certain prescription medications. The sales taxes are collected by the seller or dealer from the purchaser or consumer. Wholesalers are required to collect advance sales taxes from dealers. Wholesale invoices should separately state any advance tax payment to support the tax deduction that will be taken when the retailer sells to the consumer. Use tax in Louisiana is collected only when sales tax has not been paid and is the responsibility of the consumer. Lease and rental transaction are taxable and the tax is due in monthly installments over the life of the lease for lease purchase arrangements rather than at the inception of the transaction.

Maine

Maine imposes sales tax on all sales of tangible personal property and taxable services sold at retail in the state. The following services are taxable: rental of living quarters in any hotel, rooming house, tourist, or trailer camp; rental or lease of an automobile; telephone or telegraph services; extended cable television services; rental of videotapes and video equipment; and fabrication services. *Most sales in Maine are taxable at the rate of 5%;* however, the following goods and services are taxed at a higher rate:

- 10% on rentals of automobiles for less than one year
- 7% on all food prepared by a retailer
- 7% on liquor and prepared food in liquor establishments
- 7% on rentals of rooms or shelter
- 7% gross receipts tax (instead of sales tax) on persons engaged in the business of providing home patient care.

A tax permit is required from the State Tax Assessor (sales tax division) and can be obtained free of charge. Certain prescription medications are exempt from sales tax in Maine along with other items. In Maine, responsibility of the sales tax is on the consumer. However, the retailer is liable for payment of the tax to the state and local governments. In Maine, the retailer is required to include the tax in the sale price and may actually collect the tax from the consumer in an action at law. The use tax is collected on the use, storage, or other consumption of taxable goods or services on which sales tax has not been paid and is the responsibility of the consumer. *Leases and rent payments are not subject to the sales or use tax under Maine law unless they are lease-purchase arrangements.*

Maryland

Maryland charges a sales tax of 5% on all retail sales, including leases or rentals, of tangible personal property or a taxable service in the state. The use tax is imposed on the use of tangible personal property or on a taxable service and is not required to be paid if sales tax has already been paid. The following services are taxable under Maryland state law: fabrication, printing, or producing personal property by special order; commercial cleaning or laundry services, cellular telephone or other mobile telecommunications services; 900-type telecommunications services; custom calling services provided in connection with basic telephone services; telephone answering services, pay-per-view television services; credit reporting and security services; and the cleaning of commercial or industrial buildings. Maryland exempts certain prescription medications and items in other specific categories from sales tax. The retail vendor must register with the Office of the Comptroller for a vendor's license, which is valid indefinitely. In Maryland, the purchaser or consumer must pay the sales or use tax to the vendor, who holds the tax as a trustee for the state. Vendors do not have to collect the sales or use tax if the purchaser supplies them with an exemption certificate or a resale certificate (wholesaler license). Any buyer who does not pay the sales or use tax to the vendor is responsible for paying the tax to the state. A lease of tangible personal property is considered a taxable sale and is subject to sales and use tax. Under Maryland law, each lease payment period is considered a separate lease or sale.

Massachusetts

Massachusetts assesses a 5% sales tax on gross receipts from retail sales, including meals, leases, and rentals. The vendor is required to collect sales tax from the purchaser at the time of sale and is then remit it to the state. While the sales tax is collected by the vendor, it remains the obligation of the purchaser or consumer and may be collected directly from the consumer by the vendor in a court action. Certain prescription medications and food for human consumption are exempt items under state law. As is usually the case, Massachusetts collects use tax on taxable sales only if the sales tax is not paid; it is imposed upon the consumer. However, if a vendor does business inside the state of Massachusetts, the vendor is required to collect the use tax from the purchaser and remit it to the state. All in-state vendors must register in order to obtain a sales tax permit. Currently, there is no fee for such applications or permits and the permits are valid for three years. *The rental or lease of tangible personal property is included in the definition of sale under Massachusetts state law for tax purposes.*

Michigan

Michigan requires every retailer to collect and pay a 6% tax on all taxable sales proceeds for the privilege of carrying on a retail business. Taxable sales include: retail sales or transactions in the ordinary course of business in Michigan, including those in which title is retained for security purposes, sales of electricity and gas for heat (taxed at 4%) and light to consumers, sales of prepaid telephone calling cards, computer software offered for general sale to the public, and sales of tangible personal property by an industrial laundry under a sale, rental, or service agreement. No other services are taxable unless specifically made subject to the sales or use tax. Michigan does require retail businesses to obtain a sales tax license from the Department of Treasury. The license fee is $1. Certain prescription medications are exempt from sales tax in Michigan among other items. *The sales tax is levied on the seller. Sellers are required to reimburse themselves by adding the tax to the amount of each sale.* Use tax is levied on the consumer when sales are made outside of the state or when sales tax is not paid. In addition, Michigan levies the use tax on all lodging for one month or less and telephone, telegraph, leased wire, and similar communications. Michigan allows a lessor leasing tangible personal property either to pay a sales tax on property to be leased when it is purchased or to choose to be exempt from such sales tax at the time of purchase and collect the sales tax at the time of leasing.

Minnesota

Minnesota imposes a general sales tax of 6.5% on the gross receipts from sales at retail of tangible personal property or on its lease or rental. Certain intoxicating liquors and non-intoxicating malt liquors are taxed at the rate of 9%. In addition, Minnesota also charges sales tax on the furnishing of the following services: renting, producing, fabricating, printing, or processing of tangible personal property; preparation or serving of meals or drinks; entertainment admissions and membership fees; lodging; utilities; telecommunications; parking; cleaning; security; pet care; and lawn care. Minnesota has specific items that are exempt from sales tax—for example, certain prescription medications. Although the sales tax is on a seller's gross receipts, shifting of the tax to the purchaser is mandatory under state law. As is required by some of the other states, the sales tax must be separately stated on the invoice, billing statement, or receipt. The tax becomes a debt from the purchaser to the seller. Minnesota's use tax is complementary and is not collected if sales tax is collected on a sale. The responsibility for the payment of the use tax lies with the purchaser or consumer and is considered a debt owed from the purchaser to the seller. Minnesota defines the leasing of tangible personal property as a sale and, consequently, it is subject to the sales and use tax.

Mississippi

The Mississippi sales tax is levied on the gross proceeds of sales of tangible personal property and sales of many services at varying tax rates. The tax rates and categories of taxable items are as follows:

- **Tangible personal property.** Generally the rate of tax on services and on the sale of tangible personal property is 7%.
- **Salesman's tax.** A tax is imposed on every salesman engaged in the itinerant solicitation and taking of orders for tangible personal property by use of the highways of Mississippi for subsequent delivery to retailers or consumers in Mississippi. The tax rate is 3% of the amount of orders from consumers and 0.125% if the order is from retailers for resale.
- **Farming and/or farmers.** The tax rate is 3% on sales to farmers of qualified farm equipment.
- **Transportation equipment.** The tax rate is 3% on retail sales of aircraft, automobiles, trucks, truck-tractors, semi-trailers, and mobile homes.
- **Carriers.** The tax rate is 5% of sales of private carriers of passengers and light carriers of property.
- **Vending machines.** The tax rate is 8% of wholesale sales of food and drink to vending machine operators. The food and drink must be for sale through vending machines located apart from and not connected with other taxable businesses.
- **Utilities for industry and agriculture.** The tax rate is 1.5% of sales of gas, petroleum, electricity, or other fuels for industrial and agricultural purposes.
- **Construction.** The tax rate is 3.5% for construction contracts exceeding $10,000 (other than residences).
- **Manufacturing equipment.** The tax rate is 1.5% on sales of manufacturing machinery and manufacturing machine parts.
- **Amusements.** Generally the tax rate is 7% on amusements, except for those that are conducted in publicly owned, enclosed coliseums and

auditoriums, which are taxed at a 3% rate.

- **Room rental and services.** The tax rate is 7% on miscellaneous businesses and services, including room rentals.

Mississippi requires the seller to add the tax to the sale price paid by the purchaser and to add the sales tax to the price of the goods or service when the income from such goods and services is collected. The sales tax must be stated separately from the sales price on the sales invoices or receipts and must be shown separately on the seller's records. Businesses located in Mississippi are required to obtain a sales tax license from the State Tax Commission; this license is valid indefinitely. Mississippi has specific items that are exempt from sales tax, like certain prescription medications. You will want to review the rules related to tax-exempt items in Mississippi. A use tax is incurred in Mississippi for using, storing, or consuming within Mississippi any article of tangible personal property, regardless of the manner in which possession of the property was acquired, the use tax is the responsibility of the consumer. Lease and rental transactions are subject to the sales tax in Mississippi. In fact, Mississippi charges sales tax on leases involving such items as repairs, transportation, hotels, meals, and supplies.

Missouri

In Missouri, sales tax is collected on all sales of tangible personal property or taxable services at retail. The sales tax is imposed on the following services: tangible personal property; admission to places of amusement, recreation, games, and athletic events; basic rate paid or charged for electricity, water, and gas; basic rate paid or charged for telephone services and telegraph transmissions; rooms, meals, and drinks from places regularly offering such to the public; intrastate tickets for railroads, sleeping, dining, and express cars; boats, airplanes, and buses and trucks licensed by the Department of Economic Development engaged in transportation of persons; and renting or leasing tangible personal property, unless the tax was paid when the property was previously purchased. *The Missouri sales and use tax rate is 4.225% (4.125% effective November 8, 2008).* In Missouri any person or business required to collect the sales tax must obtain a license from the Missouri Director of Revenue. At this time, there is no charge for a Missouri state sales tax license. Like so many other states, Missouri exempts certain prescribed medications along with other items from the sales tax. *The seller is responsible for collecting and remitting the sales tax to the state.* However, purchasers are required to pay the sales tax to the seller. A use tax is imposed for the privilege of storing, using, or consuming within Missouri any article of tangible personal property. Use tax does not apply to items that are exempt from the sales tax under Missouri law. Under Missouri law, the use tax is the responsibility of the consumer. While leases of tangible personal property are subject to the use tax, no tax is imposed if the owner or the renter paid sales tax when the property was purchased or if the property is exempt from sales tax under Missouri law.

Montana

Montana does not impose any general sales tax upon the sale or use of all tangible personal property within the state. However, Montana does levy the following taxes: a lodging facility use tax, an accommodations and campground sales and use tax, a rental vehicle sales tax, and a new vehicle sales tax. Below is a description of each tax.

- **Lodging facility use tax.** A 4% lodging facility use tax is imposed upon the use of a lodging facility for a period of less than 30 days. The owner or operator of a facility must apply to the Montana Department of Revenue for a registration number and must collect and remit the tax to the state.
- **Accommodation and campground sales and use tax.** A 3% sales and use tax is imposed on accommodation, and campground fees. This is in addition to the 4% lodging facility use tax. A seller's permit is required to be obtained from the Department of Revenue and the owner of the facility must collect and remit the tax to the state.
- **Rental vehicle sales tax.** A 4% sales tax is imposed on the base rental charge of rental vehicles. Rental vehicles that are subject to the tax include: automobiles, motorcycles, motorboats, sailboats, off-road recreational vehicles, and trucks with a gross weight less than 22,000 pounds. Farm vehicles, travel trailers, motor homes, airplanes, snow-

mobiles, golf carts, and sail boards are not subject to the tax. Vendors subject to the tax must apply for a seller's permit from the Montana Department of Revenue.

- **New vehicle sales tax.** A tax is imposed on all sales of new motor vehicles for which a state license is sought and an original application for title is made. The purchaser of the new motor vehicle is required to pay the tax when applying for a license from the county treasurer. The tax is based on the list price of the vehicle and is imposed at the rate of 1.5% of list price if purchased in the first quarter, 1.125% in the second quarter, 0.75% in the third quarter, and 0.375 in the fourth quarter. The rate is 0.75% of list price for new vehicles registered as a fleet.

Montana allows some local communities to impose a resort tax, which cannot exceed 3% of the retail value of goods and services sold. This tax must be approved by voters in the community or area where the tax is to be collected and administered. The tax applies to sales by lodging establishments, restaurants, and other public establishments that serve alcoholic beverages by the drink, destination ski resorts and other destination recreational facilities, and establishments that sell luxuries.

Nebraska

Nebraska charges a sales tax on the retail sales of property; the furnishing, installing, or connecting of utilities or community antenna television service; retailers of intellectual or entertainment properties; admission tickets; and warranties or maintenance agreements when the items covered are subject to sales tax. In addition, the tax applies to the renting of hotel or motel rooms for less than 30 days. *The Nebraska sales and use tax rate is 5.5%.* In Nebraska, a seller must apply for a permit for each place of business. An application for a permit is made on the form prescribed by the Nebraska Commissioner; and there is a $10 fee. *The consumer is responsible for the sales tax, but the seller is required to collect the tax and remit it to the state.* Nebraska exempts some items—for example, certain prescription medications. Nebraska's use tax rules imposes a tax of 5.5%

on property purchased, leased, or rented on which sales tax was due but not paid and the responsibility for the tax lies with the consumer.

Nebraska charges sales tax on the lease or rental of personal property. Specifically, Nebraska imposes the tax on what it calls a "conditional" sale (lease-purchase arrangement at the time the contract is signed). A contract is considered a conditional sale if one or more of the following conditions are found to exist:

- the lease is required to be classified as a capital lease rather than an operating lease under generally accepted accounting principles;
- portions of the payments are made specifically applicable to an equity to be acquired by the lessee;
- the lease binds the lessee for a fixed term and the lessee is to obtain title at the end of the term upon completion of the payments or has the option to purchase the property for the lesser of $100 or 1% of the total contract price;
- the total amount that the lessee is required to pay for a relatively short period of use constitutes an inordinately large proportion of the total sum required to be paid to secure the transfer of title;
- the agreed periodic payments materially exceed the current fair rental value; or
- some portion of the payments is specifically designated as interest or is otherwise readily recognizable as the equivalent of interest.

Nevada

Nevada charges a 6.5% general sales tax on all retailers for the sale of tangible personal property. The following transactions are specifically subject to the tax:

- producing or processing of tangible personal property for consumers who furnish the materials used in such producing, fabricating, processing, printing, or imprinting
- furnishing and distributing of personal property for a consideration by social clubs
- furnishing, preparing, or serving of food, meals, or drinks for a consideration

- transactions in which possession of property is transferred but the seller retains the title as security for the payment of the price
- transfers for consideration of the title or possession of tangible personal property that has been produced, fabricated, or printed to the special order of the customer, or of any publication
- sale of company assets when the business is a registered seller

Generally, there is no sales tax on services in Nevada. A tax permit is required in Nevada for a fee of $15 and there are exempt items, including but not limited to certain prescription medications. Because the tax is imposed for the privilege of selling tangible personal property; the tax is the responsibility of the seller; however, the seller may collect the tax from the consumer when possible. *Nevada imposes a use tax on all property that is purchased out of state if the transaction would have been subject to sales tax had the sale occurred in the state of Nevada.* A lease or rental of tangible personal property is considered a taxable sale in Nevada if the Tax Commission finds that the transaction is in place of a transfer of title, exchange, or barter.

New Hampshire

New Hampshire does not impose a general sales tax upon the sale or use of tangible personal property within the state. However, it does impose an 8% "sales" tax on meals, room occupancies, and motor vehicle rentals. The tax on meals generally will apply to restaurants only, not prepackaged foods or meals served by religious or charitable organizations. The tax is collected from the purchaser by the business owner. Any business that sells meals, rents room, or rents vehicles must obtain a license from the Department of Revenue Administration.

New Jersey

New Jersey charges a sales tax of 7% on all receipts from:

- retail sales of tangible personal property, including leases and rentals
- sales to construction contractors
- sales of restaurant and catered meals and ready-to-eat meals or food, including sandwiches, for off-premises consumption, except food

(other than sandwiches) sold in an unheated state if commonly sold in the same form and condition in food stores other than those principally engaged in selling prepared foods

- admission charges exceeding $0.75 (except for certain boxing, wrestling, kick boxing, or combative sports contests otherwise taxable)
- hotel and motel accommodations when the daily charge exceeds $2 and the occupancy is not for more than 90 consecutive days
- services such as producing, fabricating, storing, maintaining, repairing, processing, and installing (except when performed at a residence or on exempt personal property)
- most advertising services, other than advertising in newspapers and magazines, and direct-mail advertising sent to out-of-state recipients

In New Jersey, both retailers and wholesalers must register with the Director of the Division of Taxation. There is no fee for a sales tax permit. Once again, certain prescription medications are exempt from sales tax and a review of exempt items would be prudent. In New Jersey, the sales tax is collected by the retailer from the consumer. New Jersey has the best of both worlds in that it can hold the retailer or business owner to be personally liable for the tax collected or required to be collected or it may go directly to the consumer and require payment on any tax due but not paid at the time of the sales transaction. The use tax is imposed on the consumer only if the sales tax due was not paid. If an out-of-state sales tax was paid, the consumer owes the difference between the out-of-state rate and the New Jersey rate of 7%. If the sales tax paid to another state is higher than 7%, no use tax is due to New Jersey.

New Mexico

In New Mexico, a state sales tax rate of 5% must be paid on the gross receipts from all taxable sales. A taxable sale includes: selling property in New Mexico, leasing property used in New Mexico, selling services performed outside New Mexico, the product of which is initially used in New Mexico, performing services in New Mexico, and any receipts from sales of tangible personal property handled on consignment. Virtually all businesses in New Mexico must register with the

Taxation and Revenue Department to obtain a sales tax permit. New Mexico exempts the sale of automobile warranty contracts from its sales tax, among other things. As a result, each business should check the rules on exempt items. *Under New Mexico law, the seller of goods, the lessor of property, and the seller of services is solely responsible for the tax, not just collecting the tax on behalf of the state.* New Mexico's use tax is imposed on persons using services in New Mexico that were not initially subject to the sales tax but that, because of the buyer's subsequent use, should have been subject to the use tax. In addition, the use tax is imposed when property is manufactured by a person using the property in New Mexico, when property is acquired outside the state in a transaction that would have been subject to the sales tax had it occurred in the state, and when property is acquired as the result of a transaction not giving rise to the payment of tax but that, due to the eventual use of the property, would have required payment of the tax. The use tax is levied against the user of the property or the consumer. However, payment of the sales tax to the seller releases the consumer from liability for the use tax. All receipts from renting or leasing property are taxable in New Mexico.

New York

New York state charges a state sales tax of 4% on the receipts from the following retail sales and services: retail sales of tangible personal property; gas, utilities, and telephone and telegraph services; food and drink sold by restaurants and caterers; room occupancy; processing and printing services; installation, repair, and maintenance services performed upon tangible personal property; storage and safe deposit rental; real estate maintenance service, or repair; motor vehicle parking and garaging services; interior decorating and designing services; protective and detective services; telephonic and telegraphic entertainment and information services; and certain admissions charges; social or athletic club dues; and roof garden or cabaret charges. An additional tax of 5% is imposed on the receipts from telephonic or telegraphic entertainment and information services. *Collecting and remitting the sales tax to the state is the responsibility of the seller, lessor, or the service provider.* While New York can hold sellers personally liable for the tax, if a purchaser does not pay the tax the state can transfer such liability to the purchaser. *New York imposes a use tax on purchases made outside New York for use in New York. The use tax is in place of sales tax. A credit is allowed for any sales or use tax paid to another state. The seller is responsible for collecting the use tax.* New York specifically imposes the use tax on the following items and services: use of tangible personal property in New York; use of tangible personal property manufactured, processed, or assembled by the user; use of information services, protective and detective services; use of tangible personal property upon which certain taxable services are performed such as processing or printing; installation, repair, and maintenance services performed on tangible personal property; interior decorating and designing services; use of telephone answering services; and use of computer software written or otherwise created by a user in the regular course of business. In addition, passenger car rentals of less than a year are subject to a special use tax. In New York, if property and services are not subject to sales tax, then they're not subject to use tax either. The following items are exempt from the New York use tax: purchases by a user who is not a resident of New York; retail sales of tangible personal property; gas, utilities, and telephone and telegraph services; and taxable services. New York also has some exemptions related to newspaper, periodical publications, and certain exemptions for the sale of racehorses.

North Carolina

North Carolina imposes a 4.5% state sales tax on the retail sales of tangible personal property and on the following services: hotel and motel rentals; dry cleaning, laundry, and similar services; sales of gas and electricity, and telecommunication services. *The state sales tax rate decreases to 4% on July 1, 2007.* North Carolina imposes a use tax, which is assessed against the consumer of tangible personal property in North Carolina that was purchased out-of-state. If the out-of-state seller is a registered retailer in North Carolina, the tax should be paid to the retailer. If the retailer is not registered in North Carolina, it should be paid to the state. In addition, North Carolina assesses the use tax against all persons who store, use, or otherwise consume tangible personal property in North Carolina that was transferred to them by out-of-state service providers. Finally, in North Carolina all leases and rental agreements involving tangible personal property are treated as taxable sales.

North Dakota

North Dakota taxes the gross receipts of the following sales and activities: goods, wares, or merchandise; steam or communication services; admissions to amusements, entertainment, or athletic events (this tax applies to only 80% of gross receipts from coin-operated amusement devices); magazines and other periodicals; hotel, motel, and tourist court accommodations; the leasing or renting of tangible personal property, the transfer of title to which has not been subject to sales or use tax; sales of alcoholic beverages and tobacco products; and gross receipts from sales of tangible personal property costing $0.16 or more through coin-operated vending machines. *The general tax rate is 5%*, however the following rates apply to certain specific types of sales or activities: 3% on residential or business mobile homes except for those exempt from tax; 3% on retail sales, leases, or rentals of farm machinery, farm machinery repair parts, and agricultural irrigation equipment; 7% on alcoholic beverages; and 2% on retail sales of natural gas to retail consumers or users. North Dakota retailers must obtain a permit from the State Tax Commissioner, and there are items that are exempt from the sales tax like certain prescription medications. *The sales tax is imposed upon purchasers, but retailers are responsible for collecting and remitting the tax to the state.* A use tax is imposed on the storage, use, or consumption of tangible personal property. *Property or services on which sales tax is paid generally are not subject to the use tax.* Use tax is imposed on the consumer, but the retailer is responsible for collecting and remitting the tax unless the retailer has no physical presence within the state. The lease or rental of tangible personal property for any purpose other than processing or resale is subject to sales tax in the state of North Dakota.

Ohio

In Ohio a 5.5% tax is imposed on the retail sale and rental of tangible personal property. The tax is also imposed on lodgings furnished to guests for less than 30 days and on the following services:

- repairs and installation of taxable property
- motor vehicle washing, waxing, painting
- industrial laundry cleaning services

- automatic data processing and computer services for business
- landscaping and lawn care services
- private investigation and security
- 900-number telephone number calls
- building maintenance and janitorial services
- employment placement services
- exterminating services
- physical fitness, recreation, and sports club services
- producing or reproducing written or graphic matter
- production or fabrication of tangible personal property for a consideration for consumers who furnish the materials used
- some telecommunications services
- warranties, maintenance, or service contracts

Ohio requires that tax be paid by the consumer to the vendor. *The vendor is personally responsible to the state if the tax is collected but not paid to the state.* In addition, Ohio may collect any unpaid sales tax from either the vendor or the consumer as both are personally liable for any uncollected sales tax. Ohio requires a business to obtain a license from the Tax Commission for each location or each vehicle from which sales are made. The license fee is $25. Once again, certain prescription medications are exempt along with other items. Ohio levies a use tax on the storage, use, or other consumption in Ohio of tangible personal property and any services provided in Ohio. The use tax is the responsibility of the consumer. Rentals or leases are considered taxable sales in Ohio. There are some special rules for leases related to: motor vehicles designed to carry a load of less than one ton, watercraft, outboard motors, aircraft, and business equipment.

Oklahoma

Oklahoma charges a 4.5% sales tax on the gross receipts derived from all sales of the following:

- tangible personal property, except newspapers and periodicals
- utilities or other public service, except water, sewage, and refuse

- transportation for hire of persons by qualified common carriers
- telecommunications services that originate or terminate in Oklahoma
- printing of all kinds and most printing services
- service of furnishing rooms by hotels, public rooming houses, and tourist camps
- service of furnishing storage by auto hotels or parking lots
- food, confection, or drinks prepared by dispensers and sold for immediate consumption
- advertising of all kinds
- computer hardware or software
- dues or fees to clubs
- tickets, fees, or admission charges to recreational events
- charges made for the privilege of entering or engaging in any kind of activity when spectators are not charged for admission
- charges made for the privilege of using items of recreational activity
- rental of equipment for recreational activities
- sales through vending machines
- rental or lease of tangible personal property
- floral items sold by persons engaged in florist or nursery business
- taxable services and tangible personal property sold to contractors for developing and improving real estate
- taxable services and tangible personal property sold to persons who are primarily engaged in selling their services

Oklahoma exempts specific items that are exempt from sales tax—for example, certain prescription medications. You'll want to check and see if your business qualifies for the exemption. Oklahoma vendors are required to obtain a permit, which is valid for three years for each business location. The initial permit is $20 and there is a $10 fee for each additional location. *The sales tax is imposed on the consumer or user and must be paid to the vendor. Vendors are personally liable for any sales tax due to the state. In fact, principal officers of corporations and managers or members of limited liability companies may be held personally liable for the sales tax owed to Oklahoma.* A use tax is imposed on the storage, use, or other consumption in Oklahoma of tangible personal property brought into Oklahoma. The use tax does not apply to property intended for use in other states but stored in Oklahoma, or property retained for fabrication, maintenance, and service purposes. The use tax is imposed on the person storing, using, or otherwise consuming the tangible personal property. If the use tax is not paid to the vendor, the consumer must pay the tax directly to the Oklahoma Tax Commission. The lease or rental of tangible personal property resulting in the transfer of the title to or possession of the property is subject to the sales and use tax in Oklahoma.

Oregon

Oregon does not impose any form of sales, gross receipts, occupational license, use, or consumption tax based upon the sale or use of tangible personal property. However, Oregon law allows local governments to assess a limited sales tax on transient lodgings, food, and beverages. Contact your local government to see if you are subject to any local taxes.

Pennsylvania

Pennsylvania levies a tax at the rate of 6% that is imposed upon the sale at retail and the use within the state of tangible personal property. This sales tax includes goods, wares, and merchandise. Accommodation rentals for less than 30 consecutive days are also taxable. The sales tax applies to the gross receipts from all of the following services:

- repairing, altering, mending, pressing, fitting, dyeing, laundering, dry-cleaning, or cleaning tangible personal property other than clothing or footwear
- applying or installing tangible personal property as a repair or replacement part of other tangible personal property
- labor or services billed by the vendor for delivering, installing, or applying tangible personal property sold by the vendor even if such services are contracted for separately
- inspecting, altering, cleaning, lubricating, polishing, repairing, or waxing motor vehicles

- printing or imprinting tangible personal property for persons furnishing the materials used in such operations
- lobbying services
- adjustment services, collection services, or credit reporting services
- secretarial or editing services
- disinfecting or pest control, building maintenance, or cleaning services
- employment agency services or help supply services
- lawn-care services
- self-storage services

Examples of exempt items in Pennsylvania include certain food products and prescription medication. You should check to see if your business is exempt from the tax. Pennsylvania sales and use taxes are collected by the vendor from the purchaser and then remitted to the state of by the vendor. *If sales tax is not paid to a vendor, the purchaser must pay the use tax to the state.* Pennsylvania imposes the use tax on the purchase of taxable tangible personal property or services outside of Pennsylvania that are subsequently used in Pennsylvania. In addition, the use tax is incurred by the purchaser if a vendor is not paid the required sales tax. Pennsylvania requires all sellers to apply for a license with the Department of Revenue before beginning business. The license does not need to be renewed and there is no license fee charged by the state. The leasing or rental of tangible personal property is a sale subject to the Pennsylvania sales and use tax.

Rhode Island

Rhode Island imposes a 7% tax on sales or rentals of tangible personal property, plus an additional 5% on transient room rentals. The following services are also subject to the sales tax provisions: producing, fabricating, processing, printing, or imprinting tangible personal property for consumers who furnish the materials used; furnishing tangible personal property for a consideration by social or athletic clubs; preparing or serving meals, food, and drinks (including cover charges, minimums, or similar entertainment charges); transfers of possession of tangible personal property where the seller retains title as security for payment; and the rental of living quarters in a hotel, rooming house, or tourist camp (12%). In Rhode Island every person engaging in the business of making sales at retail or engaging in the business of renting living quarters must obtain a permit for each place of business. The annual $10 permit is obtained from the Tax Administrator by February 1. Certain prescription medications are exempt from Rhode Island sales tax, along with other items. *The retailer is responsible for paying any sales tax to the state*; however, the retailer is required to collect the tax from the purchaser at the time of the sale. Any sales tax due becomes a debt of the purchaser to the retailer. If sales tax is not paid, a use tax will be imposed for the use, storage, or consumption of tangible personal property in the state. Retailers have an obligation to collect any use tax from the consumer. Lease or rental payments of tangible personal property are taxed as individual sales.

South Carolina

South Carolina imposes a 5% sales tax on persons selling at retail or furnishing or leasing any tangible personal property. The following services are taxable in South Carolina: the rental of transient sleeping accommodations for less than 90 days (taxed at 7%); property manufactured in the state for in-state use or consumption; sales of electricity; telephone services; and furnishing laundry, cleaning, dyeing, or pressing services. If the purchaser is over 85 years of age, they qualify for a 1% sales tax exemption and is issued an identity card. Retailers are required to obtain a license for each permanent location from the South Carolina Department of Revenue and Taxation; the fee is $50, reduced to $20 for artists and craftspeople selling their products at shows. South Carolina exempts certain prescription medications and other items from the sales tax. *Retailers are responsible for paying the tax to the state regardless of whether they collect the tax from the purchaser.* South Carolina imposes a use tax on the storage, use, or consumption of tangible personal property. The liability for use tax lies with the persons storing, using, or consuming in South Carolina tangible personal property purchased at retail. If the retailer collects the use tax, the consumer is relieved of liability if he or she obtains a receipt from a retailer. In South Carolina, the gross receipts received from the rental or lease of tangible personal property are subject to sales or use tax rules.

South Dakota

South Dakota has a general 4% retail sales and service tax imposed on all retailers. The tax is imposed on all retail sales of tangible personal property and all services, unless the property or service is expressly exempted by the state. For example, professional services relating to health and certain prescription medications are exempted. In addition, South Dakota imposes a 2% excise tax upon the gross receipts of all prime contractors with a building contract valued at over $100,000. Some farm machinery and irrigation equipment used exclusively for agricultural purposes is taxed at a reduced rate of 3%. The 3% reduced rate also applies to oil and gas field services. The sales tax is imposed on the retailer, and may be added to the price of the product or service sold. The Department of Revenue requires that a permit be obtained for each location; the permit is valid until cancelled or revoked. A use tax is imposed on the privilege of using, storing, and consuming tangible personal property and taxable services. However, if the property is more than seven years old when it is brought into South Dakota, it is exempt from the use tax. Use tax in South Dakota is not required if sales tax was paid on the goods or services. The liability for the use tax is imposed on the consumer, who will remain liable for the tax until it is paid either to a retailer or to the Secretary of Revenue. Finally all rentals of tangible personal property are subject to the sales and use taxes. Any property sold after it has been leased is also subject to sales tax.

Tennessee

Tennessee charges a general 7% retailers' sales and use tax on the sale of tangible personal property. The sales and use tax is imposed on every person who engages in the business of selling tangible personal property at retail in the state; uses or consumes in Tennessee any item or article of tangible personal property, irrespective of ownership; receives property or services subject to the sales or use tax; rents or furnishes any property or services subject to the sales or use tax; stores for use or consumption in Tennessee any item or article of tangible personal property; leases or rents tangible personal property, either as lessor or lessee, within Tennessee; charges taxable admission, dues, or fees; or sells space to transient dealers or vendors. In addition, Tennessee imposes sales and use tax on the following services:

- sale, rental, or charges for accommodations furnished to transients
- garage and parking lot services
- telecommunications
- repair services performed with respect to tangible personal property
- laundering and dry cleaning
- bathing and grooming of animals
- installations of tangible personal property
- charges for warranty or service contracts

The following rates are for the specific item types:

- 1% for water sold to or used by manufacturers
- 1.5% for energy fuels sold to or used by manufacturers
- 4.5% for aviation fuel
- 1.5% for electricity and liquefied gas, sold to or used by farmers and nursery businesses, and coal, wood products, or fuel oil used as energy fuel in the production of nursery and greenhouse crops
- persons operating vending machines may register at a fee of $2, plus $1 per machine and pay 1.5% of gross receipts from the machines instead of privilege and sales taxes, except that the tax on gross receipts from tobacco-dispensing machines is 2.5%

Each place of business must obtain a certificate of registration from the Tennessee Commissioner; there is no fee for the certificate of registration. *Although sellers are responsible for the tax, they are required to collect the tax from the consumer.* Sellers are required to post a sign or place a statement on the receipt giving the consumers notice that sales tax is included in their purchase. Tennessee imposes a use tax on the consumer for all personal property and taxable services used or consumed in the state. The sales and use taxes provide a uniform tax upon either the sale or the use of taxable goods and services in Tennessee, regardless of where they are purchased. In Tennessee, the lease or rental payment on tangible personal property is subject to sales or use tax.

Texas

In Texas a tax is imposed on the sale at retail of taxable items and upon the storage, use, or other consumption in the state of taxable items purchased, leased, or rented from any retailer for consumption in Texas. *The sales and use tax rate is 6.25% at the state level.* The retailer is required to collect the tax but may deduct .05% of the tax as reimbursement for collecting the tax and an additional 1.25% discount is allowed if you make prepayments of the tax based upon a reasonable estimate of the liability for a particular tax period. Taxable items include tangible personal property and taxable services listed below:

- amusement services
- cable television services
- personal services
- motor vehicle parking and storage services
- repair, remodeling, maintenance, and restoration of tangible personal property
- telecommunications services
- credit reporting services
- debt collection services
- insurance services
- information services
- real property services
- security services
- data processing services
- real property repair and remodeling services
- telephone answering services

A permit is required from the Comptroller of Public Accounts for each place of business: the permit is free and is valid indefinitely. Texas places the responsibility for the sales tax on both the seller and the purchaser. This means that Texas may proceed against either party for any unpaid sales tax. *Generally, the seller is responsible for collecting and remitting the tax to the state.* However, a seller's failure to collect the tax from the purchaser does not relieve the purchaser of tax liability. The sales tax is added to the sales price and becomes a debt from the purchaser to the seller. Texas exempts from sales and use tax water and most foods for human consumption. You should review of the exemptions. Retailers are generally responsible for collecting and remitting the use tax to the state. However, it appears that either the seller or the purchaser can be held liable to the state for any unpaid use tax. Lease and rental payments are subject to the use tax for the entire term of the lease, regardless of where the property is used, if the lessee takes delivery of the property in the state.

Utah

In Utah a sales and use tax of 4.75% is levied on the purchaser for all retail sales of tangible personal property; amounts paid to common carriers or telephone or telegraph corporations; gas, electricity, heat, coal, fuel oil, or other fuels sold or furnished for commercial or residential use; meals, admissions, or user fees for entertainment, recreation, cultural, or athletic activities; services for repairs, renovations, or installation of tangible personal property; cleaning or washing of tangible personal property; hotel or trailer court accommodations and services for less than 30 consecutive days; laundry and dry cleaning services; leases and rentals of tangible personal property; tangible personal property stored, used, or consumed in Utah; and prepaid telephone calling cards. The tax rate for residential use of utility services is 6.75%. Application for a sales and use tax license is filed with the Utah Tax Commission. *The purchaser is liable for paying the sales tax, but vendors are responsible for collecting the tax and remitting it to the state.* Among other items, certain prescription medications are exempt from the sales and use tax under Utah state law. The use tax in Utah is a complementary tax that applies when the sales tax does not; the consumer is responsible for the use tax. The rental or lease of the tangible personal property is also considered a taxable sale.

Vermont

Vermont imposes a general 6% tax on receipts from: retail sales or leases of tangible personal property, sales at retail of public utility services, including gas and electricity, but excluding water, telephone, and transportation; charges for producing, fabricating, printing, or imprinting tangible personal property for a consideration for consumers who furnish, directly or indirectly, the materials used; amusement charges; bottle deposits; and telecommunications services. *The tax rate on meals is 9% and the tax rate for alcoholic beverages is 10%.* Vermont requires retailers to register with the Commissioner of Taxes. No registration fee is required. As with many other states, Vermont exempts some items from the sales tax, such as certain prescription medications. In Vermont, the sales tax is imposed on the purchaser, and the seller is required to collect the sales tax and remit it to the state. The consumer is required to pay use tax on property used, stored, or consumed in Vermont, if the sales tax is not paid. Rental and lease payments for tangible personal property are taxable in Vermont.

Virginia

Virginia levies a 4% sales and use tax on persons engaged in selling at retail or distributing tangible personal property in the state. The tax is imposed on any persons engaged in renting or furnishing any taxable property or service. *Currently, every Virginia city and county imposes an additional 1% local tax. The following services are not taxable:*

- professional services involving sales as inconsequential elements, services of repair personnel for which a separate charge is made, and Internet-related services that do not involve an exchange of tangible personal property
- charges for labor or services rendered in installing or repairing property sold
- transportation charges
- charges for alterations to apparel, clothing, and garments
- charges for gift-wrapping services performed by a nonprofit corporation
- labor or services rendered in connection with the modification of prewritten programs
- custom computer programs

- charges for lodgings or accommodations for more than 90 continuous days by any hotel, motel, inn, tourist camp, tourist cabin, camping grounds, club, or any other place in which rooms, lodging, space, or accommodations are regularly furnished to transients for a consideration
- one-half of the charge for a maintenance contract providing for both parts and labor

Food purchases are taxed at a lower rate of 2%, which will be lowered to 1.5% on July 1, 2007. Virginia exempts certain prescription medications among other things from the sales and use tax. Anyone who engages in or conducts business as a dealer in Virginia must apply to the Tax Commissioner for a certificate of registration. The burden of paying the sales tax is on the purchaser; the tax is a legal debt for the purchaser. However, *the seller is legally obligated to collect and remit the tax to the state.* Virginia imposes a use tax on the use, consumption, or storage of tangible personal property in the state or the storage of such property elsewhere for use in Virginia. *Transactions taxed under the sales tax rules are not subject to the use tax.* Out-of-state mail order catalog purchases under $100 during any calendar year are specifically exempt from use tax. Lease and rental payments are subject to sales and use tax at the same rate as if the item is sold.

Washington

Washington imposes a 6.5% tax on retail sales of tangible personal property except sales for resale, materials becoming a component of property through installation, construction, etc., and material for manufacturing products. Retail sales include the following items and services:

- materials and/or labor rendered in repairing, etc. realty for consumers
- building cleaning
- automobile towing
- lodgings for less than one month
- leasing or renting tangible personal property
- telephone service
- sale of personal, business, or professional services

- amusement and recreation businesses
- abstract, title insurance, and escrow businesses
- credit bureau businesses
- automobile parking and storage garage businesses
- landscape services
- professional sporting events
- physical fitness, tanning salon, tattoo parlor, steam bath, escort, and dating services

Retail car rentals are subject to an additional 5.9% tax and various sales tax rates are charged on the retail sale of spirits or strong beer (malt beverage with an alcohol content above 8%). Businesses that engage in any taxable business in Washington are required to register with the Department of Revenue. No fee is required, but a separate permit is required for each business location. Registration with the Department of Revenue is not required if: the value of products, gross proceeds of sales, or gross income of the business, from all business activities subject to the business and occupation tax, is less than $12,000 per year; if gross income of the business from all activities subject to the public utility tax is less than $12,000 per year; the business is not required to collect or pay to the Department any other tax or fee that the Department is authorized to collect; or the business is not otherwise required to obtain a license subject to the state's master application procedure. Certain prescription medications are exempt from sales tax in Washington. The sales tax is imposed on the buyer and is generally collected by the seller and then remitted to the state or local government. Sales tax is a debt of the buyer to the seller until paid, but the state may collect the tax directly from the buyer if the buyer has failed to pay it to the seller. *The use tax supplements the sales tax by taxing retail service and all taxable tangible personal property on which sales tax has not been paid.* Washington imposes the use tax on the consumer for all taxable goods or services acquired in one of the following ways: purchased at retail, including isolated sales, acquired by lease, gift, repossession, or bailment; extracted or manufactured by the person using the article, including byproducts; through any qualified amusement or recreation services ; or otherwise furnished to a person engaged in a taxable business. All rentals and leases are taxable as retail sales.

West Virginia

In West Virginia the sales tax is referred to as the *general consumers sales and service tax* and is charged at a rate of 6%. The tax is imposed on the selling of tangible personal property and most services are taxable except for the furnishing of professional or personal services. Any person engaging in a business activity in West Virginia must obtain a business registration certificate from the Tax Commissioner. West Virginia exempts many specific items from sales tax, including certain prescription medications. *West Virginia imposes on the vendor the duty to collect sales tax and remit the tax to the state.* Use tax is due if sales tax is not paid on taxable sale, as the two taxes are intended to be complementary. West Virginia requires that any use tax that is not collected by the retailer must be paid to the Tax Commissioner directly by the purchaser. Lease and rental payments are taxable in the state of West Virginia.

Wisconsin

Wisconsin imposes a 5% tax on all retailers for the privilege of selling, leasing, or renting tangible personal property. The following services are also taxed: furnishing of rooms or lodging to transients (less than one month); admissions to amusement, athletic, or entertainment events, and access fees to clubs; sales of telecommunication services; qualified laundry, dry cleaning, pressing, and dyeing services; photographic services; processing, printing, and enlarging film; parking or providing parking space for motor vehicles, aircraft, and boats; the repair, service, or maintenance of taxable tangible personal property; producing, printing, imprinting, fabricating, or processing of tangible personal property for consumers who furnish the materials used; the sale of cable television services including installation charges; and landscaping and lawn maintenance services. The Department of Revenue issues a tax permit to any business that requests one if the business has a valid business registration certificate. *The tax is imposed on retailers and persons providing taxable services.* However, the retailer, the service provider, or the Department of Revenue can collect the sales tax from the purchaser. Wisconsin exempts specific items from sales tax, such as certain prescription medications. A use tax is imposed on the storage, use, or other consumption in Wisconsin of tangible personal property or taxable services purchased from any retailer, but will not apply if sales tax has been paid on the property or services. Use tax liability lies with the consumer unless the tax is collected by the retailer or service provider. Lease or rental payments on tangible personal property at retail in Wisconsin is subject to sales tax.

Wyoming

Wyoming taxes the following sales at a rate of 4% (except farm implements, which are taxed at 3%): retail sales; rentals; intrastate telephone and telegraph services; intrastate transportation of passengers; public utilities and gas, electricity or heat sold to consumers; meals and cover charges; transient living quarters; admissions; services performed for the repair, alteration, or improvement of tangible personal property; contract geophysical exploration operations; motor vehicles, house trailers, trailer coaches, trailers and semi-trailers; alcoholic beverages; and computer hardware and software. All Wyoming vendors are required to obtain a sales tax license form the Department of Revenue for each place of business. The license fee is $60. Certain prescription medications are exempt from the Wyoming sales tax. *The sales tax is paid by the purchaser and sellers are required to collect the tax and remit the tax to the state.* However, the purchaser would owe the Department of Revenue any tax not collected by the vendor. The use tax is imposed on all sales in Wyoming, all storage use or consumption of tangible personal property in Wyoming, tangible personal property sold by any person for delivery in Wyoming, and all computer hardware and software. Use tax is owed by the consumer, but collected by the vendor. Sales tax is imposed on rent or lease payments on tangible personal property if the transfer of possession would be taxable if a sale had occurred.

50-State Review of Franchise Tax

Alabama

Privilege Tax, Annual

$100–$15,000 depending on net worth and taxable income

If your business has taxable income of

- less than $200,000 the business will pay $1 per $1,000 of net worth
- $200,000–$499,000, you pay $1.25 per $1,000 of net worth
- $500,000–$2,499,000, you pay $1.50 per $1,000 of net worth
- over $2,500,000, you pay $1.75 per $1,000 of net worth

Alaska

Franchise Tax, Biennial
Domestic corporation: $100 every two years
Foreign corporation: $200 every two years
Nonprofit corporations are excluded.

Arizona

Report Fee, Annual
Report and $45 fee due each year. To provide updated information.

Arkansas

Franchise Tax, Annual
Figured by multiplying the number of outstanding capital shares by the par value (if no par value, $25) and then multiplying the result by "the percentage of shares applicable to Arkansas" and then by multiplying the result by 0.003. Corporations without authorized capital stock pay an annual tax of $150 regardless of valuation.
Minimum fee: $150 for corporations.
LLCs pay annual franchise tax of $150.

California

Franchise Tax, Annual
8.84% of the corporation's income generated in California.
The minimum annual franchise tax is $800. Franchise tax rate for S corporations is 1.5 percent.
The first year of business is exempt from the minimum tax. LLCs are not subject to the California Franchise tax.

Colorado

Report Fee, Annual
Report due each year. Internet filing: $10. Paper filing: $25.
To provide updated information on all corporations and LLCs.

Connecticut

Franchise Fee and Business Tax, Annual
Minimum franchise tax is $150. Business tax is income-based. (This is the state corporate income tax.) The rate is 7.5% for all corporations, with a $250 minimum each year. LLCs have a minimum entity tax of $250 per year. Annual reports are required for all domestic corporations: the fee is $75 and $300 for foreign corporations.

Delaware

Franchise Tax and Report Fee
Tax on domestic corporations based on a combined rate of the number of issued shares and the capital value:
- 3,000 or fewer shares $35
- 3,001–5,000 shares $62.50
- 5,001–10,000 shares $112.50
- over 10,000 shares $112.50 plus $62.50 for each additional 10,000 shares plus (+) Capital Value of
  $300,000 or less: $35
  $300,001–$500,000: $62.50
  $500,001–$1,000,000: $112.50
  Over $1,000,000: $112.50 plus between $62.50–$250 for each additional 1,000,000 depending on par values
- Foreign corporation must file an annual report with a filing fee of $60

District of Columbia

Report Fee, Biennial
Domestic corporations must file an annual report with the mayor in the year following their incorporation and then every two years. The biennial report fee is $750.

Florida

Franchise Tax and Report Fee

Franchise tax of 5.5% on net income each year on all corporations. Report and fee of $150. Late fee increases to $550.

Hawaii

Report Fee, Annual

Annual report with a fee of $25

Idaho

Minimum Tax and Building Tax Fund, Annual

Idaho does not have a franchise tax. It has a corporate income tax with a minimum of $20 and a $10 building fund tax of $10 for all corporations that are required to file an income tax return in Idaho.

Illinois

Franchise Tax and Report Fee, Annual

All corporations doing business in the state are required to pay a franchise tax of 0.1 percent on paid-in capital of the corporation with a minimum tax of $25 and a maximum tax of $1,000,000. An annual report is required also which has a fee of $75.

Indiana

Franchise Tax and Report Fee, Biennial

Indiana imposes a franchise tax on financial institutions only. Corporations and LLCs must file a report every two years: paper filing fee $30; Internet filing fee: $20.

Iowa

Franchise Tax and Report Fee, Biennial

Iowa has a bank corporation income tax that is sometimes referred to as a franchise tax. Otherwise, it requires a biennial report and a fee of $45 due the first even-numbered year following the calendar year in which business is formed or registered in Iowa.

Kentucky

State License Tax, Annual

Kentucky imposes a state license tax in addition to its income tax. The state license tax rate is $2.10 per $1,000 of capital employed by the business. There is a $30 minimum. If the corporation has gross income of $500,000 or less, it is entitled to $1.40 credit on the first $350,000 of capital employed.

Louisiana

Franchise Tax and Report Fee, Annual

A franchise report and tax are due each year. The tax rate is $1.50 for each $1,000 of capital employed and $3 for each $1,000 over $300,000. Also a report and fee of $25 are due each year.

Maine

Franchise Tax and Report Fee, Annual

Maine has a financial institution tax of 1% of the net income and .008 percent of the Maine assets. An annual report and fee are required for all corporations and LLCs. Domestic entities are $85 and foreign entities are $150.

Maryland

Franchise Tax, Annual

Maryland imposes a franchise tax of 2% of gross receipts on utilities only. Maryland has replaced its financial institution franchise tax with a 7% corporate income tax.

Massachusetts

Report Fee, Annual

Massachusetts imposes an annual report and fee requirement: $125 for all corporations and $500 for all limited liability companies.

Michigan

Report Fee, Annual

Michigan imposes an annual report and fee of $25 on all domestic and foreign corporations. The fee will be reduced to $15 after September 30, 2007.

Minnesota

Report Fee, Annual

Minnesota imposes an income tax on corporations that is frequently referred to as a franchise fee; however, it is an income tax computed at the rate of 9.8% of net income. Both domestic and foreign corporations are required to file annual reports. There is no filing fee for domestic corporations and a $115 filing fee for foreign corporations.

Mississippi

Franchise Tax and Report Fee, Annual

Mississippi imposes a franchise tax on all corporations registered with the state at the rate of $2.50 per $1,000 of capital employed in the state with a minimum tax of $25 per year. Also, all corporations must file an annual report with the Secretary of State and pay a filing fee of $25 each year.

Missouri

Franchise Tax and Report Fee, Annual

In Missouri all corporations must pay a .033 percent franchise tax. Domestic corporations base the tax on the par value and surplus of the outstanding stock of the corporation if it exceeds $200,000. Foreign corporations pay the same rate on the proportion of assets employed in Missouri. Also most corporations are required to file an annual corporation registration report with the Secretary of State along with a fee of $45.

Montana

Report Fee, Annual

Montana has an annual report requirement for all corporations and a fee of $15. While Montana does not have a franchise fee, it calls its income tax a

Corporation License Tax, which some people associate with franchise taxes.

Nebraska

Franchise Tax, Annual
Nebraska's franchise tax is based on the amount of authorized capital stock of the corporation. The fees for domestic corporations can be as low as $26 (less than 10,000 shares of stock) to as high as $23,990 (for over 100,000,000 shares of stock). The rates are double for foreign corporations operating in Nebraska, with a $30,000 maximum rate.

Nevada

Report Fee, Annual
Nevada does not impose a franchise tax on its foreign and domestic businesses. It has an annual report due with a filing fee of $85. When a business is formed, the state requires an initial list of officers and directors in addition to the articles of incorporation, for a fee of $165.

New Hampshire

Report Fee, Annual
New Hampshire requires all corporations to file an annual report with the Secretary of State and pay a fee of $100.

New Jersey

Report Fee, Annual
New Jersey requires all corporations to file an annual report with the Secretary of State and pay a fee of $50. The New Jersey corporate income tax is sometimes referred to as a franchise tax.

New Mexico

Franchise Tax and Report Fee, Annual
Every corporation operating in New Mexico must pay and annual franchise tax of $50. In addition, all corporations are required to file corporate reports with the Corporation Commission every two years for a fee of $25.

New York

Maintenance Fee, Annual; Report Fee, Biennial; Member/Partner Fee, Annual
New York's corporate income tax is often referred to as a franchise fee. However, the state requires domestic corporations to file an biennial report with the Secretary of State and pay a fee of $9. Foreign corporations are required to pay an annual maintenance fee of $300. This annual maintenance fee can be used as a credit against the income tax or franchise tax owed to the state. New York also imposes on all LLCs and LLPs an annual fee of $50 for each member or partner. This fee will not be less than $325 or more than $10,000.

North Carolina

Franchise Fee and Report Fee, Annual
North Carolina's franchise tax rate is .15 percent. To figure the tax, multiply the rate (.15) by each of the following numbers: 1) the corporation's paid-in capital, which includes value of stock, additional capital, and undivided and undistributed profits; 2) the investments the corporation has made in North Carolina property; 3) and 55% of the appraised value of all tangible property owned in North Carolina. Whichever of the resulting three figures is higher is the franchise tax liability. The state has a minimum tax of $35. North Carolina also requires all corporations to file an annual report with the Secretary of State and pay a fee of $20. LLCs must also file an annual report; the fee is $200.

North Dakota

Report Fee, Annual
All domestic and foreign corporations registered with the state must file an annual report with the Secretary of State and pay a fee of $25.

Ohio

None
Ohio's income tax is sometimes referred to as a franchise tax.

Oklahoma

License Tax, Annual

Oklahoma has a license tax instead of a franchise tax. This tax is imposed on all corporations. For domestic corporations, the tax is based on the value of the corporation's capital stock, undivided profits, and the amount of any indebtedness maturing three years after issuance. For foreign corporations, the tax is based on the capital employed in Oklahoma. The rate is $1.25 per $1,000 of capital used, invested, or employed in Oklahoma. The tax is not required in the first year of registration.

Oregon

Report Fee, Annual

Oregon requires all corporations and LLCs to file an annual report with the Secretary of State and pay a $50 fee.

Pennsylvania

Franchise Tax, Capital Stock Tax, Annual

Pennsylvania has a franchise tax and a capital stock tax, both of which are being phased out by 2011. Generally, Pennsylvania taxes the value of the capital stock of all foreign and domestic entities, not just corporations. Domestic entities follow the capital stock tax rules and foreign entities may elect either the franchise tax rules or the capital stock rules, but not both.

Rhode Island

Franchise Tax and Report Fee, Annual

All corporations, domestic or foreign, doing business in Rhode Island must pay an annual franchise tax of $2.50 for each $10,000 of authorized stock, with a minimum tax of $500. The franchise tax paid may be credited on the corporation's state income tax return. Also if a business is registered in Rhode Island but is not required to file an income tax return, it is still required to pay the franchise tax at a rate of $500 if the stock value does not exceed $1,000,000, with an additional $412.50 for each additional $1,000,000 of value. Rhode Island treats no-par value stock at $100 per share. All corporations and LLCs are required to file an annual report with the Secretary of State and pay a $50 filing fee.

South Carolina

License Tax, Annual
South Carolina imposes a corporate license tax of $15 plus $1 for each $1,000 of capital stock, paid-in capital, or capital surplus. The minimum tax is $25 per year and is paid to the Department of Revenue.

South Dakota

Report Fees, Annual
South Dakota calls its annual report fee a franchise tax. It is required to be paid with an annual report filed with the Secretary of State. The corporate fee is $30 and the LLC fee is $50.

Tennessee

Franchise Tax and Report Fees, Annual
A franchise tax based on the outstanding capital stock, surplus and undivided profits is imposed by Tennessee on all domestic and foreign corporations. The tax is $.25 per $100 of the stock surplus and undivided profits, with a minimum tax of $100. Also an annual report must be filed with the Secretary of State, with a filing fee of $20.

Texas

Franchise Tax, Annual
Texas imposes a franchise tax on all corporations, S corporations, and LLCs. The tax rate is based in part on the federal taxable income and comprises two parts: 0.25% of the net taxable capital; and 4.5% of the net taxable earned surplus. There are several credits that can be subtracted from the amount of the franchise tax liability due to reach the amount of tax due. If the franchise tax due, is under $100, no tax is due; however, a tax report will still be required.

Utah

Report Fees, Annual

Utah's Department of Commerce requires all domestic and foreign corporations to file an annual report and pay an annual fee of $12.

Vermont

Report Fee, Annual

Vermont requires all corporations and LLCs to file an annual report with the Secretary of State. The filing fees are $25 for domestic corporations, $150 for foreign corporations, $15 for domestic LLCs, and $100 for foreign LLCs.

Virginia

Report Fee, Annual

Virginia requires an annual registration fee and an annual report from all corporations. The annual fee is $100 for stock corporations that have 5,000 share of stock or less. For corporations with more than 5,000 shares of stock, the registration fee is $100 plus $30 for each additional 5,000 shares of stock. The maximum registration fee is $1,700. Non-stock corporations are required to pay a registration fee of $25.

Washington

License Fee and Report Fee, Annual

Washington requires an initial annual report and fee of $10 for all corporations and LLCs and an annual license renewal fee of $59, regardless of whether the entities are domestic or foreign entities.

West Virginia

Franchise Tax, License Fee, and Report Fee, Annual

West Virginia imposes a franchise tax of $50 or 0.70 percent of the value of the capital of the corporation. This applies to both C corporations and S corporations. In addition, there is a license fee of between $250 and $4,375

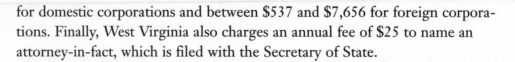

for domestic corporations and between $537 and $7,656 for foreign corporations. Finally, West Virginia also charges an annual fee of $25 to name an attorney-in-fact, which is filed with the Secretary of State.

Wisconsin

Report Fee and Excess Capital Fee, Annual

All Wisconsin corporations, domestic or foreign, must file an annual report with the Department of Financial Institutions. Domestic corporations pay $40 and foreign corporations pay $80 to file the reports. Also, every foreign corporation is required to pay an additional $2 for every $1,000 worth of new or additional capital paid to the corporation.

Wyoming

Franchise Tax, Annual

Wyoming has a franchise tax that it calls an annual license tax. The tax is based on the corporate property employed in Wyoming. The tax rate is either $50 or .0002 of the dollar value of the property or assets employed in Wyoming, whichever is greater. This tax applies not only to corporations, but also to LLCs, LLPs, and RLLPs (Registered Limited Liability Partnerships).

State Income Tax

Alabama

Corporate Income Tax Rate: 6.5%

Note: Multi-state businesses whose only activities in Alabama consist of sales and do not include owning or renting realty or personal property and whose gross sales volume for the tax year does not exceed $100,000, may pay an income tax at the rate of 0.25 percent of such sales volume.

Personal Income Tax

If you are operating your business as an S corporation, partnership, limited liability company or sole proprietorship you will be subject to the individual income tax on business income. Local income taxes apply in certain areas of Alabama, so be sure to check with your local government. The following rates are applicable to the amount of income over the exempted amount:

Single Person, Head of Family, or Married Person Filing Separately

Up to and including	Rate
First $500	2%
Next $2,500	4%
Excess over $3,000	5%

Married Persons Filing Jointly

Up to and including	Rate
First $1,000	2%
Next $5,000	4%
Excess over $6,000	5%

Alaska

Corporate Income Tax: The corporate net income tax is imposed on the entire taxable income derived from sources within Alaska as follows:

If Taxable Income Is:	The Tax Is:
Less than $10,000	1% of taxable income
$10,000 but less than $20,000	$100 plus 2% of taxable income over $10,000
$20,000 but less than $30,000	$300 plus 3% of taxable income over $20,000
$30,000 but less than $40,000	$600 plus 4% of taxable income over $30,000
$40,000 but less than $50,000	$1,000 plus 5% of taxable income over $40,000
$50,000 but less than $60,000	$1,500 plus 6% of taxable income over $50,000
$60,000 but less than $70,000	$2,100 plus 7% of taxable income over $60,000

If Taxable Income Is:	The Tax Is:
$70,000 but less than $80,000	$2,800 plus 8% of taxable income over $70,000
$80,000 but less than $90,000	$3,600 plus 9% of taxable income over $80,000
$90,000 or more	$4,500 plus 9.4% of taxable income over $90,000

Personal Income Tax

Alaska does not have a personal income tax. If you are operating an S corporation, partnership, limited liability company, or sole proprietorship you will pay only federal income taxes on the income passed through to you from your business.

Arizona

Corporate Income Tax: 6.968%

Arizona taxes C corporations at the rate of 6.968% of their taxable income.

Personal Income Tax Rates for 2007 are as follows:

Single Person or Married Person Filing Separately

Taxable Income	Tax Rate for Income Bracket
$0 - $10,000	2.59%
$10,001 - $25,000	2.88%
$25,001 - $50,000	3.36%
$50,001 - $150,000	4.24%
Over $150,000	4.54%

Married Persons Filing Jointly and Unmarried Head of Household

Taxable Income	Tax Rate for Income Bracket
$0 - $20,000	2.59%
$20,001 - $50,000	2.88%
$50,001 - $100,000	3.36%
$100,001 - $300,000	4.24%
Over $300,000	4.54%

Arkansas

Corporate Income Tax

Arkansas applies the following income tax rates to the net income of all C corporations:

Successive Amounts or Parts Thereof	Tax Rates
1st $3,000	1%
2nd $3,000	2%
Next $5,000	3%
Next $14,000	5%
Next $75,000	6%
Over $100,000	6.5%

Personal Income Tax

Income at Least	But Not More Than	Tax Rate
$0	$3,400	1%
$3,400	$6,799	2.5% minus $50.99
$6,800	$10,299	3.5% minus $118.98
$10,300	$17,099	4.5% minus $221.97
$17,100	$28,499	6% minus $478.46
$28,500 and over		7% minus $763.45

California

Corporate Tax Rate: 8.84%

California taxes only income not subject to the 8.84% franchise tax imposed by the state. California allows S corporations to pass income to shareholders, but the 1.5% franchise tax still applies. Thus, in California, if your business has income that was not generated in California, you may have a state tax savings by electing S corporation rather than a C corporation.

Personal Income Tax: 1% to 9.3%

California imposes a personal income tax on the portion of your adjusted gross income generated in California. If you are operating an S corporation, partnership, limited liability company, or sole proprietorship, you will be subject to the personal income tax on business income.

Colorado

Corporate Income Tax: 4.63%

Similar to Alabama, Colorado's alternative corporate tax rate for corporations applies only to Colorado sales. The corporation can't own or rent real estate in Colorado, and it must have annual gross sales in Colorado of less than $100,000. This alternative tax rate is 0.5 percent of gross receipts from sales in Colorado.

Personal Income Tax: 4.63%

If you are operating an S corporation, partnership, limited liability company, or sole proprietorship, you will be subject to the personal income tax rate on business income.

Connecticut

Corporate Income Tax: 7.5%

Connecticut also has an alternative capital stock tax (sometimes referred to as a franchise tax) that must be paid by qualified corporations if the capital stock tax would exceed the 7.5% income tax. This alternative tax is .31 percent of the value of the capital stock of the corporation as adjusted by surplus reserves, deficits, and stock holdings of private corporations.

Personal Tax Rates

The personal tax rate is 3% on the first $10,000 for singles and married filing separate filers, the first $16,000 for heads of households, and the first $20,000 for married filing jointly and surviving spouses. All income above these amounts is taxed at a rate of 5%.

Delaware

Corporate Income Tax Rate: 8.7%

In Delaware, C corporations are required to pay the corporate income tax only on income generated in Delaware.

Personal Income Tax

Delaware's personal income tax rates range from 2.2% (net income over $2000 but not over $5,000) to 5.95% (net income over $60,000). If you are operating an S corporation, partnership, limited liability company, or sole proprietorship, in Delaware, you will be subject to the personal income tax on business income. In addition, S corporations are be required to withhold personal income tax on all amounts paid to nonresident shareholders.

District of Columbia

Business Tax Rate: 9.75%

D.C. does not have a corporate income tax, but it has a business income tax. All businesses (corporations, partnerships, limited liability companies, and sole proprietorships, must pay tax at the rate of 9.75% on all income derived from sources within the District. The minimum tax is $100 even if your business has no income. Certain types of businesses and entities are exempt from this tax: labor organizations, insurance companies, service partnerships, nonprofit cemetery companies, fraternal benefit organizations, and nonprofit corporations and business organizations. This tax is in addition to any income passed through to individual owners of the business.

Personal Income Tax

2005 Taxable Income	2005 Rate of Tax
not over $10,000	4.5%
over $10,000, but not over $40,000	$450 plus 7% of the excess over $10,000
over $40,000	$2,550 plus 8.7% of the excess over $40,000

Florida

Corporate Income Tax (Franchise Tax on Business Income): 5.5%

Florida has what it calls a Franchise Tax on Business Income of 5.5% on the annual business income in excess of $5,000 for all C corporations doing business in Florida. Sole proprietorships, S corporations, limited liability companies, and partnerships as pass-through entities are not required to pay state income tax as Florida has no personal income tax. However, federal personal income tax will still apply on such entities.

Personal Income Tax

Florida does not impose a personal income tax on its residents.

Georgia

Corporate Income Tax: 6%

C corporations in Georgia are required to pay an annual corporate tax of 6% on the income generated in Georgia. If you are operating an S corporation, partnership, limited liability company, or sole proprietorship, you will be subject to the personal income tax on business income passed through to owners of such businesses. Also Georgia requires S corporations, partnerships, and limited liability companies to withhold personal income tax on all income earned by nonresident owners.

Personal Income Tax

Georgia personal income tax depends on the individual filing status and is imposed as follows: singles, 1% (net income not over $750) to 6% (net income over $7,000); for married filing joint and heads of household, 1% (net income not over $1,000) to 6% (net income over $10,000); and for married filing separate, 1% (net income not over $500) to 6% (net income over $5,000).

Hawaii

Corporate Income Tax

All Hawaii C corporations must pay an annual corporate tax as follows:

Taxable Income	Tax Rate
Not over $25,000	4.4%
Over $25,000 but not over $100,000	5.4%
All income over $100,000	6.4%

If you are operating an S corporation, partnership, limited liability company, or sole proprietorship, you will be subject to the personal income tax on business income that passes through to your personal income tax return.

Personal Income Tax

Taxable Income—Singles and Married

Filing Separately	*Tax Rate*
First $2,000	1.4%
$2,001 to $4,000	3.2%
$4,001 to $8,000	5.5%
$8,001 to $12,000	6.4%
$12,001 to $16,000	6.8%
$16,001 to $20,000	7.2%
$20,001 to $30,000	7.6%
$30,001 to $40,000	7.9%
Taxable income over $40,000	8.25%

Taxable Income—Married

Filing Jointly	*Tax Rate*
First $1,000	1.4%
$12,001 to $2,000	3.2%
$2,001 to $4,000	5.5%
$4,001 to $6,000	6.4%
$6,001 to $8,000	6.8%
$8,001 to $10,000	7.2%
$10,001 to $15,000	7.6%
$15,001 to $20,000	7.9%
Taxable income over $20,000	8.25%

For heads of households, the rates range from 1.4% of the first $3,000 of taxable income to 8.25% of taxable income over $60,000.

Idaho

Corporate Income Tax: 7.6%

C corporations in Idaho must pay an annual income tax of 7.5%. The minimum corporate income tax is $20. In addition, Idaho requires every C corporation to file a state income tax return and also pay a $10 permanent building fund tax. An alternative tax of 1% of gross sales may be paid instead of the income tax in the following the circumstances: if the only corporate activity in Idaho consist of sales and the corporation doesn't own or rent real estate or tangible personal property in the state and gross sales in Idaho do not exceed $100,000 for the year.

Personal Income Tax
The following rates are applicable to single

Taxable Income	*Amount of Tax*
up to $1,159 1.6%	
$1,159 to $2,318	$18.54 plus 3.6% of excess over $1,159
$2,318 to $3,477	$60.26 plus 4.1% of excess over $2,318
$3,477 to $4,636	$107.78 plus 5.1% of excess over $3,477
$4,636 to $5,794	$166.89 plus 6.1% of excess over $4,636
$5,794 to $8,692	$237.53 plus 7.1% of excess over $5,794
$8,692 to $23,178	$443.29 plus 7.4% of excess over $8,692
$23,178 and above	$1,515.25 plus 7.8% of excess over $23,178

Married filing jointly, surviving spouses, and heads of household

Taxable Income	*Amount of Tax*
up to $2,318	1.6%
$2,318 to $4,636	$37.09 plus 3.6% of excess over $2,318
$4,636 to $6,953	$120.54 plus 4.1% of excess over $4,636
$6,953 to $9,271	$215.54 plus 5.1% of excess over $6,953
$9,271 to $11,589	$333.76 plus 6.1% of excess over $9,271
$11,589 to $17,383	$475.16 plus 7.1% of excess over $11,589
$17,383 to $46,356	$886.53 plus 7.4% of excess over $17,383
$46,356 and above	$3,030.53 plus 7.8% of excess over $46,356

If you are operating an S corporation, partnership, limited liability company, or sole proprietorship, you will be subject to personal income tax on your business income passed through to your personal income tax return.

Illinois

Corporate Income Tax: 4.8%

All Illinois C corporations must pay an annual corporate income tax of 4.8% to the state on their income reported to the IRS. In addition, Illinois assesses a personal property replacement tax based on net income (2.5% for C corporations and 1.5% for S corporations, limited liability companies partnerships and sole proprietorships). The personal property replacement tax must be paid by all businesses, whether they are incorporated or not.

Personal Income Tax: 3%

Illinois imposes a 3% income tax on each individual's federal adjusted gross income. If you are operating an S corporation, partnership, limited liability company, or sole proprietorship, you will be subject to the personal income tax on your business income passed through to your personal income tax return.

Indiana

Corporate Income Tax: 8.5%

Indiana imposes an income tax of 8.5% on all C corporations doing business in the state. If you are operating an S corporation, partnership, limited liability company, or sole proprietorship, you will be subject to the personal income tax on your business income passed through to your personal income tax return.

Personal Income Tax: 3.4%

Indiana imposes a 3.4% personal income tax on an individual's federal adjusted gross income.

Iowa

Corporate Income Tax

The Iowa corporate income tax is computed as follows:

Taxable Net Income	Tax Rate
First $25,000	6%
Over $25,000 to $100,000	8%

Taxable Net Income	Tax Rate
Over $100,000 to $250,000	10%
Over $250,000	12%

In addition, banks and similar financial institutions are subject to a an additional 5% franchise tax on net income received or accrued during the tax year.

Personal Income Tax

Taxable Income	Amount of Tax
Over $0, but not over $1,269	0.36%
Over $1,269, but not over $2,538	$4.57 plus 0.72% of excess over $1,269
Over $2,538, but not over $5,076	$13.71 plus 2.43% of excess over $2,538
Over $5,076, but not over $11,421	$75.38 plus 4.50% of excess over $5,076
Over $11,421, but not over $19,035	$360.91 plus 6.12% of excess over $11,421
Over $19,035, but not over $25,380	$826.89 plus 6.48% of excess over $19,035
Over $25,380, but not over $38,070	$1,238.05 plus 6.80% of excess over $25,380
Over $38,070, but not over $57,105	$2,100.97 plus 7.92% of excess over $38,070
Over $57,105	$3,608.54 plus 8.98% of excess over $57,105

If you are operating an S corporation, partnership, limited liability company, or sole proprietorship, you will be subject to the personal income tax on your business income passed through to your personal income tax return.

Kansas

Corporate Income Tax

Kansas C corporations must pay a corporate income tax of 4% plus a surtax of 3.35% of Kansas taxable income in excess of $50,000.

Personal Income Tax

The following rates are applicable in Kansas:

Married Individuals Filing Joint Returns

Taxable Income	*Amount of Tax*
Not over $30,000	3.5% of taxable income
Over $30,000, but not over $60,000	$1,050 plus 6.25% of excess over $30,000
Over $60,000	$2,925 plus 6.45% of excess over $60,000

All Other Individuals

Taxable Income	*Amount of Tax*
Not over $15,000	3.5% of taxable income
Over $15,000, but not over $30,000	$525 plus 6.25% of excess over $15,000
Over $30,000	$1,462.50 plus 6.45% of excess over $30,000

Kentucky

Corporate Income Tax

In Kentucky all limited liability entities (C corporations, S corporations, LLCs, including single member LLCs, and limited partnerships and LLPs) pay tax based on the greater of the 1) taxable net income computation (4% - 6%); 2) the alternative minimum calculation; or 3) the minimum tax ($175). The alternative minimum tax calculation is equal to the lesser of: 9.5 cents per $100 of the taxpayer's gross receipts; or 75 cents per $100 of gross profits. Kentucky does not follow the federal rules for S corporations; in fact, general partnerships and sole proprietorships are not subject to the above corporate tax calculation.

Personal Income Tax

The following tax rates are applicable in Kentucky:

Taxable Income	Rate of Tax
up to $3,000	2%
over $3,000 to $4,000	3%
over $4,000 to $5,000	4%
over $5,000 to $8,000	5%
over $8,000 to $75,000	5.8%
over $75,000	6%

The personal income tax applies to any taxable income earned from property owned or business transacted in Kentucky. Because Kentucky does not follow the pass-through rules associated with S corporations, limited partnerships, LLPs, and limited liability companies, the owners of those entities will also be subject to a personal income tax on their business income that passes through to them. In addition, some local governments are authorized to levy a local income tax, so be sure to check with your local government.

Louisiana

Corporate Income Tax

Corporations pay a corporate income tax based the table below:

Taxable Income	Rate of Tax
First $25,000	4%
Over $25,000 to $50,000	$1,000 plus 5% on amount over $25,000
Over $50,000 to $100,000	$2,250 plus 6% on amount over $50,000
Over $100,000 to $200,000	$5,250 plus 7% on amount over $100,000
Over $200,000 $12,250 plus	8% on amount over $200,000

In Louisiana an S corporation is taxed the same as a C corporation. However, in computing the tax, an S corporation is allowed to exclude the portion of its Louisiana net income that has been passed through to shareholders who have filed a Louisiana personal income tax return and have paid the tax due. The same is true of an LLC that is taxable as a corporation. Sole proprietorships, partnerships and LLCs that are taxed as a partnerships for federal income tax purposes do not pay the Louisiana corporate income tax.

Personal Income Tax

For single, married filing separately and head of house:

Taxable Net Income	Rate of Tax
First $12,500	2%
Next $12,500	4%
Excess over $25,000	6%

For married filing jointly and qualified surviving spouses:

Taxable Net Income	Rate of Tax
First $25,000	2%
Next $25,000	4%
Excess over $50,000	6%

Maine

Corporate Income Tax

In Maine the corporate income tax is based on the following schedule:

Taxable Income	Rate of Tax
Up to $25,000	3.5%
Amount over $25,000 to $75,000	7.93%
Amount over $75,000 to $250,000	8.33%
Amount over $250,000	8.93%

S corporations and LLCs (taxed as partnerships or sole proprietorships) are not subject to the Maine corporate income tax. Remember that if you are operating an S corporation, partnership, or LLC taxed as partnership or sole proprietorship, you will be subject to the personal income tax on your business income that passes through to your personal income tax return.

Personal Income Tax
Single Individuals and Married Persons Filing Separately

Taxable Income	Amount of Tax
Less than $4,450	2%

Taxable Income	Amount of Tax
$4,450 but less than $8,850	$89 plus 4.5% of excess over $4,450
$8,850 but less than $17,700	$287 plus 7% of excess over $8,850
$17,700 or more	$907 plus 8.5% of excess over $17,700

Unmarried or Legally Separated Individuals Who Qualify as Heads of Households

Taxable Income	Amount of Tax
Less than $6,650	2%
$6,650 but less than $13,250	$133 plus 4.5% of excess over $6,650
$13,250 but less than $26,600	$430 plus 7% of excess over $13,250
$26,600 or more	$1,365 plus 8.5% of excess over $26,600

Married Taxpayers and Widows and Widowers Filing Joint Federal Returns

Taxable Income	Amount of Tax
Less than $8,900	2%
$8,900 but less than $17,700	$178 plus 4.5% of excess over $8,900
$17,700 but less than $35,450	$574 plus 7% of excess over $17,700
$35,450 or more	$1,817 plus 8.5% of excess over $35,450

Maryland

Corporate Income Tax: 7%

C corporations in Maryland pay a corporate income tax on their net income of 7%. Maryland imposes a tax of 4.75% on S corporations, partnerships, and LLCs that have nonresident members and taxable income. In Maryland, the law extends this favorable tax treatment to state corporate income tax liability for resident members, and S corporations are not subject to the corporate income tax.

Personal Income Tax

Maryland taxes personal income at the following rates:

Taxable Income	Rate
First $1,000	2%
Second $1,000	3%
Third $1,000	4%
Over $3,000	4.75%

In Maryland, if you are operating an S corporation, partnership, limited liability company, or sole proprietorship, you will be subject to the personal income tax on business income. Some Maryland counties may impose a county personal income tax, so check with your local officials.

Massachusetts

Corporate Income Tax

C corporations must pay an annual excise tax and a corporate income tax. The excise tax is the greater of $456 or the sum of $2.60 per $1,000 of the value of qualified taxable tangible property or qualified taxable net worth plus 9.5% of taxable net income (the minimum tax is $456). Massachusetts S corporations that have total receipts of more than $6 million, will have to pay tax on the net income at the rate 3% and 4.5% for receipts of more than $9 million on the net income. If you are operating an S corporation, partnership, limited liability company, or sole proprietorship, you will be subject to the personal income tax on business income.

Personal Income Tax

Massachusetts has a personal income tax rate of 5.3%. Also, short-term capital gains are taxed at 12%, and long-term capital gains are taxed at 5.3%.

Michigan

Corporate Income Tax: 1.9%

Michigan taxes all corporations, LLCs, partnerships, and sole proprietorships at the rate of 1.9% of the business's federal taxable income. This tax is called the single business tax and is set to be repealed in 2010. However, the first $45,000 is exempt from tax and the exemption amount is increased by $12,000 for each full-time employee/owner up to $48,000. In addition, the exemption is reduced by $1 for every $2 by which the taxable income exceeds the exemption amount.

Personal Income Tax: 3.9%

Michigan taxes all personal income at the rate of 3.9%. If you are operating an S corporation, partnership, LLC or sole proprietorship, in Michigan, you will be subject to the personal income tax on business income.

Minnesota

Corporate Income Tax: 9.8%

Minnesota imposes a corporate income tax (also referred to as the Minnesota franchise tax) at the rate of 9.8% of net income. In addition, all C corporation, S corporations and LLCs pay an additional tax as follows:

Sum of Property, Payroll, and Sales or Receipts	Amount of Tax
Less than $500,000	$0
At least $500,000, but less than $1 million	$100
At least $1 million, but less than $5 million	$300
At least $5 million, but less than $10 million	$1,000
At least $10 million, but less than $20 million	$2,000
$20 million, or more	$5,000

Personal Income Tax

Minnesota imposes the following personal income tax rates:

Married Filing Jointly

Taxable Income	Amount of Tax
Over $0, but not over $29,980	5.35%
Over $29,980, but not over $119,100	7.05% of excess over $29,980
Over $119,100	7.85% of excess over $119,100

Head of Household

Taxable Income	Amount of Tax
Over $0, but not over $25,250	5.35%
Over $25,250, but not over $101,450	7.05% of excess over $25,250
Over $101,450	7.85% of excess over $101,450

Married Filing Separately

Taxable Income	Amount of Tax
Over $0, but not over $14,990	5.35%
Over $14,990, but not over $59,550	7.05% of excess over $14,990
Over $59,550	7.85% of excess over $59,550

Single

Taxable Income	Amount of Tax
Over $0, but not over $20,510	5.35%
Over $20,510, but not over $67,360	7.05% of excess over $19,440
Over $67,360	7.85% of excess over $67,360

Mississippi

Corporate Income Tax

Mississippi has the following corporate income tax rates on C corporations:

Taxable Net Income	Tax Rate
First $5,000	3%
The next $5,000	4%
In excess of $10,000	5%

While Mississippi does not require S corporations to pay corporate income taxes, there is a special state election that must be made when the entity elects S corporation status.

Personal Income Tax

Mississippi charges the following personal income tax rates:

Taxable Net Income	Tax Rate
First $5,000	3%
The next $5,000	4%
In excess of $10,000	5%

If you are operating an S corporation, partnership, limited liability company, or sole proprietorship, you will be subject to Mississippi's personal income tax on your business income.

Missouri

Corporate Income Tax: 6.25%

The Missouri corporate tax rate for most corporations is 6.25% of taxable income. However, banks and similar financial institutions are subject to a separate tax computed on income and capital.) In Missouri, local governments are allowed to impose a local income tax, so check with your local government.

Personal Income Tax

Missouri imposes the following personal income tax rates:

Taxable Income	Amount of Tax
Over $0 but not over $1,000	1.5%
Over $1,000, but not over $2,000	$15 plus 2.0% of excess over $1,000
Over $2,000, but not over $3,000	$35 plus 2.5% of excess over $2,000
Over $3,000, but not over $4,000	$60 plus 3.0% of excess over $3,000
Over $4,000, but not over $5,000	$90 plus 3.5% of excess over $4,000
Over $5,000, but not over $6,000	$125 plus 4.0% of excess over $5,000
Over $6,000, but not over $7,000	$165 plus 4.5% of excess over $6,000
Over $7,000, but not over $8,000	$210 plus 5.0% of excess over $7,000
Over $8,000, but not over $9,000	$260 plus 5.5% of excess over $8,000
Over $9,000	$315 plus 6.0% of excess over $9,000

If you are operating an S corporation, partnership, limited liability company, or sole proprietorship, you will be subject to Missouri's personal income tax on your business income.

Montana

Corporate Income Tax: 6.75%

The Montana corporate tax rate is 6.75% of taxable net income with a minimum tax of $50. If your corporation sales volume in Montana does not exceed $100,000, you may elect to pay an alternative tax of 0.5% of Montana gross sales. As with most alternative taxes, your corporation's activity in Montana must be sales only, and the corporation cannot own or rent property in Montana. S corporations must pay a minimum fee of $10 but are not otherwise required to pay the corporate income tax.

Personal Income Tax

Montana personal income tax rates apply as follows:

Taxable Income	Amount of Tax
Over $0, but not over $2,300	1%
Over $2,300, but not over $4,100	2% less $23
Over $4,100, but not over $6,200	3% less $64
Over $6,200, but not over $8,400	4% less $126
Over $8,400, but not over $10,800	5% less $210
Over $10,800, but not over $13,900	6% less $318
$13,900 and over	6.9% less $443

If you are operating an S corporation, partnership, limited liability company, or sole proprietorship, you will be subject to the personal income tax on your business income that passes through to your personal tax return.

Nebraska

Corporate Income Tax

Nebraska imposes a corporate income tax on the income of all C corporations of 5.58% of the first $50,000 of taxable income and 7.81% of the taxable income over $50,000.

Personal Income Tax

Nebraska's personal income tax rates are as follows:

Married Taxpayers Filing Joint Returns and Surviving Spouses

Taxable Income	Tax Rate
Not over $4,000	2.56%
Over $4,000 but not over $30,000	$102.40 plus 3.57% of excess over $4,000

Taxable Income	Tax Rate
Over $30,000 but not over $46,750	$1,030.60 plus 5.12% of excess over $30,000
Over $46,750	$1,888.20 plus 6.84% of excess over $46,750

Married Taxpayers Filing Separately

Taxable Income	Tax Rate
Not over $2,000	2.56%
Over $2,000 but not over $15,000	$51.20 plus 3.57% of excess over $2,000
Over $15,000 but not over $23,375	$515.30 plus 5.12% of excess over $15,000
Over $23,375	$944.10 plus 6.84% of excess over $23,375

Head of Household

Taxable Income	Tax Rate
Not over $3,800	2.56%
Over $3,800 but not over $24,000	$97.28 plus 3.57% of excess over $3,800
Over $24,000 but not over $35,000	$818.42 plus 5.12% of excess over $24,000
Over $35,000	$1,381.62 plus 6.84% of excess over $35,000

Single Taxpayer

Taxable Income	Tax Rate
Not over $2,400	2.56%
Over $2,400 but not over $17,000	$61.44 plus 3.57% of excess over $2,400
Over $17,000 but not over $26,500	$582.66 plus 5.12% of excess over $17,000
Over $26,500	$1,069.06 plus 6.84% of excess over $26,500

If you are operating an S corporation, partnership, limited liability company, or sole proprietorship, you will be subject to the personal income tax on your business income that passes through to your personal tax return.

Nevada

Corporate Income Tax

Nevada has several taxes that may apply to your business: A quarterly modified business tax (MBT) is imposed as an excise tax on Nevada employers. This tax is based on employee gross wages after certain qualified deductions for health insurance benefits. The tax rate is 0.63% and is currently effective through June 30, 2007. In addition, Nevada has several types of taxes and license fees related to the gambling industry. In addition, Nevada has a 10% casino entertainment tax on admissions, food, refreshments, and merchandise sold at a licensed gaming establishment where music and dance privileges or any other entertainment takes place.

Personal Income Tax

Nevada has no personal income tax.

New Hampshire

Corporate Income Tax

New Hampshire has a business enterprise tax and a business profits tax. The business enterprise tax of .075 applies if your business enterprise has business receipts in excess of $150,000 or a business enterprise value of more than $75,000. The business profits tax is imposed on profits from your business organization at the rate of 8.5%. Both taxes apply to all business entities (all corporations, LLCs, and partnerships), including S corporations, as New Hampshire does not recognize that business form. If you are operating an S corporation, partnership, limited liability company, or sole proprietorship, you will be subject to the personal income tax on your business income that passes through to your personal tax return.

Personal Income Tax

New Hampshire does not have a personal income tax, however, interest and dividends, and distributions are taxed by the state at the rate of 5%. The first $2,400 of interest, dividends, and distributions is not taxable ($4,800 for married filing jointly, and an additional $1,200 exclusion for those who are blind or over 64 years old).

New Jersey

Corporate Income Tax: 9%

New Jersey's corporate tax structure consists of a flat 9% on corporate income. However, corporations with total net income of $100,000 or less pay 7.5%. Moreover, corporations with total net incomes of $50,000 or under pay 6.5%. The minimum tax is $500. Through June 30, 2007, New Jersey will require S corporations to pay a corporate income tax of .67%. If an S corporation has income of $100,000 no tax is due. After July 1, 2007 there will be no corporate tax imposed on S corporations.

Personal Income Tax

New Jersey imposes the following personal income tax rates:

Married Individuals Filing Joint Returns, Heads of Households and Surviving Spouses

Taxable Income	Amount of Tax
Not over $20,000	1.40%
Over $20,000, but not over $50,000	$280 plus 1.75% of excess over $20,000
Over $50,000, but not over $70,000	$805 plus 2.45% of excess over $50,000
Over $70,000, but not over $80,000	$1,295.50 plus 3.5% of excess over $70,000
Over $80,000, but not over $150,000	$1,645 plus 5.525% of excess over $80,000
Over $150,000, but not over $500,000	$5,512.50 plus 6.37% of excess over $150,000
Over $500,000	$27,807.50 plus 8.97% of excess over $500,000

Married Individuals Filing Separately, All Other Unmarried Individuals and Estates and Trusts

Taxable Income	Amount of Tax
Not over $20,000	1.40%
Over $20,000, but not over $35,000	$280 plus 1.75% of excess over $20,000
Over $35,000, but not over $40,000	$542.50 plus 3.5% of excess over $35,000
Over $40,000, but not over $75,000	$717.50 plus 5.525% of excess over $40,000
Over $75,000, but not over $500,000	$2,651.25 plus 6.37% of excess over $75,000
Over $500,000	$29,723.75 plus 8.97% of excess over $500,000

In New Jersey, if you are operating an S corporation, partnership, limited liability company, or sole proprietorship, you will be subject to the personal income tax on your business income that passes through to your personal tax return.

New Mexico

Corporate Income Tax

New Mexico imposes a corporate income tax on C corporations as follows:

Taxable Net Income	Tax
Not over $500,000	4.8%
Over $500,000, but not over $1,000,000	$24,000 plus 6.4% of excess over $500,000
Over $1,000,000	$56,000 plus 7.6% of excess over $1,000,000

New Mexico has an alternative tax of .75% for corporations that have state sales of less than $100,000 and do not own or rent real estate in the state.

Personal Income Tax

New Mexico has the following personal income tax rates:

Single Individuals, Estates and Trusts

Taxable Income	Amount of Tax
Not over $5,500	1.7% of taxable income
Over $5,500, but not over $11,000	$93.50 plus 3.2% of excess over $5,500
Over $11,000, but not over $16,000	$269.50 plus 4.7% of excess over $11,000
Over $16,000	$504.50 plus 5.3% of excess over $16,000

Heads of Household, Surviving Spouses and Married Individuals Filing Jointly

Taxable Income	Amount of Tax
Not over $8,000	1.7% of taxable income
Over $8,000, but not over $16,000	$136 plus 3.2% of excess over $8,000
Over $16,000, but not over $24,000	$392 plus 4.7% of excess over $16,000
Over $24,000	$768 plus 5.3% of excess over $24,000

Married Individuals Filing Separately

Taxable Income	Amount of Tax
Not over $4,000	1.7% of taxable income
Over $4,000, but not over $8,000	$68 plus 3.2% of excess over $4,000
Over $8,000, but not over $12,000	$196 plus 4.7% of excess over $8,000
Over $12,000	$384 plus 5.3% of excess over $12,000

If you are operating an S corporation, partnership, limited liability company, or sole proprietorship, you will be subject to New Mexico's personal income tax on your business income that passes through to your personal tax return.

New York

Corporate Income Tax: 7.5%

Currently, New York has a flat corporate tax rate of 7.5% on S corporations and C corporations.

Personal Income Tax

Single Individuals, Married Couples Filing Separately, Estates and Trusts

If NY taxable income is:	*The tax is:*
Not over $8,000	4% of NY taxable income
Over $8,000 but not over $11,000	$320 plus 4.5% of excess over $8,000
Over $11,000 but not over $13,000	$455 plus 5.25% of excess over $11,000
Over $13,000 but not over $20,000	$560 plus 5.9% of excess over $13,000
Over $20,000 but not over $100,000	$973 plus 6.85% of excess over $20,000
Over $100,000 but not over $500,000	$6,453 plus 7.25% of excess over $100,000
Over $500,000	$35,453 plus 7.7% of excess over $500,000

Married Couples Filing Jointly and Surviving Spouses

If NY taxable income is:	*The tax is:*
Not over $16,000	4% of NY taxable income
Over $16,000 but not over $22,000	$640 plus 4.5% of excess over $16,000
Over $22,000 but not over $26,000	$910 plus 5.25% of excess over $22,000
Over $26,000 but not over $40,000	$1,120 plus 5.9% of excess over $26,000
Over $40,000 but not over $150,000	$1,946 plus 6.85% of excess over $40,000
Over $150,000 but not over $500,000	$9,481 plus 7.25% of excess over $150,000
Over $500,000	$35,856 plus 7.7% of excess over $500,000

Head of Household Taxpayers

If NY taxable income is:	*The tax is:*
Not over $11,000	4% of NY taxable income
Over $11,000 but not over $15,000	$440 plus 4.5% of excess over $11,000
Over $15,000 but not over $17,000	$620 plus 5.25% of excess over $15,000
Over $17,000 but not over $30,000	$725 plus 5.9% of excess over $17,000
Over $30,000 but not over $125,000	$1,492 plus 6.85% of excess over $30,000
Over $125,000 but not over $500,000	$8,000 plus 7.25% of excess over $125,000
Over $500,000	$35,187 plus 7.7% of excess over $500,000

In New York, if you are operating an S corporation, partnership, limited liability company, or sole proprietorship, you will be subject to the personal income tax on your business income that passes through to your personal tax return.

New York City income tax. Residents of New York City pay an additional income tax on their individual income. The tax rate ranges from 2.907% to 4.45% and will depend on your income and filing status.

North Carolina

Corporate Income Tax: 6.9%

All North Carolina C corporations are required to pay a corporate tax of 6.9% on the amount of income that the corporation reports to the IRS.

Personal Income Tax

The applicable personal income tax rates for North Carolina are as follows:

Single Individuals

Taxable Income	*Amount of Tax*
Up to $12,750	6% of taxable income
Over $12,750 to $60,000	$765 plus 7% of excess over $12,750
Over $60,000 to $120,000	$4,072.50 plus 7.75% of excess over $60,000

Taxable Income	Amount of Tax
Over $120,000	$8,722.50 plus 8% of excess over $120,000

Married Filing Jointly and Qualifying Widow(er)

Taxable Income	Amount of Tax
Up to $21,250	6% of taxable income
Over $21,250 to $100,000	$1,275 plus 7% of excess over $21,250
Over $100,000 to $200,000	$6,787.50 plus 7.75% of excess over $100,000
Over $200,000	$14,537.50 plus 8% of excess over $200,000

Married Filing Separately

Taxable Income	Amount of Tax
Up to $10,625	6% of taxable income
Over $10,625 to $50,000	$637.50 plus 7% of excess over $10,625
Over $50,000 to $100,000	$3,393.75 plus 7.75% of excess over $50,000
Over $100,000	$7,268.75 plus 8% of excess over $100,000

Head of Household

Taxable Income	Amount of Tax
Up to $17,000	6% of taxable income
Over $17,000 to $80,000	$1,020 plus 7% of excess over $17,000
Over $80,000 to $160,000	$5,430 plus 7.75% of excess over $80,000
Over $160,000	$11,630 plus 8% of excess over $160,000

In North Carolina, if you are operating an S corporation, partnership, limited liability company, or sole proprietorship, you will be subject to the personal income tax on your business income that passes through to your personal tax return.

North Dakota

Corporate Income Tax

North Dakota imposes a corporate income tax on C corporations as follows:

Taxable Net Income	Tax Rate
First $3,000	2.6%
Over $3,000 to $8,000	$78 plus 4.1% of excess over $3,000
Over $8,000 to $20,000	$283 plus 5.6% of excess over $8,000
Over $20,000 to $30,000	$955 plus 6.4% of excess over $20,000
Over $30,000	$1,595 plus 7% of excess over $30,000

North Dakota has an alternative gross receipts tax based on gross sales in the state if the gross sales don't exceed $100,000 and the only activity in the state is sales. In addition, the corporation cannot own or rent any real or tangible personal property in the state. This alternative tax is computed at the following rates:

Gross Sales	Tax Rate
First $20,000	0.6%
Next $35,000	0.8%
Between $55,000 to $100,000	1.0%

Personal Income Tax

North Dakota has the following personal income tax rates:

Single Individuals

Taxable Income	Amount of Tax
Up to $29,700	2.1% of taxable income
Over $29,700 to $71,950	$623.70 plus 3.92% of excess over $29,700
Over $71,950 to $150,150	$2,279.90 plus 4.34% of excess over $71,950
Over $150,150 to $326,450	$5,673.78 plus 5.04% of excess over $150,150
Over $326,450	$14,559.30 plus 5.54% of excess over $326,450

Married Filing Jointly and Qualifying Widow(er)

Taxable Income	*Amount of Tax*
Up to $49,600	2.1% of taxable income
Over $49,600 to $119,950	$1,041.60 plus 3.92% of excess over $49,600
Over $119,950 to $182,800	$3,799.32 plus 4.34% of excess over $119,950
Over $182,800 to $326,450	$6,527.01 plus 5.04% of excess over $182,800
Over $326,450	$13,766.97 plus 5.54% of excess over $326,450

Married Filing Separately

Taxable Income	*Amount of Tax*
Up to $24,800	2.1% of taxable income
Over $24,800 to $59,975	$520.80 plus 3.92% of excess over $24,800
Over $59,975 to $91,400	$1,899.66 plus 4.34% of excess over $59,975
Over $91,400 to $163,225	$3,263.51 plus 5.04% of excess over $91,400
Over $163,225	$6,883.49 plus 5.54% of excess over $163,225

Head of Household

Taxable Income	*Amount of Tax*
Up to $39,800	2.1% of taxable income
Over $39,800 to $102,800	835.80 plus 3.92% of excess over $39,800
Over $102,800 to $166,450	$3,305.40 plus 4.34% of excess over $102,800
Over $166,450 to $326,450	$6,067.81 plus 5.04% of excess over $166,450
Over $326,451	$14,131.81 plus 5.54% of excess over $326,450

In North Dakota, if you are operating an S corporation, partnership, limited liability company, or sole proprietorship, you will be subject to the personal income tax on your business income that passes through to your personal tax return.

Ohio

Corporate Income Tax

In Ohio the corporate tax rate on C corporations is computed as follows: $50 (the minimum tax)

For some larger corporations the minimum tax is $1,000 or 5.1% of the first $50,000 of the value of a taxpayer's outstanding shares of stock determined according to net income plus 8.5% of the value over $50,000; or .004 times the value of the taxpayer's total value of capital, surplus, undivided profits, and reserves.

There is an additional corporate tax (known as the "tier I litter tax") of 0.11% to 0.22% of the computation above. The maximum amount for the tier I litter tax is $5,000. Also, if your corporation manufactures or sells "litter stream" products (beverage and fast food containers, cigarettes, candy, etc.), there is another tax (known as the "tier II litter tax" of another 0.11% to 0.22%. The maximum amount for the tier II litter tax is $5,000. Ohio authorizes qualified areas to levy a local income tax, so be sure to check with your local government.

Personal Income Tax

Ohio has the following personal income tax rates:

Taxable Income	Amount of Tax
Up to $5,000	0.712%
Over $5,000 to $10,000	$35.60 plus 1.424% of excess over $5,000
Over $10,000 to $15,000	$106.80 plus 2.847% of excess over $10,000
Over $15,000 to $20,000	$249.15 plus 3.559% of excess over $15,000

Taxable Income	*Amount of Tax*
Over $20,000 to $40,000	$427.10 plus 4.27% of excess over $20,000
Over $40,000 to $80,000	$1,281.10 plus 4.983% of excess over $40,000
Over $80,000 to $100,000	$3,274.30 plus 5.693% of excess over $80,000
Over $100,000 to $200,000	$4,412.90 plus 6.61% of excess over $100,000
Over $200,000	$11,022.90 plus 7.185% of excess over $200,000

In Ohio, if you are operating an S corporation, partnership, limited liability company, or sole proprietorship, you will be subject to the personal income tax on your business income that passes through to your personal tax return.

Oklahoma

Corporate Income Tax: 6%

Oklahoma taxes C corporations net income at a flat 6% rate.

Personal Income Tax

Oklahoma imposes the following personal tax rates:

Single Person and for Husband and Wife Filing Separate Returns Not Deducting Federal Income Tax

Taxable Income	*Tax*
First $1,000	0.5% of Taxable Income
Next $1,500	Taxed at 1%
Next $1,250	2%
Next $1,150	3%
Next $1,300	4%
Next $1,500	5%
Next $2,300	6%
Remainder	6.65% (6.25% after 2005)

Single Person and for Husband and Wife Filing Separate Returns Deducting Federal Income Tax

Taxable Income	*Tax*
$0 up to $1,000	Pay 0.5% of Taxable Income
Next $1,000	Taxed at 1%
Next $1,250	2%
Next $1,150	3%
Next $1,200	4%
Next $1,400	5%
Next $1,500	6%
Next $1,500	7%
Next $2,000	8%
Next $3,500	9%
Remainder	10%

Husband and Wife Filing Joint Returns, Qualifying widow(er) with Dependent Child, and Head of Household Not Deducting Federal Income Tax

Taxable Income	*Tax*
$0 up to $2,000	Pay 0.5% of Taxable Income
Next $3,000	1%
Next $2,500	2%
Next $2,300	3%
Next $2,400	4%
Next $2,800	5%
Next $6,000	6%
Remainder	6.65% (6.25% after 2005)

Husband and Wife Filing Joint Returns, Qualifying widow(er) with Dependent Child, and Head of Household Deducting Federal Income Tax

Taxable Income	*Tax*
$0 up to $2,000	Pay 0.5% of Taxable Income
Next $3,000	1%
Next $2,500	2%

Taxable Income	Tax
Next $1,400	3%
Next $1,500	4%
Next $1,600	5%
Next $1,250	6%
Next $1,750	7%
Next $3,000	8%
Next $6,000	9%
Remainder	10%

Qualification for 65 and Over Exemption

Filing Status	Federal AGI Must Not Exceed
Married and Filing Jointly	$25,000
Married and Filing Separately	$12,500
Single	$15,000
Qualifying Head of Household	$19,000

Oregon

Corporate Income Tax

Oregon imposes a flat corporate income tax rate of 6.6% on all C corporations with a minimum tax of $10. If a corporation's only activities in Oregon consist of sales and the corporation does not own or rent any property in the state, they can elect to pay an alternative tax. In order to be eligible, annual gross sales made in Oregon for the tax year must not exceed $100,000. The alternative tax is 0.25%, but may be 0.125% if the return on sales is less than 5% of your dollar volume. Some local governments in Oregon also assess a business income tax, so check with your local authorities..

Personal Income Tax

Oregon imposes the following personal income tax rates:

Single Individuals and Married Individuals Filing Separately

Taxable Income	Tax Rate
First $2,650	5%

Taxable Income	Tax Rate
Over $2,650, but not over $6,650	$133 plus 7% of excess over $2,650
Over $6,650	$413 plus 9% of excess over $6,650

Married Filing Jointly, Head of Household, and Qualifying Widow(er)

Taxable Income	Tax Rate
First $5,300	5%
Over $5,300, but not over $13,300	$266 plus 7% of excess over $5,300
Over $13,300	$826 plus 9% of excess over $13,300

If you are operating an S corporation, partnership, limited liability company, or sole proprietorship, you will be subject to the personal income tax on your business income that passes through to your personal tax return.

Pennsylvania

Corporate Income Tax: 9.99%

Pennsylvania imposes a corporate tax on C corporation at the rate of 9.99%. However, you should check with your local government. Some cities are authorized to impose a tax on persons engaging in any business within the city.

Personal Income Tax

Pennsylvania's personal income tax is computed at the rate of 3.07% of taxable income. Certain areas of Pennsylvania also impose a personal income tax, so be sure to check with your local government. In Pennsylvania, if you are operating an S corporation, partnership, limited liability company, or sole proprietorship, you will be subject to the personal income tax on your business income that passes through to your personal tax return.

Rhode Island

Corporate Income Tax: 9%

Rhode Island has a corporate income tax on C corporations of 9% of the net income, with a minimum tax of $500. Corporate income tax can be reduced with various qualified credits.

Personal Income Tax

Personal income tax rates for individuals are as follows:

Single Individuals

Taxable Income	Amount of Tax
Up to $29,700	3.75% of taxable income
Over $29,700 to $71,950	$1,113.75 plus 7% of excess over $29,700
Over $71,950 to $150,150	$4,071.25 plus 7.75% of excess over $71,950
Over $150,150 to $326,450	$9,901.38 plus 9% of excess over $150,150
Over $326,450	$25,998.75 plus 9.9% of excess over $326,450

Married Filing Jointly and Qualifying Widow(er)

Taxable Income	Amount of Tax
Up to $49,650	3.75% of taxable income
Over $49,650 to $119,950	$1,861.88 plus 7% of excess over $49,650
Over $119,950 to $182,800	$6,782.88 plus 7.75% of excess over $119,950
Over $182,800 to $326,450	$11,653.75 plus 9% of excess over $182,800
Over $326,450	$24,582.25 plus 9.9% of excess over $326,450

Married Filing Separately

Taxable Income	Amount of Tax
Up to $24,825	3.75% of taxable income
Over $24,825 to $59,975	$930.94 plus 7% of excess over $24,825
Over $59,975 to $91,400	$3,391.44 plus 7.75% of excess over $59,975
Over $91,400 to $163,225	$5,826.88 plus 9% of excess over $91,400
Over $163,225	$12,291.13 plus 9.9% of excess over $163,225

Heads of Households

Taxable Income	Amount of Tax
Up to $39,800	3.75% of taxable income
Over $39,800 to $102,800	$1,492.50 plus 7% of excess over $39,800
Over $102,800 to $166,450	$5,902.50 plus 7.75% of excess over $102,800
Over $166,450 to $326,450	$10,835.38 plus 9% of excess over $166,450
Over $326,450	$25,235.38 plus 9.9% of excess over $326,450

If you are operating an S corporation, partnership, limited liability company, or sole proprietorship in Rhode Island, you will be subject to the personal income tax on your business income that passes through to your personal tax return.

South Carolina

Corporate Income Tax: 5% South Carolina imposes a corporate income tax on C corporations of 5% on taxable net income

Personal Income Tax

South Carolina imposes the following personal income tax on individuals:

Taxable Income	*Amount of Tax*
Over $0, not over $2,530	2.5%
Over $2,530, not over $5,060	$63 plus 3% of excess over $2,530
Over $5,060, not over $7,590	$139 plus 4% of excess over $5,060
Over $7,590, not over $10,120	$240 plus 5% of excess over $7,590
Over $10,120, not over $12,650	$367 plus 6% of excess over $10,120
Over $12,650	$519 plus 7% of excess over $12,650

If you are operating an S corporation, partnership, limited liability company, or sole proprietorship in South Carolina, you will be subject to the personal income tax on your business income that passes through to your personal tax return.

South Dakota

Corporate Income Tax

South Dakota does not have a general income tax on corporations. Only banks and financial institutions pay income tax at he rate of 6% on net income less than $400 million and 0.25% on income greater than $1.26 billion (minimum tax is $200 per business location).

Personal Income Tax

South Dakota does not impose a personal income tax on individuals.

Tennessee

Corporate Income Tax: 6.5%

Tennessee taxes C corporations and S corporations at the flat rate of 6.5%.

Personal Income Tax

Tennessee imposes an income tax of 6% on qualified income. Under Tennessee law qualified income consists of dividends from stocks and interest from qualified bonds and other obligations. Tennessee does not tax salaries and wages. If you doing business as a partnership, limited liability company, or sole proprietorship in Tennessee, you will be subject to the personal income tax on your business income that is considered qualified income.

Texas

Corporate Income Tax

Texas does not impose a tax on business income.

Personal Income Tax

Texas does not imposes a personal income tax, but it does have a franchise tax.

Utah

Corporate Income Tax

Utah imposes a income tax is 5% of taxable income on all C corporations with a minimum tax of $100.

Personal Income Tax

Utah has the following individual income tax rates:

Married Persons Filing Jointly or Head of Household

Taxable Income	Rate of Tax
Not over $1,726	2.3%
Over $1,726 to $3,450	$40 plus 3.3% of excess over $1,726
Over $3,450 to $5,176	$97 plus 4.2% of excess over $3,450
Over $5,176 to $6,900	$169 plus 5.2% of excess over $5,176
Over $6,900 to $8,626	$259 plus 6% of excess over $6,900
Over $8,626	$362 plus 7% of excess over $8,626

Single Taxpayers, Estates, Trusts, and Married Couples Filing Separately

Taxable Income	Rate of Tax
Not over $863	2.3%
Over $863 to $1,726	$20 plus 3.3% of excess over $863
Over $1,726 to $2,588	$48 plus 4.2% of excess over $1,726
Over $2,588 to $3,450	$85 plus 5.2% of excess over $2,588
Over $3,450 to $4,313	$129 plus 6% of excess over $3,450
Over $4,313	$181 plus 7% of excess over $4,313

If you are operating an S corporation, partnership, limited liability company, or sole proprietorship in Utah, you will be subject to the personal income tax on your business income that passes through to your personal tax return

Vermont

Corporate Income Tax

Vermont imposes the following corporate tax on the net income of C corporations, with a minimum tax of $250:

Taxable Net Income	Tax
$0 to $10,000	7%
$10,001 to $25,000	$700 plus 8.1% of excess over $10,000
$25,001 to $250,000	$1,915 plus 9.2% of excess over $25,000
$250,001 or more	$22,615 plus 9.75% of excess over $250,000

S corporations in Vermont must pay an annual minimum tax of $150, and must also pay tax on income distributed to nonresident shareholders.

Personal Income Tax

Below are the personal income tax rates for Vermont:

Single Individuals

Taxable Income	Amount of Tax
Up to $29,700	3.6% of taxable income

Taxable Income	Amount of Tax
Over $29,700 to $71,950	$1,069 plus 7.2% of excess over $29,700
Over $71,950 to $75,000	$4,111 plus 8.5% of excess over $71,950
Over $75,000 to $150,150	$4,370 plus 8.5% of excess over $75,000
Over $150,150 to $326,450	$10,758 plus 9% of excess over $150,150
Over $326,450	$26,625 plus 9.5% of excess over $326,450

Married Filing Jointly and Qualifying Widow(er)

Taxable Income	Amount of Tax
Up to $49,650	3.6% of taxable income
Over $49,650 to $75,000	$1,787 plus 7.2% of excess over $49,650
Over $75,000 to $119,950	$3,613 plus 7.2% of excess over $75,000
Over $119,950 to $182,800	$6,849 plus 8.5% of excess over $119,950
Over $182,800 to $326,450	$12,191 plus 9% of excess over $182,800
Over $326,450	$25,120 plus 9.5% of excess over $326,450

Married Filing Separately

Taxable Income	Amount of Tax
Up to $24,825	3.6% of taxable income
Over $24,825 to $59,975	$894 plus 7.2% of excess over $24,825
Over $59,975 to $75,000	$3,425 plus 8.5% of excess over $59,975
Over $75,000 to $91,400	$4,702 plus 8.5% of excess over $75,000
Over $91,400 to $163,225	$6,096 plus 9% of excess over $91,400
Over $163,225	$12,560 plus 9.5% of excess over $163,225

Heads of Households

Taxable Income	Amount of Tax
Up to $39,800	3.6% of taxable income

Taxable Income	Amount of Tax
Over $39,800 to $75,000	$1,433 plus 7.2% of excess over $39,800
Over $75,000 to $102,800	$3,967 plus 7.2% of excess over $75,000
Over $102,800 to $166,450	$5,969 plus 8.5% of excess over $102,800
Over $166,450 to $326,450	$11,379 plus 9% of excess over $166,450
Over $326,450	$25,779 plus 9.5% of excess over $326,450

In Vermont, owners of S corporations, partnerships, limited liability companies and sole proprietorships will be subject to the personal income tax on the business income that passes through to their personal tax returns.

Virginia

Corporate Income Tax: 6%

Virginia has a corporate income tax rate of 6% on the taxable income of C corporations. Also, qualified local areas are authorized to levy a local income tax, so be sure to check with your local authorities.

Personal Income Tax

Virginia imposes the following personal income taxes:

Taxable Income	Rate
Up to $3,000	2%
Over $3,000, but not over $5,000	$60 plus 3% of excess over $3,000
Over $5,000, but not over $17,000	$120 plus 5% of excess over $5,000
Over $17,000	$720 plus 5.75% of excess over $17,000

Owners of S corporations, partnerships, limited liability companies and sole proprietorships will be subject to Virginia's personal income tax on the business income that passes through to their personal tax returns.

Washington

Corporate Income Tax

Washington does not assess an income tax on C corporations, S corporations, LLCs, or any individual business owner. However, Washington does have what it calls a business and occupation tax. The business and occupation tax is calculated by a specific tax rate multiplied by either the value of products, gross proceeds of sales, or gross income of the business. There are many specific activities that are exempt from the tax, for example, certain farm and horticultural products. You'll want to check to see if you are exempt and to determine your tax rate for your type of business and your area. Washington allows a credit for small businesses in the maximum amount of $35 multiplied by the number of months in the reporting period to reduce the business and occupation tax.

Personal Income Tax

A personal income tax is not assessed in Washington.

West Virginia

Corporate Income Tax: 9%

The West Virginia corporate income tax on C corporations is assessed at the rate of 9%.

Personal Income Tax

West Virginia imposes the following personal income taxes:

All Resident Individuals (Except Married Persons Filing Separately), Estates and Trusts

Taxable Income	Amount of Tax
Not over $10,000	3% of taxable income
Over $10,000, but not over $25,000	$300 plus 4% of excess over $10,000
Over $25,000, but not over $40,000	$900 plus 4.5% of excess over $25,000
Over $40,000, but not over $60,000	$1,575 plus 6% of excess over $40,000
Over $60,000	$2,775 plus 6.5% of excess over $60,000

All Resident Married Individuals Filing Separately

Taxable Income	*Amount of Tax*
Not over $5,000	3% of taxable income
Over $5,000, but not over $12,500	$150 plus 4% of excess over $5,000
Over $12,500, but not over $20,000	$450 plus 4.5% of excess over $12,500
Over $20,000, but not over $30,000	$787.50 plus 6% of excess over $20,000
Over $30,000	$1,387.50 plus 6.5% of excess over $30,000

Owners of S corporations, partnerships, limited liability companies and sole proprietorships will be subject to West Virginia's personal income tax on the business income that passes through to their personal tax returns.

Wisconsin

Corporate income Tax: 7.9%

The corporate income tax on C corporations in Wisconsin is a flat rate of 7.9% of net income.

Personal Income Tax

Wisconsin imposes the following personal income taxes:

Married Persons Filing Jointly

Taxable Income	*Tax Rate*
$0 to $11,780	4.6%
Over $11,780 to $23,570	$541.88 plus 6.15% on all taxable income over $11,780
Over $23,570 to $176,770	$1,266.97 plus 6.5% on all taxable income over $23,570
Over $176,770	$11,224.97 plus 6.75% on all taxable income over $176,770

Married Persons Filing Separately

Taxable Income	*Tax Rate*
$0 to $5,890	4.6%
Over $5,890 to $11,780	$270.94 plus 6.15% on all taxable income over $5,890

Taxable Income	*Tax Rate*
Over $11,780 to $88,390	$633.18 plus 6.5% on all taxable income over $11,780
Over $88,390	$5,612.83 plus 6.75% on all taxable income over $88,390

Single Individuals, Fiduciaries, and Heads of Households

Taxable Income	*Tax Rate*
$0 to $8,840	4.6%
Over $8,840 to $17,680	$406.64 plus 6.15% on all taxable income over $8,840
Over $17,680 to $132,580	$950.30 plus 6.5% on all taxable income over $17,680
Over $132,580	$8,418.80 plus 6.75% on all taxable income over $132,580

In Wisconsin, owners of S corporations, partnerships, limited liability companies and sole proprietorships will be subject to the personal income tax on the business income that passes through to their personal tax returns.

Wyoming

Corporate Income Tax

There is no income tax on corporate or other business income in Wyoming.

Personal Income Tax

There is no personal income tax in Wyoming.

Glossary

Accrual Basis Method of accounting that requires income to be recorded in a company's books at the time it is earned (but not necessarily received) and expenses to be recorded when they are incurred (but not necessarily paid).

Amortization of a Loan An amortization schedule will show how much of each payment is principal and how much is interest, and what the balance remains. The concept of paying both principal and interest of a loan with equal periodic payments.

At-will Employment An employment relationship where either party can terminate the relationship at any time for any reason. This doctrine does has a few limitations, such as an employer cannot terminate the employment relationship because of race, color, religion, sex, national origin, age, or handicap status. Also many states have chipped away at this doctrine over the years and now it would be prudent for an employer to have good cause to terminate the employment relationship.

Balance Sheet A balance sheet is a financial statement of the book value of a business or other organization or a person at a particular date, often at the end of the calendar or fiscal year. A balance sheet is often described as a "snapshot" of a business's financial condition on a given date.

Biannual Twice in one year.

Biennial Once every two years.

C Corporation In general, a C corporation is an entity separate from its shareholders that is formed under state law by the filing of articles of incorporation with the state. The C corporation files and pays taxes and its shareholders' may be subject to double taxation when a dividend is paid.

Calendar year Any year that begins on January 1 and ends on December 31.

Capital Contribution A contribution of cash, assets, property, or services contributed to a business entity in exchange for an ownership interest.

Cash Basis Method of accounting that recognizes revenues and expenses at the time cash is actually received or paid out.

Common-Law Employee A person working for another if the person paying has the right to control what work will be done and how.

Contract An agreement with specific terms between two or more persons or entities in which there is a promise to do something in return for a valuable benefit known as consideration. Since the law of contracts is at the heart of most business dealings, it is one of the three or four most significant areas of legal concern and can involve variations on circumstances and complexities. The existence of a contract requires finding the following factual elements: a) an offer; b) an acceptance of that offer that results in a meeting of the minds; c) a promise to perform; d) a valuable consideration (which can be a promise or payment in some form); e) a time or event when performance must be made (meet commitments); f) terms and conditions for performance, including fulfilling promises; and g) performance. Contracts can be either written or oral, but oral contracts are more difficult to prove and in most jurisdictions the time to sue on the contract is shorter.

Cost of Goods Sold (COGS) The total cost of buying raw materials or inventory, and paying for all the factors that go into producing finished goods for sale, including labor and shipping costs.

Depreciation A method of accounting for the reduction of the value (and a write-off for tax purposes) of a capital asset over its useful life.

Discretionary Cash Flow The cash available to a business after paying all operating expenses.

Distributions Nonwage payment of profits made to S corporation shareholders.

Dividends A per-share payment of some of the profits to the shareholders of a C corporation. Most dividends are taxable income to the shareholders.

Employee Every individual performing services if the relationship between that individual and the person for whom he or she performs such services is the legal relationship of company and those who are paid wages or salary to work for it.

Entity Isolation The practice of creating a Web-based business that is separate from the retail locations within a state to avoid sales and use taxes on Internet sales.

FICA Taxes Federal employment related taxes on the gross wages of an employee that are partially withheld from the employee's wages (7.65%) and partially paid by an employer on the gross wages of an employee. Social Security taxes are 12.4% and Medicare taxes are 2.9%.

Fiscal Year Any business year comprised of 12 months that does not begin on January 1 and end on December 31.

Fiduciary An individual who is required by law to act in the best interest of another person or persons. A fiduciary cannot put his or her personal interests before the duty, and must not profit from being a fiduciary, unless the principal or beneficiary consents. The fiduciary relationship is governed by good faith, loyalty, and trust.

General Partnership An arrangement by which two or more persons or businesses conduct business jointly for profit. General partners have unlimited liability, which means their personal assets are liable for the partnership's obligations. Because all partners have unlimited liability, even innocent partners can be held responsible when another partner commits inappropriate or illegal actions. This fact alone demonstrates how an investor should heed caution when deciding on whether to become a general partner.

Ghost Asset An asset that no longer exists physically within the organization, yet remains on the books.

Gross Profit The profit before selling, and general and administrative costs, like depreciation and interest. It is the sales less direct cost of goods sold (COGS) prior to operating expenses or overhead.

Income Statement *See* Profit and loss statement.

Indemnification An agreement to compensate a person or a business for actual loss or damage that may arise.

Independent Contractor A person working for another if the one paying for the work does not have the right to control the day-to-day working but merely to direct the desired result.

Joint and Several Liability A common law liability, whereby a person or entity (plaintiff) may recover all the damages from any of the negligent defendants regardless of their individual share of the liability. Joint and several liability is premised on the theory that the defendants are in the best position to apportion damages amongst themselves; therefore, the plaintiff can collect all or a portion of the damages from any one or more of the defendants.

Lease Option A legal document that combines a basic lease with an option to purchase the leased property at the end of the lease. Also known as a lease-purchase contract.

Lien A security position against an item of property or the assets of an individual or entity that secures the payment of a debt or obligation.

Limited Liability Company (LLC) An entity formed under state law that allows for the flexibility of the sole proprietorship or general partnership structure within a framework of limited liability for all its members (owners). A type of LLC available in some jurisdictions (usually limited to licensed professionals such as architects, lawyers, physicians, or engineers) is the professional limited liability company (P.L.L.C. or PLLC). The LLC is a pass-through entity and may be taxed like a sole proprietor, a partnership, or a corporation depending on the specifics of ownership.

Limited Partnership (LP) A special type of partnership that includes one or more partners who have limited liability protection and who do not participate in the daily operations of the business. A limited partnership must have at least one general partner who runs the daily operation and who *does not* have limited liability protection.

Limited Liability Limited Partnership (LLLP) The limited liability limited partnership is a new form of business organization that allows the general partners limited liability protections as set forth under state statute. The LLLP is so new that its use is not yet widespread and they are most commonly used in the real estate business.

Limited Liability Partnership (LLP) A limited liability partnership is a form of business organization combining elements of partnerships and corporations. In an LLP, all partners have some form of limited liability protection, depending on state law. However, the partners have the right to manage the business directly. The LLP is taxed like a partnership and is therefore a pass-through entity.

Limited Liability Protection A type of liability that does not exceed the initial amount a person invested into a business. Limited liability protects the owner's personal assets from being liquidated should the company become insolvent.

Net income A business's total earnings, after revenues are adjusted for costs of doing business, cost of goods sold, inventory costs, wages, depreciation, interest, taxes and other operating expenses.

Nexus A substantial physical presence within a state. Usually a business would need to have an office location, a warehouse, a distribution center, or employees within a state to create a nexus.

Operating Expenses The amount paid for asset maintenance or the cost of doing business, excluding depreciation. Profits may be distributed after cost of goods sold and operating expenses have been deducted.

Par Value Stated value or face value, often used to describe the minimum amount that must be paid for a share of stock of a corporation. A par value is no longer required to be stated in most jurisdictions.

Pass-through Entity Business entity that does not pay its own income tax, but rather passes the tax liability on to its individual owners. In some cases the pass-through entity (S corporations, partnerships, and LLCs electing S corporation status) must file an informational return for tax purposes. The informational return then generates a K-1 that contain eacg individual owner's proportionate share of income and deductions.

Personal Garanty (or Personal Guarantee) An agreement by which an individual agrees to be responsible for the debt or obligation of another person or business if such person or business fails to perform its obligations.

Pierce the Corporate Veil A corporate law concept describing a legal decision where a shareholder, officer, director or manager of a corporation or LLC is held personally liable for the obligations of the entity despite the general principle that those persons have limited liability protection.

Profit The sales of a business less the expenses related to running the business such as wages, rent, fuel, inventory costs, raw materials, supplies, interest on loans, and depreciation.

Profit and Loss Statement (P&L) A statement that indicates how revenue (money received from the sale of products and services before expenses are taken out, also known as the "top line") is transformed into net income or profit (after all revenue and expenses have been accounted for, also known as the "bottom line"). The purpose of the income statement is to show managers and investors whether or not the company made or lost money during the period being reported. Also called an Income Statement.

Promissory Note A contract detailing the terms of a promise by one party (borrower) to pay back a sum of money loaned or otherwise financed by the other (note holder).

Receivable Turnover Period The time between delivering a product or service and collecting payment for such product or service. *See* Sales Cycle.

Registered Agent The person or entity which agrees to accept service of process on behalf of a corporation, or other legal entity.

Return of Investment The return of an initial capital or other capital investment to the investor.

Return on Investment The earnings enjoyed as the result of a capital investment in addition to the actual capital investment made.

S Corporation An eligible domestic corporation that can avoid double taxation by electing to be treated as an S corporation. Generally, an S corporation is exempt from federal income tax other than tax on certain capital gains and passive income. On their tax returns, the S corporation's shareholders include their share of the corporation's separately stated items of income, deduction, loss, and credit, and their share of non-separately stated income or loss. Such information is then passed through the S corporation to the individual shareholder's personal tax returns.

Sales Cycle The period of time between selling goods or providing services and collecting payment for such goods or services.

Self Employment Tax A federal tax of 15.3% imposed on self-employed individuals, who must pay this tax in order to receive Social Security benefits upon retirement. Note: The self-employment tax may be reduced if the person also pays Social Security and Medicare taxes through another employer.

Sole Proprietorship An entity that is unincorporated, has only one owner, and is created for the purpose of making a profit.

Service of Process The procedure employed to give legal notice to a person (defendant, et al) of a court or government agency's jurisdiction over that person or entity so as to enable that person to respond to the proceeding before the court or other tribunal. Usually, notice is furnished by delivering a set of court documents to the person to be served or to the registered agent of an entity.

Statute of Frauds A statute or state law provision that requires certain kinds of contracts to be in writing and be signed by the party against whom enforcement is sought to be valid.

Statute of Limitations A statute or law that sets forth the maximum period of time, after certain events, that legal proceedings based on those events may be initiated.

Tangible Personal Property All assets (things, including animals) which are not real property, money, or investments.

Tax Deduction An expense paid by a taxpayer that is subtracted from gross revenue and results in a lower overall profit or taxable income.

Tort Liability A tort is a civil wrong, other than a breach of contract, for which the law provides a remedy. Tort law serves to protect a person's interest in his or her bodily security, tangible property, financial resources, or reputation. The law of torts therefore aims to restore the injured person to the position he or she was in before the tort was committed.

Index

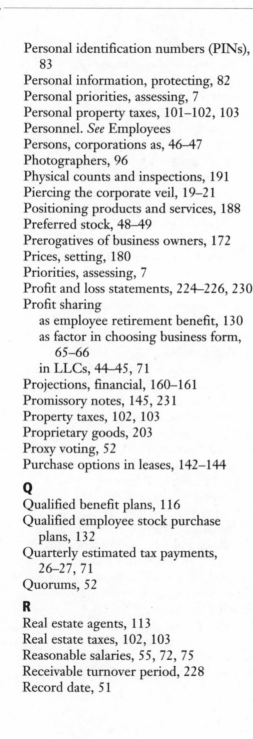